'I HAVE BEEN WAITING':
RACE AND U.S. HIGHER EDUCATION

While much progress has been made towards the quest for racial equality in the education system, there is still much work to be done. In *'I Have Been Waiting,'* Jennifer Simpson looks at the ways in which systems of higher education have excluded people of color, and how white students and teachers might better address issues of race and racism in educational settings.

Simpson's discussion is wide-ranging and incisive. She examines the role of history and the link between racial agency and racial memories; she probes epistemology, claims to authority, and the limits of a knowledge base that draws primarily on what white people know; she analyzes cross-racial dialogues to reveal the prevalence of assimilationist approaches; and she reiterates the importance of making whiteness visible.

Methodologically, Simpson draws heavily on autoethnography and social analysis. She provides a historical overview of the issues central to race and higher education, as well as a rigorous examination of theoretical discourse from a variety of fields. *'I Have Been Waiting'* argues that sustained attention to issues of race in higher education is both difficult and necessary. Each chapter addresses a particular challenge in the area of race and education, and offers practical suggestions and guidelines for constructive change. An appendix provides discussion questions, exercises, and assignments.

JENNIFER S. SIMPSON is an assistant professor of communication at Indiana University – Purdue University Fort Wayne.

'I HAVE BEEN WAITING'

Race and U.S. Higher Education

Jennifer S. Simpson

UNIVERSITY OF TORONTO PRESS
Toronto Buffalo London

© University of Toronto Press Incorporated 2003
Toronto Buffalo London
Printed in Canada

ISBN 0-8020-8779-5 (cloth)
ISBN 0-8020-8569-5 (paper)

Printed on acid-free paper

National Library of Canada Cataloguing in Publication

Simpson, Jennifer S.
    'I have been waiting' : race and U.S. higher education / Jennifer
S. Simpson.

    Includes bibliographical references and index.
    ISBN 0-8020-8779-5 (bound).   ISBN 0-8020-8569-5 (pbk.)

    1. Discrimination in higher education – United States.
    2. Minorities – Education (Higher) – United States.
    3. United States – Race relations.   I. Title.

LC212.42.I5 2003   306.43   C2003-901367-7

University of Toronto Press acknowledges the financial assistance to its
publishing program of the Canada Council for the Arts and the Ontario
Arts Council.

University of Toronto Press acknowledges the financial support for its
publishing activities of the Government of Canada through the Book
Publishing Industry Development Program (BPIDP).

In memory of my grandparents
Gladys and William Johnson
Marguerite and Howard Simpson

Contents

Preface

Placing myself within the reality of race and racism has been and is an ongoing process. Learning to recognize the presence of racism in my life and choices is a daunting and elusive task. Racism is present in my own actions, rises up in my relationships and the contexts in which I locate myself. I first began to feel the press of its weight at a Midwestern Protestant seminary in the late 1980s. In the wake of a faculty hiring process, it was clear that faculty and administration were choosing not to act on a spoken and written commitment to diversity. Fortunately, a group of about fifty students decided to draw attention to the discrepancy between words and actions.

As conversation and contention continued over the quarter, a few white students, myself included, began to notice the importance of race and the regularity of racism at the seminary. Disagreements had revealed layers of conflict, including the possibility of race and gender exclusion. Student demands resulted in a meeting for students, faculty, administration, staff, and board members to discuss the hiring process specifically, and the climate at the school more generally. For the administration, this meeting was an attempt to respond to concerns they hoped would go quietly away. But over the course of the term, I was fortunate to work with a group of students wrestling with each other and with the shape of our resistance.

I walked into that meeting keenly aware of racism at the seminary. The possibility of racism under my own skin was distant and comfortably vague; it was much easier to focus on the more 'obvious' racism among faculty and administration at the seminary than to consider how racism might be present in my interactions with people of color at the seminary. While I walked into that meeting certain that white people made racist choices, I chose to distance myself from 'those whites.' Racism did indeed lurk under white skin, but not under mine.

One statement cracked open that false distance. In the midst of the tension edging that meeting, an African American woman student stood up, and slowly, carefully, insistently put words together. It is the order of her words, the crafting of her knowing, that place me inside her subject. 'I have been waiting for the day when white folks start to deal with their own racism.'

Her words press and linger. I know she means to draw me inside that circle of 'white folks' and 'their own racism,' and locating myself inside the picture she drew continues to challenge my understanding of race. Her words mattered to me, because the two of us had worked long hours together with a small group of students on a faculty search. I knew I was located at the beginning of her sentence and at the end: White folks had started to deal with racism. Had I? Her choice to stand up and voice her weary hope is the first clear recollection I have of placing myself inside race, of connecting racism with my choices and actions.

Because of the events at school, my then-recent interest in feminism collided with the reality of race, bumping toward cooperation, reaching for space and place in my constructions of knowing. The often-cantankerous conversation between my whitewashed feminism and my elusive understanding of my white body as raced began in the late 1980s at that Midwestern Protestant seminary. Now, that conversation continues, as I hope for a deepened understanding of racism and anti-racism in the academy.

'I have been waiting for the day when white folks start to deal with their own racism.' That sentence continues to follow me; it surfaces in classrooms and in conversations with friends, as I read, teach, write, and consider new knowledge. Its significance did not fade like the struggles at the seminary. This book, an exploration of race issues in higher education, and in particular European American racial agency, is intricately tied to my memory of that African American woman's long-suffering hope. It is one response to 'I have been waiting,' part of an ongoing effort to acknowledge racism in my context, to name its presence in the academy and in feminist thought and movement, and to participate in its undoing.

Acknowledgments

It has been a pleasure to work with my editor, Virgil Duff, and his colleagues at the University of Toronto Press. I appreciate the helpful feedback from an anonymous reviewer, as well as the instructive editing of Allyson N. May.

I am grateful to my parents for instilling in me the value of learning. I also benefit from the support offered by my colleagues in the Communication Department at Indiana University–Purdue University Fort Wayne.

I will always value the early insights, constructive challenges, and engagement that Professor Dwight Conquergood, Marta Effinger, Marisa Nordstrom, Deborah Parédez, Professor Sandra Richards, and Professor Richard Tholin provided.

María L.G. Gettman and Professor Sandra Richards reminded me, always in timely fashion, to stick with it. Romaine Harris has offered humor and passion to our conversations about race. The thoughtful feedback of Jean Stefancic and Richard Delgado have been central to my completion of the book.

Since the early stages of the book, Njoki Kamau has extended valuable insights regarding her sense of race and education, and consistently helped me discern my connection to the topic. Dr Toinette M. Eugene provided an early focus for many of the ideas central to this book. I will always appreciate her ongoing advice, wisdom, and consideration. Anne-Maria Schultheis has from the project's start to finish shared her belief in the book and sensible advice regarding its completion. Her patience and generous spirit have been constant.

'I HAVE BEEN WAITING':
RACE AND U.S. HIGHER EDUCATION

CHAPTER ONE

Introduction: Race and Higher Education

When discussing how race is or is not present in our scholarship and in our classrooms, agreement rarely comes easily. Students and teachers alike have a range of views on the relationship of race to learning objectives and topics. People in higher education have not resolved issues such as affirmative action, identity politics, cultural competence, and racial representation on faculties and in classrooms. Such issues invite a range of often intense and always conflicting responses, and discussion about these topics in public settings, such as classrooms and meetings, can be strained. Often, the most honest and lengthy conversations continue after class in small groups, or in hallways among two or three faculty. Feelings of blame, guilt, and defensiveness are frequently present. Tensions erupt as people insist that racism is a thing of the past, that we are doing all we can, or that what we are doing is never enough.

Constructive approaches to addressing race are fundamental both to combatting racism and to constructing more diverse classrooms and meeting rooms. In the face of change in higher education around issues of culture and race, strong opinions and feelings remain among students and faculty. It is clear that students and faculty of color are present in higher education in greater numbers than they were two or three decades ago. At the same time, discussion of race issues in the classroom can meet with strong resistance from large numbers of students, and from faculty as well. Such resistance blocks learning. Further, in the absence of constructive ways to address that resistance, students are often profoundly reluctant to consider race issues outside of the classroom.

Within the context of higher education, how might faculty and students work at constructive dialogue in cross-racial groups? How might teachers facilitate discussions in the classroom that pick up race and racism in all of their complexity, and that leave students with deeper understandings and a commitment to work at change? What does personal experience of race and racism have to do with the relationship of racial location and knowledge in the classes we teach and the knowledge we produce?

More particularly, how do knowledge and understandings of race and racism differ among racial groups? In higher education, white people have had near-exclusive control of disciplinary development and university norms and expectations. How does this control leave room for or exclude alternative approaches to education? Any significant and broad-based change in higher education must at some point include white people. How do whites encourage or prohibit cross-racial dialogue and change? Further, how can teachers address race issues with white students, who may have a profound lack of connection to any sense of racial identity or responsibility?

This book assumes that racism is still present in higher education, and that understandings of race are centrally important to what we know and how we teach and produce knowledge. It considers the questions set out above at both practical and theoretical levels, and draws on examples and routine interactions to provide angles into analysis. Finally, it draws on work across the disciplines to locate particular articulations of race and racism.

Contemporary white feminist scholarship and the critique offered by U.S. women of color provides particularly valuable insights into issues of race and racism. Concerns central to race matters in higher education – the relationship between knowledge and one's racial location, who is in control of specific disciplinary discourses, and the place of race in the classroom and in the production of knowledge – have been central to many of the differences between European American feminists and feminists of color. Likewise, this discourse provides an angle from which to analyze race and racism in higher education. White feminists are increasingly interested in developing working relationships with women of color in which they directly address race and racism. At the same time, for most white feminists, initiating and sustaining practical and theoretical work with women of color scholars that addresses race head on is a difficult task. Cross-racial interactions in the academy more generally are similarly elusive.

Cross-racial dialogue in the academy continues to be difficult.[1] In particular, working relationships among cross-racial groups of faculty and cross-racial groups of students that take on issues of race and racism in a concrete and sustained manner are rare. Again, the issues in feminism run parallel to broader issues in higher education. What is the role of white feminists in cross-racial feminism in the academy? How do white women enter cross-racial feminism, with what relationship to history, and with what priorities for the feminist work we pursue and practice? As women of color have pointed out, obstacles to cross-racial work among women are frequently embedded in the work and scholarship of white feminists. That is, the assumptions, norms, and practices white feminists take for granted are often problematic. White women unknowingly and as a matter of course make scholarly choices that indicate both a lack of knowledge of scholarship by women of color and a reluctance to engage that knowledge. Similarly, routine decisions of European American faculty and students are burdened with racist assumptions. How do the choices made by white people contribute to or prohibit dialogue and working relationships with people of color?

White U.S. feminists have recently begun to address the significance of race to feminist work,[7] and many white feminists might now agree with the assertion that 'race shapes white women's lives.'[3] White feminists have begun to explore how the complications of race challenge analyses of gender. But we rarely engage with any serious depth the questions of how and to what extent race has marked and marks our existence. Consequently, we are often unaware of and inattentive to the ways in which race has marked and marks our scholarship. White feminist considerations of race often dance around the edges of race privilege and discrimination, barely touching the meaning of race and racism. Indeed, the weight of racism may well prove too heavy a burden for many of us. Unfortunately, 'There are not many examples of white feminists embracing women of Color's writings without cannibalizing them.'[4]

A related and significant implication of European American feminists' reluctance to think carefully about race and our own participation in white supremacy is the sometimes vast divide between and even hostility among white feminists, and American Indian, Asian American, Latin American, and African American men. Writers and activists have perhaps given the most attention to the divide between European American women and African American men. As one author writes, 'To many black folks feminism continues to be seen as synonymous with bourgeois white women.'[5] European American feminists' insistent focus on gender and inattention to race and class, as well as the attention paid by some radical white feminists to gender separatism, often results in European American feminists asking feminists of color to choose between gender and race. Likewise, men of color are aware that they have no place in most versions of white feminism.

This is unfortunate and can be contrary to feminism's aims. Men of color are rightfully suspicious of white women who identify as feminists, and European American feminists lose potential allies in the struggle against oppression in relation to gender and race. We also lose potential alliances with women of color who choose to work with men of color. White women's refusal to address white supremacy in feminism and beyond can actively contribute to antagonisms with men and women of color.

As with white people more generally, white feminists demonstrate a variety of agendas, and many have chosen not to respond to the challenges offered by U.S. women of color. I am concerned with dominant scholarship that *is* responsive to U.S. women of color and to their scholarship. While many white people choose to ignore, devalue, or misrepresent the critique of U.S. women of color, the central struggle of this book is to establish the meaning of that critique in the context of higher education. White feminist scholarship that speaks to the challenges U.S. women of color offer is of particular value in moving toward cross-racial work.

A history and persistence of racist choices, an active reluctance of whites to view their bodies as racially significant, and a tendency toward theoretical elitism and irrelevance are issues that white people must address in pursuit of anti-racist and pluralist scholarship.[6] This book offers one way through the terrain of racism past and of current work by U.S. women of color, an analysis of how white people's choices affect cross-racial discourse in the academy. Chapter 2 situates European American feminism and race in an historical setting. Current dynamics among cross-racial groups in the academy emerge out of concrete historical relationships and processes. Racial memory, defined as frameworks of interpretation used to remember the past, is always intertwined with knowledge of race history. I propose sustained racial memory as one way for white people to acknowledge their histories as racial and their bodies as raced.

Chapter 3 looks closely at epistemology, or the ways in which we claim knowledge. Scholarship committed to cross-racial change must consider the ways in which racial location affects the knowledge we produce, and the ends and communities that knowledge serves. Feminist work has established the importance of knowing gender, but from what angles and perspectives do white women know race, and how does this affect their work? Examination of three major European American feminist frameworks for knowing – feminist empiricism, feminist standpoint, and postmodern feminism – demonstrates that none of these three epistemologies, in and of themselves, offers resources adequate to producing anti-racist white feminist scholarship. The epistemological implications, both practical and theoretical, of recent feminist scholarship, as well as the components necessary for European American feminist scholarship that is anti-racist, are also topics central to this chapter.

Dialogue is a primary aspect of cross-racial change, and the focus of chapter 4. How do faculty and students in higher education achieve dialogues about race and racism that do not end in frustration and expressions of guilt, but move instead toward deeper understanding and change? Knowledge of the recent history of cross-racial dialogue among women in higher education, of significant barriers to dialogue in the academy, and of the necessary components of dialogue for white people committed to anti-racism in the academy will contribute to a determination of how those in higher education might achieve dialogue in particular cross-racial settings.

The final chapter addresses race in the classroom. A history of assimilationist approaches to education, at almost all levels of higher education, has resulted in a near inability to address racial injustice thoroughly across the curriculum. Most white people prefer to manage diversity rather than confront the ways in which the values and frameworks of people of color call for us to change our own. Attending to whiteness in the classroom, as well as combining social analysis and affective reflection, are two concrete ways to squarely confront racism in classroom contexts.

I explicitly link my own racial agency with the knowledge I produce and with anti-racist practice. As a white feminist addressing racism, I critique a cultural practice, racism, from which I benefit and in which I participate. I am a part of the subjects I address, and I choose not to remove myself from those subjects. Further, facing race in all of its complexity requires a cross-disciplinary approach. It calls for ways of writing and thinking that balance past and present, theory and practice, hurt and possibility, damage done and new ways of being.

I am interested in making plain the ways in which race and racism move under my white skin, the shapes white privilege and racism take in relationships, and the way to reach through racism to cross-racial dialogue. White privilege is rarely clear cut or always visible; it shimmers and slips, occupies the status of norm, and is as prevalent as air. In light of this, writing that can hold both theory and the lived materiality of race, racism, and white privilege, and that makes it explicit for others is particularly useful.

This book offers strategies and tools for collaboration with people of color that is respectful, mutual, and not entirely on European American terms or within white frameworks. It offers a way for white people in higher education and beyond to listen to what people of color are saying and writing, and to move forward in ways that both reflect and challenge what we know.

Race and White Feminism

Recent work by white feminists in the United States on race advances three arguments. It asserts that European American women have made and continue to make choices that exclude and misrepresent the lives and scholarship of women of color. In some cases, white women's choices have been racist, and race and racism are an integral part of women's history in the United States. Second, this scholarship posits that all women are racially marked. White women are located within the category of race; they are always and everywhere racial beings. A final claim is that white feminism is often an obstacle to cross-racial work among women.

Historically, white people rarely entered into relationships with people of color on a mutual and respectful basis. Following white genocide of American Indian peoples and cultures European Americans forced people of African, Asian, and Latin American descent into the United States in large part as cheap labor and to further white economic interests.[7] White people with the economic means brought women of African descent to the United States to work as slaves.[8] Labor demands have largely dictated the presence of Asian women in the United States.[9] Additionally, 'Many of the mechanisms that institutionalized racism, sexism, and working-class status as Chicanos were incorporated into North American society' still exist.[10] Racism has always been present in U.S. women's cross-racial relationships, and it has often framed white women's interactions with women of color.

Throughout most of the history of the United States, whites have viewed U.S. women of color as breeders, slaves, menial workers, and sexual objects, and ultimately expendable. European American feminists have not adequately addressed the legacy and meaning of this history to cross-racial work among women.

The idea that 'Race shapes white women's lives' has profound implications for white feminist work, and constitutes the second of three arguments these scholars make. White women have a race; all women live racially significant lives.[11] Contrary to a long-standing and often subtle assumption of white feminist theorists, gender is not the only or even primary marker of difference.[12] My intent in this book is to interrupt and decenter white feminist theory that makes gender primary and that writes European American women beyond or outside of race.

Finally, white feminist theory often serves as an obstacle to cross-racial work among women. Historical and current racism on the part of white feminists, and European American feminists' frequent insistence that white women are not racial, contribute to scholarship and theory that are explicitly and profoundly elitist and exclusionary. White feminist theory's refusal to thoroughly acknowledge women's differences 'lies at the heart of feminism's implicit politics of domination.'[13]

It is important to note that such exclusivity in white feminist scholarship has ramifications other than inattention to race. While this book discusses the barriers to and possibilities for tending to race in white feminist scholarship and in higher education more generally, feminist scholars have also neglected issues of social class. Likewise, this inattention and its significance for feminist scholarship and higher education are specific to social class. Considering race is not the same as considering class. Scholarly work on the relationship of social class to knowledge produced in the academy is increasing.[14]

White women have, however, begun to address race issues. Recent work by white feminists draws attention to race, women's racial histories, white women's historical complicity with racism, and the relevance of white women's cross-racial histories to the possibility of a cross-racial present.[15] Writing by white women also acknowledges that race affects the experience of white women.[16] Being white is for many European Americans an unmarked privilege and underpins the assumption that our lives constitute a norm and standard by which all should be measured and to which everything else must be compared. Recent scholarship addresses as well the possibility of cross-racial feminism. In a few cases, white women have been working on race issues in groups and over time. The knowledge communicated by such groups demonstrates the complicated layers of white women's privilege, details the difficulty of marking that privilege and stepping outside of it, and offers much-needed guidance for other white women working on racism and anti-racist movement.[17]

Challenges to White Feminism

Tensions between white women and U.S. women of color have existed at least since contact between the two groups, and U.S. women of color have articulated a critique of white women's elitism and exclusionary practices in a variety of forms since the 1800s.[18] Historically, racist choices on the part of white people have forced genocide, slavery, lynching, limited education, destructive immigration policies, loss of land, boarding schools, pervasive stereotyping, assimilation into white culture, punishment for speaking their languages, and sterilization onto women of color. While issues such as lynching and land rights may seem external to current feminist work in the academy, it is inappropriate for white women to dismiss these concerns as secondary or even peripheral to feminist movement. Work by U.S. women of color has made it clear that white people's inability and reluctance to grapple with the far-reaching effects of racism, as a matter of course and as a legacy that is in many ways ours, is profoundly problematic in the context of cross-racial women's relationships.

Feminist work by women of color has been readily accessible to, and in a few cases included in, white academic contexts for at least twenty years. Work by U.S. women of color is filling many university libraries and academic journals and increasing numbers of popular and scholarly bookstores. The themes and positions that this body of work presents have strong parallels. Women of color scholars point out that European American women are rarely interested in the realities and lives of women of color, or in the scholarship and theories of women of color.[19] This lack of interest leads directly to white women's continuation of racism within the feminist movement. Women of color also assert that addressing and eliminating racism in European American feminism is white women's work, rather than the task or responsibility of women of color. Finally, women of color make clear that white women's good intentions, however honest and sincere, do not necessarily result in anti-racist feminism. Women of color have noticed a long-standing and pervasive inattention to and disregard for their scholarship, priorities, and lives on the part of white women. As one scholar puts it, 'white feminist scholars pay hardly more than lip service to race as they continue to analyze their own experience in ever more sophisticated forms.'[20]

The reluctance on the part of white feminists to engage with work by U.S. women of color effectively results in racist scholarship. European American women routinely make choices that indicate a lack of understanding of race and racism in a feminist context. White women claim that they cannot speak beyond their experiences and openly choose not to address the work or lives of U.S. women of color; foreground theoretical work by white women and experiential work by U.S. women of color; or bring in U.S. women of color as authorities on race and European American women as experts on all other topics.[21] Additional ways of dismissing work by U.S. women of color include leaving it out completely, judging it useless because it adopts different forms of presentation and organization than work by white women, or deciding it is not relevant because it deals with issues that European American feminists have deemed unimportant.[22] Such choices have broader implications: they indicate white women's inability to work mutually and respectfully with women of color, and demonstrate the extent of their ignorance when it comes to race. Such choices rarely encourage women of color to seek out white women in the hope of building cross-racial feminist practice.

Finally, as a white feminist drawing on the resources offered by women of color, I risk appropriation, misuse, and disrespect of the work I engage. I do not want to paint the scholarship of U.S. women of color onto white feminism; I am more interested in investigating the meaning of their work for European American anti-racist feminism. Further, because the work of U.S. women of color is often largely context-based, severing their scholarship and writing from particular locations strips their theories of meaning. In order to respectfully engage the work of U.S. women of color, European American feminists must examine that scholarship in its own context, and then determine how it informs a white feminist context.[23]

The Historical Significance of Race and the Possibilities of Racial Memory

The lack of widespread and public resistance to racism, specifically in the academy and on the part of white women, has historical origins.

Current exclusionary practices are connected to European American women's racism in the suffrage movement, to ongoing ignorance regarding the past and present lives of U.S. women of color, and to feminist theory that requires U.S. women of color to 'do lots of acrobatics – like a contortionist or tight-rope walker' to see their lives in feminist theory.[24] White women are frequently unaware of how race factors into women's histories and have rarely considered their own complicity with widespread white supremacy and racism. Moreover, when they do begin to acknowledge that the scope of women's history may carry the burden of white women's racist choices, they are eager to minimize the significance of those choices, to deny their relevance to current feminist work, or to simplify the ways those choices have marked women's cross-racial relationships.

Remember the comment made by an African American woman in a meeting that occurred during my graduate studies: 'I have been waiting for the day when white folks start to deal with their own racism.' Her succinct 'I have been waiting' holds the crux and complexity of women's cross-racial relationships in relation to history. 'I have been waiting' lets me know that someone has been waiting on me. It communicates the burden of white women's choices, and the historical layer of our responsibility. It reminds me of European American women's ignorance on race matters, and of my own connection to white privilege. White people can be relieved that this woman is, in fact, still waiting.

A Conversation on the History of Choosing Not to Deal

The conversation set out below, based on a classroom exchange, illustrates tensions among cross-racial groups of people with respect to race.[25] Direct conversation posits agency and performed identities as central in analyses of cross-racial relationships. That is, European Americans and people of color signify race awareness or lack of it everyday, and this signifying matters to cross-racial relationships. This conversation took place among a cross-racial group of graduate and undergraduate students, and demonstrates the missed understandings among women, the tendency of white women to hope for the best, and the generosity of women of color when we reveal our ignorance.

WHITE WOMAN: You mean the word 'feminist' doesn't include everyone?
MULTI-RACIAL WOMAN: What do you mean? You guys decided long
    ago that the category of 'woman' is an exclusive, whites-only club.

WHITE WOMAN: But what's the matter with being for women? I mean, I thought we all agreed on that.

AFRICAN AMERICAN WOMAN: All agree? You never even asked me if I have an opinion!

MULTI-RACIAL WOMAN: Most white women didn't even want Sojourner Truth to speak at an 1851 women's rights meeting in Ohio. She had to invite herself up to the podium, and many of the white women attending wanted her to sit down. White women didn't even want us to have the vote. For most of you, Susan B. Anthony and Elizabeth Cady Stanton are heroes. Black women weren't even allowed to form a chapter in the main women's suffrage movement.

WHITE WOMAN: Oh ... I guess I didn't realize ...

The gap in knowing demonstrated in this conversation is not unusual in racially mixed groups. As evidenced by this exchange, history is neither over nor forgotten. The ruptures that surface in this conversation, and parallel fractures among white people and people of color in relation to history, must be attended to before cross-racial work can occur. Much scholarly work by women of color assumes the foundational importance of gender, race, and class. In contrast, work by European American women readily acknowledges gender as relevant, but often pays scant attention to race. In other words, white women rarely know race in the same ways that they know gender. We can quickly and convincingly speak of our experiences as women; we rarely achieve the same ease or familiarity when we speak of our experiences as white. Whereas women of color are often asked to choose between, for example, being Asian American or being female, and consistently respond that they will come to the table whole or not at all, European American women routinely opt for the privilege of leaving their race behind.

While white feminists have frequently identified women's experiences as gendered, we have not identified that same experience as raced. This has affected how and what European American feminists know. Not knowing race influences our knowledge claims. Much of white feminist work is 'irrevocably rooted in women's concrete and diverse practical and everyday experiences of oppressions.'[26] What European American feminists know about race, how we know race, and if we know white as a race are all crucial issues. The processes of knowing and knowledge production, specifically in regards to race and white privilege, are central to this book.

Bending Bodies and Layered Language

Language is crucial to all writing. In applying words to complicated bodies, definitions quickly disintegrate in the face of real life. Peoples' experiences always push beyond the edges of words, even when the uses of those words are dynamic and expansive. 'The ambiguities and limitations of language can be startling when people resist the categories imposed on them.'[27]

Defining Race

Race, most simply, is a means of classification, often by skin color. Race is a 'concept which signifies and symbolizes social conflicts and interests by referring to different types of human bodies.'[28] Race is simultaneously socially constructed and socially significant. That is, race is a categorical system of privilege and discrimination invented and sustained by individuals and institutions rather than a natural part of the world. People can thus unlearn racism. At the same time, despite racism being a practice people choose, it is still always and everywhere materially present. For most of the history of the United States white thinkers in particular have conceived of race as fixed and exclusively biological, a categorization system with clear lines and certain boundaries.[29] But in recent years, scholars have come to view racial formation and race itself as constantly changing.[30]

The increasing acceptance of social constructionist arguments in understanding and theorizing race is connected to the disturbing and socially naive position that because race has no scientific foundations, we need not address the politics of race or even the power of racism. In articles in the *Chronicle of Higher Education*, in the 1995 annual meeting of the American Association for the Advancement of Science, and in conversations among European American colleagues, white writers and thinkers in particular have argued, often implicitly, that the non-essential nature of race leads to the declining significance of racism.[31] But racism exists and race matters.

Racism differentiates between varying 'types of human bodies.' Essentialist ideas of race, as found, for example, in the assertion that all Asian Americans have above-average scientific intelligence, lead to racism. Racism is 'a fundamental characteristic of social projects which create or reproduce structures of domination based on essentialist categories of race.'[32] Racism occurs in courts, classrooms, grocery stores, religious conventions, all-white suburbs, in the media, on the job, at fast food and fine restaurants. It is routine and often subtle, especially to white eyes. Racism engages ideologies and structures, depends on both ideas and behaviors, and 'is all around us.'[33] Finally, racism is individual and structural. In racialized societies, 'Actors in superordinant positions (dominant race) develop a set of social practices (a racial praxis if you will) and an ideology to maintain the advantages they receive based on their racial classification.'[34]

Within the realities of race and racism, white is a race. 'White' is a racial category that refers to all people of European descent. Another term that identifies this group of people is European American. Multiracial people are not white, nor are people who appear white necessarily European American. In selecting racial identifiers, such as white, multi-racial, and person of color, I have relied on terms that people employ themselves. Throughout this book, I use the terms 'white' and 'European American' to refer to people of European descent in the United States.

The category of white, and precisely who qualifies as a white person, has never been fixed. Historically, Irish, Italian, and Hungarian immigrants were not necessarily considered white. Likewise, migrants from southern and eastern Europe, as well as Jewish people, were not always categorized as white. While 'the "good Jew" was sometimes counted as white,' Jews who were poor 'were slurred as Black with special frequency.'[35] As recently as 1987, a U.S. Supreme Court decision relied on the history of Jews having been viewed as a racial group in the nineteenth century 'as precedent to allow a Jewish group to sue under racial discrimination statutes.'[36]

It is possible to trace a strong link between European immigrants seeking to become more Americanized and an 'acquired ... sense of whiteness and of white supremacy.'[37] Indeed, it was useful for European immigrants to draw attention away from the concept of 'nativity' – they would never be 'natives' – and toward race, a category within which they could distinguish themselves as white. White people are thus not simply put by others into the category of white, but also choose whiteness for themselves. Definitions and perceptions of who is white fit closely with power and what an individual or group had and has to gain. Choosing whiteness has always had concrete and immediate rewards. Choosing whiteness 'enabled [European immigrants] to live more easily with the white American population [and] to live more easily with themselves and with the vast changes industrialist capitalist America required of them.'[38]

The term 'white' cannot and should not be simplified or flattened out. Different groups within the category of white, based on gender, religion, sexuality, and socio-economic class, have different material relationships to power and resources. At the same time, white identifies a category that is racially privileged, even though 'not all members of the dominant race receive the same level of rewards.'[39]

In the context of racism and white people, 'white privilege' and 'white supremacy' are useful terms. 'White privilege' refers to the range of benefits that institutions and individuals afford to people who are or who appear white. European Americans, for example, are regularly able to see countless images of intelligent, complex, and well-spoken white people on television and in other media. They are rarely, if ever, asked to represent their entire race: people seldom ask European Americans for the 'white perspective.' Store owners and employees rarely, if ever, assume that European Americans are in a store to steal rather than to browse or to buy.[40]

'White supremacy' is a broader term than 'white privilege.' The privileges all European Americans experience are an integral component of systematic and institutional white supremacy. White supremacy is 'the ideology that most determines how white people in this society (irrespective of their political leanings to the right or left) perceive and relate to black people and other people of color.'[41] The term 'white supremacy,' which is often used to identify extreme forms of racism, marks the structure of interactions, institutional and personal, that dominate cross-racial relations in the United States. White supremacy encompasses not only the choices and actions of overtly racist individuals and groups, but the choices and actions of white people who consider themselves above overt racism yet continue to act on racist assumptions. Put another way, 'racism and white supremacy are manifested in blatant ways, but they also work in covert and subtle ways, and the latter are much more common in today's society than the former.'[42]

Particularly in academic contexts, in which liberal white people often consider themselves incapable of racism, the term white supremacy asserts the systematic and overarching nature of racism. While many European American liberals have learned to notice overt racism, it is common for 'deeply ingrained notions of white supremacy to remain intact.' 'When liberal whites fail to understand how they can and/or do embody white supremacist values and beliefs even though they may not embrace racism as prejudice or domination ... they cannot recognize the ways their actions support and affirm the very structure of racist domination and oppression that they profess to wish to see eradicated.'[43] The term white supremacy is useful because it encourages an understanding of racism that does not reduce racist choices to overt or obvious acts. It also moves the possibility of racism closer to white feminists who imagined or hoped themselves to operate outside of racist choices.

Further Definitions

Terms used regularly in this study are defined here for the reader's convenience. 'White feminist theory' refers primarily to feminist work produced in the academy across the disciplines. 'European American feminist theory' names the range of work that has both made space for women's studies in the academy and that has been most attentive to the realities of middle-class, white, and heterosexual women living in the United States, while rarely naming the results of that exclusion. It is most often written by middle-class, white, heterosexual women.[44]

'U.S. women of color' refers to women of African, Asian, and 'Latin American descent and American Indian women living in the United States.[45] American Indian women and women of African, Asian, and Latin American descent have a range of histories, experiences, priorities, and values, although parallels can be found across racial and ethnic lines. Neither white feminist theory nor the challenge from U.S. women of color is monolithic, with clear-cut boundaries. They are not always diametrically opposed, and there are exceptions to the tendencies described in this book. 'Our' and 'we' as used below refer to white people committed to anti-racism and to addressing the critique by U.S. women of color.

'Anti-racist acts' are intentional and interrupt essentialist categories of race. They publicly challenge stereotypes, assumptions, choices, and practices white people endorse regarding U.S. men, women, and children of color. Anti-racism also encompasses noticing and responding to people of color in the academy.

Language, like life, is complicated. Language is routinely 'defied by the subjectivity of the human mind.'[46] While racial language is common, languaging race is difficult, and language that furthers cross-racial change must encourage European Americans to locate themselves inside race, a choice necessary to anti-racism.

The Place of Values

Rejecting the traditional academic notion of value-free inquiry, feminists have highlighted the importance of values in all academic work and knowledge production. The very foundations of feminist theory rest on the importance of valuing women's experiences and knowledge. As part of a decision to value women, feminists make further choices regarding which women to value, and in which ways.[47] Three primary values endorsed in this book are anti-racism, rooted and connected scholarship and theory, and pluralist feminism. Anti-racism is a necessary value in working toward cross-racial dialogue and change because racism exists in the academy and hurts people in the academy and outside of it. In academic white feminism, adherence to narrow definitions of what constitutes theory, inattention to the scholarship of U.S. women of color, and lack of explicit acknowledgment of the partial nature of all scholarship contribute to racism.

Racism in the academy exists on structural levels and in interpersonal relationships. In 1999, about 14 per cent of college and university faculty in the United States were people of color, while 50 per cent were white men and 35 per cent were white women.[48] Further, 'Black, Hispanic, and American Indian/Alaska Native faculty members are less likely than White faculty to have tenure.'[49] These statistics describe tendencies, and should not detract attention from connected issues such as the racial distribution of faculty across disciplines and across institutional hierarchies, including faculty versus administration and full professor versus associate professor. In responding to the statistics, many cite a lack of people of color to hire into faculty positions. A commitment to changing the current situation requires hard work at several levels. It is easy to state that the pool is too small. How one finds and defines the pool, or how a group might change the make-up of the pool, merit further investigation.

Mary Romero and Debbie Storrs interviewed women of color in PhD programs and concluded that women of color have less access to resources than white women and continue to encounter racial and sexual stereotypes on a regular basis. One woman's committee member told her, '"You act too much like a [member of a particular ethnicity] and not enough like a sociologist,"' which 'served the function of socializing [the student] to view race and ethnicity as illegitimate areas in the study of sociology.'[50] Another example of racism in the academy involves the reactions of white students when they learn that people of color critically assess white people. 'Often their rage erupts because they believe that all ways of looking that highlight difference subvert the liberal conviction that it is the assertion of universal subjectivity (we are all just people) that will make racism disappear.'[51] Racism exists in many forms in the academy, and requires a range of anti-racist strategies.[52]

Rooted and connected scholarship is a second value necessary for cross-racial dialogue and change. Where academia continues to legitimize academic work that makes claims to objectivity, the work by U.S. women of color challenges these processes of legitimation. In both method and content, the scholarship of U.S. women of color models a connection to academic work that displaces an either objective/universalist or subjective/relativist framework.[53] The work of U.S. women of color encourages careful consideration of the reasons for and priorities of all academic work. Further, knowledge assumes various forms; rationality, emotions, intuition, and theory often come in connected layers.

Analysis of various levels of the academy, including the politics of publishing, the near-exclusivity of text-based forms of scholarly representation, and widespread resistance to heterogeneous theories and paradigms,[54] reveals a lingering resistance that often implicitly values distance and detachment. It is rare in academic settings for white people to identify race as written on their bodies; whites are often most comfortable talking about race as a purely intellectual reality.[55] European American academics, moreover, frequently locate race somewhere else. This occurs on personal levels – only people of color have race – and in topical discussions, such as those which deal exclusively with anti-immigrant public policy or other, similar issues that exist largely outside of the academy rather than addressing race matters in our midst.

The third value critical to cross-racial work among women is pluralist feminism. Pluralist feminism is the topic of an essay by María C. Lugones addressed specifically to white women. Pluralist feminism is interactive and builds on differences, and Lugones does not understand European American feminism as pluralist: 'they [white women]

theorized as if all women were the same.'[56] Pluralist feminism challenges European American feminism, which can be destructive in its
theorizing, primarily because it does not adequately tend to differences and complexity.

White women are reluctant to engage the presence of differences
among women with seriousness and in an in-depth manner. White
women do 'recognize the problem of difference. Whether they *recognize* difference is another matter.' As Lugones explains, when she reads
articles about 'universal' topics such as motherhood, morals, and the
self, she is often outside of the discourse. Further, feminist theories
describe and prescribe, and rarely in the interests of women of color.
'But a prescription for whom? How is one who lies outside the limits to
correct the prescription? ... Why does the author think that all we need
to do is correct the prescription? ... Why does [the writer] think she is
justified in doing that?' Unfortunately, white women have cared more
about the theory than actual women. 'I say this because even when
they heard this claim [regarding the importance of difference], they did
not notice us.'[57]

Ethics and European American Feminist Theory

'They did not notice us' and 'I have been waiting for the day when
white folks start to deal with their own racism' are statements that
immediately establish a connection among particular women, however tenuous, fragile, and conflicted. Another student had been waiting on me; I did not notice a particular group of women. What we do
with that waiting, with the charge of choosing not to notice, is fundamentally ethical. Ethics, most simply, is how we choose to be with each
other, and more precisely, how particular people choose to negotiate
specific relationships.

Feminists addressing ethics exhibit a range of concerns in their writing. In the academy, whose scholarship we take seriously enough to
critique and address, whose knowledge we consider authoritative, and
what kind of writing we consider theoretical are all ethical issues. In a
feminist context, if and how we choose to engage Cixous or Collins,
Anzaldúa or Irigaray, Harstock or Higgenbotham, or neither or both,
pose ethical questions. Our working idea of feminist theory, who we
consider feminist theorists, and which feminists' work we know well,
are all ethical choices.

*An Ongoing Conversation on the Existence of Ethics in
Feminist Scholarship*

The three conversations reproduced below took place over the course
of three weeks in a graduate feminist theory seminar in 1996. In a
group of fifteen women, a quarter of the women were African American, mixed race, Asian, and African. The rest of us were European
American. These three discussions are intentionally located and specific. They do not represent all feminist discourse, nor do they provide
a general view of the current state of women's studies courses. They
are useful because they offer up sites of contention in direct relation to
white feminist work and the critique women of color offer.

Conversation Number One: Truth

WHITE WOMAN NUMBER ONE: Don't we have to have standards that
make things right or wrong, good or bad? I mean, isn't it possible to
know if something is a fact or not, to know if something really happened?
AFRICAN AMERICAN WOMAN: Maybe we should start with different
questions. Such as who benefits? Who suffers? How does an event
variously impact differently identified groups?
WHITE WOMAN NUMBER ONE: I don't see how we can get anywhere if
we can't decide on some things as purely objective, you know,
truth.
WHITE WOMAN NUMBER TWO: Where do you want to go, anyway? And
whose truth are you going there with?

Conversation Number Two: Woman

WHITE WOMAN NUMBER ONE: Can't we come together simply as
women? That used to work.
WHITE WOMAN NUMBER TWO: Work for whom?
AFRICAN AMERICAN WOMAN: Whenever you play that game, you white
women pretend I'm not 'woman' anymore. I'm black.
WHITE WOMAN NUMBER THREE: Well, how about sexual harassment?
Can't we all agree that violence against women is simply wrong?
Then we can all come together as *women* [smiling hopefully].
AFRICAN WOMAN: You might think of sexual harassment as impacting

'women.' I know sexual harassment is about gender, race, and class. Please don't divide me into pieces.

WHITE WOMAN NUMBER TWO: This dream of coming together as women seems way too big for me. We can't even agree in this class. Women come together in particular contexts. I'm interested in a little smaller scale.

Conversation Number Three: Knowledge

WHITE WOMAN NUMBER TWO: I've been thinking about epistemology. Patricia Hill Collins, for example, is one feminist who is explicit about her epistemology, and it got me wondering about how I know, how I decide who has authority in my work. [Long silence]

WHITE WOMAN NUMBER ONE: Well, I just don't think it's possible to talk about those things.

WHITE WOMAN NUMBER THREE: I don't have one. It's the same as my methodology.

WHITE WOMAN NUMBER TWO: What do you mean? When you do research, how do you decide on sources? I think it's connected to values. It's an ethical issue.

WHITE WOMAN NUMBER FOUR: Values? Ethics? Part of epistemology? Un-uh [laughing]. Why do we need to talk about values and epistemology anyway? I'd rather talk about question two on the take-home exam.

WHITE WOMAN NUMBER TWO: What are you going to say when you have the power and responsibility to assign books for a course and a student asks why?

WHITE WOMAN NUMBER FOUR: I'll say I'm the teacher.

These conversations raise several issues and questions relevant for European American feminists in the academy. The forms of our epistemologies, their embeddedness in and differentiation from traditional epistemologies, the place of values, and the possibility and scope of objectivity all affect our writing and representation of knowledge. Whether we address it or not, epistemology is, indeed, crucial to our work. Further, the scholarship of many U.S. women of color directly critiques writing by white feminists and articulates epistemologies that are radically different from white epistemologies.

Who we know affects how and what we know. The inability of a white woman to accept the authority of an Asian American woman scholar is connected to the ways in which that European American woman writes an outline for a research project, or chooses resources for that project. White women often comment that the work of U.S. women of color is not theoretical enough for their projects. We also admit our collective ignorance when we admit that we have not heard of or read even one of the countless scholarly texts by women of color.

Another frequent comment made by white women regarding the work of U.S. women of color is, 'I'm not used to their style. It was difficult to get into.' I see these same women spend hours with texts by Donna Haraway or Hélène Cixous, two white feminists who often write in a style that is both complicated and not immediately relevant to practice. What this suggests is that European American feminists choose what we read based on not only how a piece is written, but what that piece says, and how traditional academic circles receive the author.

The increasing legitimacy of acontextual white feminist theory in the academy and our inattention to U.S. women of color have contributed to a lack of accountability in our theories. That is, in the attempt to bring women's lives to the forefront in the academy, we have not always been clear about which women and whose lives, even as we have made choices about both. Which women is our feminism for, and why, are important considerations. There has been extensive and serious resistance to courses in women's studies and to feminist theories in the academy. At the same time, most universities offer courses in European American feminist theory, and the existence of several academic journals reflects the academy's acknowledgment of the discipline. We must ask, in the interests of furthering women's studies, which women have we left out? And in leaving women out, what does feminist theory lack or misrepresent?

While white feminists tend carefully to the difference gender makes, we do not always notice the difference race, class, sexuality, or nation make. This inattention is often accepted without question, and our resulting theories become authoritative despite what they leave out. This book, in its foundations and aims, is one response to 'I have been waiting,' one reply to 'They did not notice us.' It is part of a growing conversation among white women regarding our own racism, and one effort at supporting cross-racial dialogue in the academy. The African American student's statement of wearied hope was both gift and risk. For European American women to be able to communicate cross-racially about race and racism, we will also need to risk, and to learn how to notice and accept gifts of connection when offered by U.S. women of color.

'I have been waiting,' she said. I sit with the knowledge that someone is waiting on me; that the learned habits and assumptions of white supremacy are not permanent; that the racism imbedded in my thoughts, actions, language, and choices is not inevitable, and that it can crack, splinter, and crumble depending on my choices and actions. This book is one response to that waiting.

Resisting 'Sympathy and Yet Distance':[1] The Connection of Race, Memory, and History

Current cross-racial work always exists in the context of cross-racial history. That is, relationships among cross-racial groups of people are not isolated from the past; they never stand alone, beyond the reach of history. Rather, the reality of racism, historical and present, is present in our relationships with people of color in the best of situations: when we have known a particular person of color for years and socialize with her regularly; when we have coffee with a man of color who is a colleague in our department; and in routine interactions with people of color at our university, at the bank, or in the grocery store. The choice to recognize the weight of racism, past and present, in our interactions with people of color is an acknowledgment of what is, and a necessary first step in anti-racism. Recognizing the presence of racism past may or may not be about what we have done. It is always about something of which we are a part.

This chapter assumes that white people who work with people of color on issues of race and racism must acknowledge that history matters. Anti-racist work on the part of whites does not begin with the desire to start fresh, or to move forward unburdened. It begins with the willingness to engage the histories inherent in cross-racial relationships. White people must accept the unwelcome guest of racism past and present with clarity, frankness, and responsibility, rather than guilt, before mutual relationships with people of color can occur.

When we learn about or discuss the presence of racism historically, we immediately and often subconsciously distance ourselves from the white people who made racist choices. The grandmother who routinely talked down to her African American domestic servant; the neighbor who decried all Latin Americans as lazy; white women suffragists who opted for white suffrage at the expense of people of color; and the many European Americans who, less than fifty years ago, were adamantly and systematically opposed to school integration are 'not like us.' Further, we often dismiss those peoples' choices as the result of ignorance, subtly excusing their actions and indirectly implying their choices were inevitable.

In the particular context of white women's histories and race, European American women today are often immediately and insistently other than, removed from, and beyond those white women. In our eagerness to deny the possibility that our own choices in any way parallel the choices of those white women, now so obviously racist, we dislocate ourselves from white supremacy. In our own minds, we are significantly different from the European Americans who opposed integration, or from white women suffragists who excluded African American women from meetings. It is profoundly convenient to sever ourselves from the possibility of having more in common with white women who made racist choices than not.

Such severing and dislocation are arrogant and acontextual choices. Further, distancing ourselves from white women's historical race matters denies the ongoing nature of white supremacy and institutional white privilege. It assumes whites can exist outside of race, can place ourselves beyond the reach of white supremacy. In categorizing European Americans opposing integration as ignorant, ill-informed, and misguided, we fail to acknowledge that these people may have been thoughtful, intentional, and mindful in their racist choices. In distancing ourselves from white women's historical racism, we act as if racial agency does not exist. If we can excuse the past racism of white people as ignorance, or a passing mistake, we allow ourselves a similar escape route.

White people can engage in mutual relationships with people of color only when we understand racist choices, past and present, as the product of racial agency and responsibility. For instance, we might consider the rationale of white women who were vehemently opposed to school integration: what did they have to gain, what did they have to lose, and what led them to consciously oppose integration? Seeking to understand European American race history from a location of agency is critical to forming cross-racial relationships. Racial agency involves the roles white people play as racial doers. Racial agency assumes that all white people are moral actors in relation to race matters. European Americans who opposed school integration and actively made choices about race for which they were responsible were racial agents. Likewise, when, throughout most of the twentieth century, white people repeatedly passed laws restricting Asian immigration, sometimes in ways that clearly hurt families' abilities to stay together, they were racial agents. These white people had opinions about race, they were themselves racially significant, and they made deliberate choices that were inextricably linked to notions of racial inferiority and superiority.

In the context of history and cross-racial relationships among women, this chapter makes three points. First, European American history – all of it – is racial. White history is always about race. Second, knowing my own racial identity and my racial agency helps me locate white choices and responsibility in cross-racial women's histories. Once European Americans sense our own raciality as skin close, racial history is not always about racial other. It is also about the racial implications and privileges embedded in white supremacy and actions. Finally, memory can serve as a link for white people between personal racial agency – that is, our negotiation of our own raciality over time – and the racial agency of white people historically. Once we begin to link our own racial agency with the history of white supremacy, we can begin to form relationships with people of color that acknowledge the history and presence of racism.

With respect to the example of European American resistance to school integration, these three arguments mean that historical accounts of white actions in regard to school integration are necessarily about race; that once European Americans understand ourselves as racial actors, we are more likely to consider whites who opposed school integration as racial agents; and that white acknowledgment of racial agency might serve as a link to current discussions of European American racism in the context of school integration. Moving toward cross-racial work in higher education requires an ongoing engagement with the past.[2]

White Women, History, and Race

Scholarship on white women, race, and history makes three broad points. First, racism, as an institutionalized social, economic, and political reality, is part of the larger backdrop against which women's histories and the growth of feminist thought and practice have played out. Second, racism has long pervaded U.S. society, and race marks all women. Women's relationships to institutional power and representation have been and are in part racially based. White women's failure to consider how white privilege offers European American women a different relationship to institutional power and representation than that to which women of color have access continues to undermine women's cross-racial relationships. Finally, in the context of racism and women's cross-racial relationships, white women are moral agents. We have been making racially significant choices for years.

European American feminism has always coexisted with racism. While white women occupied themselves with the issues of suffrage, women's roles in public and private spheres, and work conditions for women, white people forced American Indians into boarding schools, lynched African American men, prohibited the immigration of Asian American women and limited that of Asian American men, and exploited the labor of all women of color in menial work roles.

In short, white women have not always been allies of women of color in their struggle against racist and sexist oppression. As European American women began shaping and defining activism and the feminist movement, women of color were doing the same in their own communities. White women's participation in, ignorance of, and resistance toward racism as it has played out against women affects women's cross-racial relationships. For example, white women who banded together in the 1970s in local communities around issues of gender oppression in the context of the family rarely considered the racism women of color confronted every time they entered their workplace. This disregard for race necessarily affected how feminist consciousness-raising groups framed issues and addressed the issues of women of color or not.

In the late 1800s and early 1900s, relationships among women were particularly affected by race matters. The fight of disenfranchised groups to secure the vote demonstrates the complexities of women's relationships. As middle- and upper-class white women developed strategies to achieve suffrage, they intentionally and deliberately chose a policy of expediency. Under the leadership of Susan B. Anthony and Elizabeth Cady Stanton, white women suffragists sought to 'prove that the enfranchisement of White women would further, rather than impede, the power of a white ruling class that was fearful of Black and immigrant domination.'[3] White women knew that to gain the support of southern white men, they would need to speak publicly against granting the vote to all people of color.[4]

The European American practice of lynching was another point of tension among women of color and white women. African American women understood that European American men were responsible for the widespread lynching of African American men. African American women activists challenged white women to speak out against lynching. In recognizing white women's access to European American men, Mary Church Terrell encouraged white women to 'arise in the purity and power of their womanhood to implore their fathers, husbands, and sons [to] no longer stain their hands with the black man's blood.'[5] Unfortunately, this plea met with little if any response on the part of European American women.

Another example of the ways in which white women have made choices about their interactions with women of color is the response of white women to the concerns and priorities of American Indian women. One author points out that some American Indian women see white feminists as supporters of white supremacist and colonialist systems that oppress Indian women.[6] Devon A. Mihesuah states that while white feminists criticized the domestic roles assumed by American Indian women during the 1973 takeover at Wounded Knee, American Indian women were more concerned with 'combating racism' than with 'personal gain.' Despite the white feminist criticism, American Indian women were able to take 'charge of their lives.'[7]

In the late 1800s, two white women, Amelia Stone Quinton and Mary Lucinda Bonney, formed the Women's National Indian Association, which 'helped subsidize reservation schools and assisted older pupils in getting further education in the East.' These schools had particular goals that were specifically aimed at American Indian women, including conversion to Christianity and a curriculum that would '"uplift" American Indians to the standards of Anglo-Americans.'[8] In this case, even as white women may have become 'sensitized, in small ways, to the struggle of American Indians,'[9] they were active participants in denying American Indian people their language, culture, and connections with families.

Women's relationships have always developed within the rhythms and practice of choices squarely connected to race. Further, despite the good intentions of white women who now choose to interact with women of color, our history is heavy with missed opportunities. European American women failed to challenge slavery, boarding schools and other efforts to force assimilation on American Indians, unjust immigration policies, and the prevalence of women of color in domestic positions in the first half of the twentieth century, all historical processes that white people largely controlled. Feminist thought and movement never exist separately from the complications of race.

In more current contexts, how white women speak in organized and intentional ways against racism and sexism indicates our ability and willingness, or lack thereof, to forge cross-racial working relationships with women of color. What do we say and do about police brutality against people of color in the communities in which we live, about the high level of environmental toxins in neighborhoods in which people of color are the primary inhabitants, and about the low number of women of color in positions of power and influence in the institutions in which we work? White women interested in cross-racial work must learn to see feminism and feminist thought not as independent or pure entities, but as a set of choices embedded in the dynamics of racial difference and white supremacy.

The second point European American feminist scholarship on women, race, and history makes is that race privilege and race discrimination mark women's lives. For example, white women's almost total silence with respect to the lynching of African American men indicates our earlier willingness to accept blatant racism. It also marks our historic privilege. In the case of lynching, white men's choices and white women's near silence resulted in the deaths of African American men. European American women must acknowledge that the racial privileges historically afforded to white women, and our reluctance to acknowledge these privileges, have created a divide among white women and women of color.

It is also important to emphasize that white women have always been and are marked by our race as well as our gender. For example, white women who taught in American Indian boarding schools were appropriate teachers by virtue of both gender and race. As white women they would be able to communicate the moral and cultural guidance to American Indian students that white men desired them to teach.[10] Their racial identity also gave them concrete forms of power, both in terms of their own agency, and in terms of their relationship with people of color.

Finally, European American women have always made and continue to make choices that have racial implications. Given this reality, neutrality is impossible. In the case of suffrage, white women chose to seek the support of white southern men at the expense of allying themselves with women of color. Historically, European American women have not been powerless in regards to race and anti-racism; we have regularly faced choices about race, and in some cases, we made racist choices.

Women, History, and Race: Scholarship by Women of Color

Work by women of color on issues of history, race, and women contains both critical analyses of the histories and lives of U.S. people of color and challenges to the method and content of European American women's histories.[11] In addition to examining historical processes and dynamics, women of color demonstrate that any scholarly work that dismisses or ignores the relevance of the past is often overly simplistic. Theoretical work by women of color argues for the necessity of all scholarship to address the historical context in which an issue is embedded, and to view historical realities, events, and processes as operative within current structures of relationships. White feminists might ask ourselves: how does European American women's ignorance of race matters affect current cross-racial relationships among women? How does white women's refusal to systematically explore a history filled with racist choices contribute to a lack of trust among cross-racial groups of women?

History by women of color in the form of oral histories, biographies, autobiographies, interviews, fiction, collections of primary sources, personal narratives, anthologies, and historical monographs are all increasingly accessible in academic contexts.[12] This work theoretically and substantively challenges the ways in which European Americans represent history. It also challenges the ways in which European American women identify current racial dynamics among women. Women of color historians assert the centrality of multiplicity in women's histories, point out the relevance of conflict and disagreement in women's cross-racial relationships and in historical representation, and emphasize the theoretical significance of institutional and structural differences among women in representing women's histories.

Work by women of color examines the existence of multiple frameworks, perspectives, and understandings of the world. White women asserted that women tell history from their perspective; women of color urge that people in a variety of locations, including people of color, tell history. The acknowledgment of multiple directions encourages a focus on how those directions are related and on the dynamics of power relationships among women. Scholarship by women of color examines the historical intersections of privilege and discrimination among women. History is always histories, a variety of stories that are in dialogue with each other. If a historian writes about middle-class women, does she acknowledge that 'middle class women live the lives they do precisely because working class women live the lives they do?'[13] A history of cross-racial women's relationships in the first half of the 1900s might examine the structures of privilege that enabled European American middle- and upper-class women to hire women of color as domestic workers, and the socio-economic factors that afforded women of color few employment-related opportunities. Studies like this might encourage an analysis of power from many angles; history moves beyond simple constructions of all women compared to all men to contextual critiques that can illuminate the complicated layers of peoples' lives.

Marking the cross-currents of women's relationships with each other opens up history to conflict, disagreement, and competing agendas. If we write women's histories with an eye toward cross-racial conflict, the complications of women's relationships surface. The history of women does not emerge clean-cut and shiny, nor does it exist exclusively within a gender-based analysis, in which scholars compare large groups of women to large groups of men. Acknowledging conflict and disagreement among women adds a layer of ambiguity to current interactions among them. For example, once we realize that white women actively participated in attempts to deny American Indians their language, culture, spirituality, and familial connections, we may better understand why developing trust between cross-racial groups of women is often fraught with difficulty.

Much of the history of women continues to emphasize similarities among women rather than difference or disagreement. In other words, 'the rhetoric of community despite the reality of conflict' often obscures differences among women.[14] It is much easier and usually more satisfying for white women to speak about the general ability of all women to overcome oppression than to address how a Latina woman who cleans white women's homes overcomes the privilege of the white women whose homes she cleans. Even when an author addresses a particular group of women, thus choosing to be specific, it is rare to discover how women's historical choices affected other women, or how one woman's privilege is intimately linked to another woman's lack of privilege. In most European American women's scholarship, the histories of women of color come 'across as exotic or deviant, providing no clue to the larger history of American woman-hood.'[15] Fortunately, there are increasing numbers of exceptions to this tendency to avoid concrete attention to white women's historical racial agency and choices surrounding racial issues. Books and articles written in the last few years have begun to examine white women's participation as racial actors.[16]

Women of color historians clearly advocate a different way into the histories of women than most white women have chosen. Situating women's history on a male/female axis denies or pushes into the background the other lines that run through women's lives. Further, 'adding diversity in,' or making additions without changing the framework and method for writing history, 'merely sprinkles color on a white background.' In contrast, when history is written with an eye toward 'difference in social structural terms, in terms of interests, of privileges, and of deprivations,'[17] women are not only gendered, but represented in terms of race, class, and nation as well.

The scholarship by women of color on history and race, as well as the small but growing body of work by white women on white women's racial history, is instructive to European American feminists. For the most part, white feminism has been built on the idea that gender matters. Women experience life differently than men, suffer discrimination, and have a different view of reality and different routes to knowledge. Many European American feminists have come to these premises first hand through their own experiences. We have constructed theories and methodologies with extremely close and detailed attention to gender.

These theories and methodologies have shed light on how women live, and in turn, have turned a more critical eye toward how men live as well. At the same time, they have left women out. Further, as women of color have made plain what white feminism has left out, white women continue to respond from a position of defensiveness, distancing themselves from any possible oversight and exclusion. In defending our lack of analysis of differences among women, we might assert that European American men have had the most power, that white women could not change the structures that limited employment opportunities for women of color, or that European American women have had to deal with a considerable amount of gender oppression, rather than assessing the power, access to resources, and choices we have had and how we used them in ways that privileged us and potentially hurt people of color.

Likewise, when we have picked up the critique women of color offer, we have done so superficially, and rarely from a location of agency. We have been able to locate our oppression as women, but we have not, with a parallel commitment and thoroughness, located our-selves as white women who have the power to oppress. Ignoring the angles of race and class, or treating them with the same superficial attention of which we have accused white men of treating gender, flat-tens analyses of gender. All women, including European American women, live more than gendered lives. Writing about women as if only gender matters, or as if it matters the most, misrepresents how women live.

Too often, white women address race and history from a location of detachment. In considering white women in the suffrage movement, or their participation as teachers in boarding schools, when we choose to acknowledge their actions at all, we almost imagine their racism to be irrelevant. We can easily rationalize that their accomplishments supersede their oversights. Or, if we do acknowledge their racism, we might reason that 'they just didn't know ... they were products of their time and place ...' We are in no way like these women; we thoroughly deny any connection with them.

Analyses of whiteness and white supremacy for European American women can best begin from an understanding of racial agency. White people have a tremendous capacity for 'sympathy and yet distance.'[18] Once we acknowledge that race matters, it is far too easy to remove ourselves from the picture rather than struggle with our place in it. For example, it is common to hear pleas of 'that's not my fault,' 'isn't that all over,' and 'there's no way I'm going to shoulder all that history' from European Americans when anyone raises the historical compo-nents of cross-racial relationships.

This position does not support transformative scholarship or cross-racial work. It is much more difficult and rare for European Americans to accept the white privilege exercised by white people historically and to wrestle with the implications of a racist past for a cross-racial present. For example, it would be fairly exceptional for a white woman historian to consider the series of events and the mindset that led white women to invite African American men into their homes, and then led their husbands to lynch those men. In contrast, Patricia Carter's article on white women teachers in boarding schools does consider the moral relevance of white women's choices.

In the process of systematically shedding our connection to European Americans and racist choices, we (1) disconnect ourselves from a history that we need to claim and unravel for cross-racial work to occur; and (2) deny our own very specific and real relationship to historical and institutional white supremacy. But history is not over, and theoretical approaches to history affect current understandings of race. Racial history involves complex structures of power and discrimination, and women's history is racial. Anti-racist white feminist scholarship must be able to address racism in women's histories and its current relevance if our scholarship is to be meaningful to women of color. How do white people in the academy move beyond 'sympathy and yet distance' when it comes to matters of race? How do we consider the weight and import of racist choices made by white women in the past, what led up to these choices, and how these choices affected peoples' lives? How do we locate our own racial agency, and what does this location have to do with our scholarship?

Location of racial agency can serve as a link between racial present and past; it allows white women to address women's cross-racial histories from a position of being white, and from the inside of race. In the case of history, memory is a primary location of racial agency. Through memory, we understand our own racial past, and we can then begin to frame history through lenses that refract racial realities. That is, if I begin to thoroughly consider how my own socialization has racially marked my experiences and reality over time, I may be better able to understand that all of the choices white women made in their fight for the vote, or in their decision to teach in boarding schools, were in some way about race, and that these women exercised racial agency. The remainder of this chapter explores the relevance of memory to history, and more specifically, the ties between white racial memory and women's histories. Sustained and rigorous racial memory is a beginning for white people interested in anti-racist scholarship and in working relationships with people of color.

Race, Memory, and History

Anti-racist white feminist scholarship requires a closeness to both our race and our scholarship that the academy often eschews. This chapter articulates intentional racial memory[19] as one way for European Americans to move beyond 'sympathy and yet distance.' An awareness of the frameworks we use to understand race encourage understanding race and racism from the position of racial agency. Once our lenses for the past know white as racial, European Americans become active in racial dynamics. We know history through frameworks that make sense to us. The frameworks that hold racial layers of our past matter. If we cannot cast a critical racial eye on our own experience and knowledge, on which critical tools will we draw to understand the historical racial dynamics of others? If I cannot think carefully about my own experiences as a white person in a high school with a significant number of Mexican American students that was filled with racial tension (primarily related to white kids' provocation of the Mexican Americans and European American adults' intolerance of Mexican Americans), how will I ever understand any cross-racial history in ways that lead to cross-racial dialogue? If we cannot understand our own bodies as having racial significance and agency, how will we understand white people historically as racial agents who made intentional choices about race?

Racial memory, most simply, is how we remember race. Racial memory involves frameworks of interpretation that bring together current understandings of race with memories of racial situations. Racial memory involves the ways in which I bring forward the past in regard to race: the ways in which I remember a southern California suburb in which I grew up and the racial division of that suburb; the talk about an African American woman vice-principal at my high school; the friendship in college with an Asian-European woman within which I never once considered the relevance of her racial identity to her life and to our friendship. What I know and think about race now directly affects how I interpret all of these experiences.

Racial memory is centrally about how we locate race, including our own, in our negotiation of relationships and the choices we have made. Careful attention to our own racial memory draws us inside race and connects us to race history. How we frame race in our memory, and the ways in which we know our own history to be racial, in large part constitute the lenses through which we view racial history.

Memory is active in historical representations and dynamic in the construction of meaning.[20] Scholarship on memory complicates history. The relationship between the two is neither purely complementary nor oppositional. Likewise, memory connects us to history. Representations of race history are not separate from choices regarding racial memory. The ways in which European Americans remember our own racial significance affect our scholarship. White people who are able to discuss their own racial agency are more likely to see racial agency in other white people. Lack of critical awareness of racial memory on the part of European Americans sustains a convenient distance from race history and impedes, if not prohibits, anti-racist scholarship.

Recent scholarship on memory demonstrates the relevance of memory to history.[21] Historians 'actively engage in remembering and producing texts based on memory.'[22] Choosing to be intentional about our memory, to carefully and consistently consider how we know our past, can result in a changed understanding of history. Memory, more than simply making the past present, involves a process of developing frameworks of interpretation. In remembering, we rely on structures of meaning that make sense. If we change how and what we remember, and thus shift the frameworks for interpreting what we know, we will change how we know history.

For example, I might acknowledge that much of the tension in my high school, and indeed, what provoked the presence of the police on campus, was due to white boys verbally and sometimes physically taunting Mexican American students and white girls looking on. I might admit that this tension and the police presence was not due to the mere presence of Mexican Americans. If I can see this, I might think differently about, for instance, the conflict in Los Angeles following the Rodney King verdict. Identifying the role of white people in that tension at my high school enlarges and complicates the picture. The problem is not reduced to the presence of Mexican Americans, or the presence of Rodney King and people of color who protested the verdict. The problem expands to encompass issues of white verbal and physical taunting and institutional control. When European Americans remember our race and our whiteness, we interrupt that history of 'sympathy and yet distance.'

In academic contexts, distance between the knower and the object of knowing is widely accepted. When we choose distance, the academy readily approves of our knowing. We may be able to discuss the offensiveness of hate crimes, the injustice of racial profiling, and the destruction that occurred when white people forced American Indians into boarding schools. But when we assert our personal connection to our topic, import our compassion and conviction into the same academic space, there is a holding of breath, a collective question mark – 'Where is this going? How long will it take?' – and a desire to move on. In contexts of higher education, a discussion of racial profiling in our own community or neighborhood can be much more difficult than discussing the problem at national levels. Marking racism's destruction on located bodies, including our own, is messy.

In current discourse, 'the development of new modes of inquiry into memory has had the most direct effect on the one academic field traditionally privileged to tell the story of the past – history.'[23] Memory is not necessarily predictable, linear, logical, or rational. Memory is partial; it is useful (or not) 'as a tool to defend different aims and agendas.'[24] Connecting memory and history again raises the issue of agency. History is not a given; our choice of what and how to remember has moral implications for the history we tell. In a women's studies course, I can choose to remember the racism of white women or not.

Bringing together sites of memory with women's histories can demonstrate that knowing history through intentional memory reframes history, and that remembering race makes 'sympathy and yet distance' difficult. Current directions in memory studies profoundly complicate history. Ways in which scholars choose to care about the past matter. Memory and agency engage each other, reveal choices of interaction and their racial significance. Remembering my acceptance of my classmates' taunting may help me understand how European American women's endorsement of lynching was part of the problem. White people choose their memories and through that choice know history. In choosing how we know history, we variously position ourselves in relation to the lives and work of people of color. Memory, history, and our agency complicate the past and clamour for our attention. Negotiating memory, history, and agency is ethical and repels distance. Once I know that I make choices about race, it is difficult to deny the racial agency I possessed as a high school student and act on now.

Remembering Race

Remembering race is difficult. Considering race, analyzing its relevance, requires sustained effort. It is quite easy for me to simply forget, to dismember the pieces of my history that are racial from the history that is supposedly beyond race. For many European American scholars, race may not always be distant, but neither is it regularly close to our bodies; remembering race demands rigorous attention to the racial layer of bodies, politics, and scholarship. Lack of sustained racial memory is not quickly or easily corrected.

My history is racial. All of it, previously cast in the prevailing tone of 'I am white and therefore racially unmarked,' takes on different shades of meaning as I accept and acknowledge my own raciality. As I struggle with the significance of my racial memories, newly layered understandings recast my knowledge. What I know about myself, about history, about feminist theory, and about ethics increases in complexity. Shifted realities and more layered knowing complicate and alter my rhythms of learning. Working with the skin-quality of whiteness, its constant and permanent presence, changes history.

I know race history through racial memory. That is, how I remember race shapes my understanding of race history. It informs how I think about suffrage and slavery, forced assimilation, lost land and languages, the dynamics of domestic work, the expediency of exclusion acts, the indecency of internment camps and immigration laws, and about the resistance of people of color to all of these forms of oppression. Through my own racial memories, I demonstrate connections between memory and history, and reveal the limitations of understanding race history with 'sympathy and yet distance.'

At a small southern California high school in the mid-1980s, I am a student. I attend a high school where most of us are white and many are brown, in a suburban coastal community of under 50,000, which for the most part ignores the racial tensions that cause a quiet and steady static. As a high school senior, I sense the static but do not yet realize my place in its persistence.

I remember one afternoon when I am with a friend, Miguel, getting our pictures taken for the yearbook. Our class chose Miguel as the recipient of an award related to high-school achievement. Miguel, the person a family member asks about – 'Jennifer, how many of those Mexicans are at your school now?' Miguel, whose brown body contrasts to my white one, needs a ride home. I remember offering, without thought or hesitation, 'My mom can take you.' Suddenly, I am filled with anxiety. 'What have I done?!' The static fills my head, pushing out any pre-existing calm. A Mexican in the car with my white mom? Subtle and powerful lessons of bodies and belonging pour through me, filling me with discomfort that seems strangely out of place in my seventeen-year-old body on a sunny afternoon. I am alarmed by the implications of my offer in my white world. What will my white mom say? Unarticulated and not yet understood uneasiness suffuses my teenage body.

I remember my white mom driving up, her four-door car with plenty of room stopping in front of us, her familiar face smiling through the windshield. Before I tend to introductions, I rush at her with my words, funneling them through the square opening of the rolled-down window: 'Mom, can you take Miguel home?' I wait for her answer, aware of my rudeness, intensely upset by my own disease. Later, when my white mom asks, 'Why were you in such a hurry? You could have at least introduced us. Really, taking him home was no big deal,' I have no words. I stammer my frustration and confusion.

Six years later, I am standing in a farmers' market in Germany. It is a sunny Saturday morning, and the market is crowded and busy. The market is held in a neighborhood that is, in the last five to ten years, composed equally of people of color and white people, a neighborhood where white Germans assert their own racial prejudices publicly and without shame, by making claims, drawing lines, stating ownership. As I walk through the mix of people, vegetables, flowers, voices, bodies, sunlight, and crisp air, I hear clearly, sharply, as if the voice has a microphone hooked up to my speaker-ears: 'What are all these people doing at my market?'

I remember his words twisting into my Saturday morning, singular and still among movement. I turn around, look at a white German man with a white woman. I am standing there with him, noise and movement and color and business gone, leaving the plain crassness of his words, his body filled with the destruction of perceived ownership, my Saturday morning dissolved into his words and my hearing.

'What are all these people doing at my market?'

I stand there, still and silent, staring at his shadow and his words. I remember colors, bodies, movement, vegetables, business, the sunlight and the crisp air. I remember race hatred.

The border checkpoint about thirty miles north of my growing-up place carries a range of memories. I have been through that checkpoint, moving south to north, many times over the years, by myself, with friends, parents, and sisters, at night, in the morning, in cars and on Greyhound buses.

In my high school days, it was a place of slow passage through uniformed, mostly white men, eye contact, a wave, foot on accelerator and border check left behind. Side glances at vans, brown bodies, cars pulled over and uniformed, mostly white men searching. Foot on accelerator and brown bodies left behind.

I remember later, after college, passing through for the first time on a Greyhound. The bus stops, uniformed, mostly white men with guns move into my vision and pass through the narrow aisle, ask for driver's licenses, move on, tell several brown men to get off. I sit near the too-close aisle, show my license, drop my eyes to the gun that is now level with my vision. Foot on accelerator and memories braked in my travels.

Southern California border check appears, during my graduate work, in my midwestern present. The news is full of stories about bodies bolting across freeways, about cars meeting bodies, about drivers killing brown people, about vans, chased by Immigration and Naturalization Service officials, careening out of control and more dead bodies. I swallow hard, remember growing up, beach and ocean, freeway, cars, braking and accelerating. I wonder about the choice to move, about the choice to drive on that freeway to work, to shop, to visit, about cars moving, driving, smashing into moving bodies trying to find safety.

In the early 1990s, Claudia Smith worked for the immigrant rights group, California Rural Legal Assistance. In her work, she had to cross through border checks. She said of immigrants running across the freeway, 'They are disoriented. They are tired. And they are crossing sixteen lanes of freeway. It's a terrible situation. I won't drive down the freeway to San Ysidro now. I take the train instead.'[25]

I return to southern California, and after news of bolting bodies and careening cars, I again get in a car and choose to drive on that freeway. I remember driving, moving on the freeway, going south to north, accelerating with side views of hills and ocean. I sit in unresolved tension, with sharp memories that brake and accelerate independently of my feet. I try to shift my mind to other topics, to move my memory away from border checks and people from south of the border who die on this freeway.

Foot on accelerator, I notice new side views: the government has installed signs of men, women, and children, hands together, running. Black bodies on a yellow square, posted on the freeway so that drivers like myself will consider the possibility of braking for bodies and not only for border checks.

I remember growing up, traffic, ocean, beach, hills, braking, side views of brown bodies, searches, a wave, and accelerating. My foot grows tired, weighted, jerks. My memory hangs, suspended between braking and accelerating and certain of the need to make contact.

Remembering these stories as racial is a choice. Understanding myself as white and placing myself inside these racial narratives affects how I know race history.[26] It is memories of Miguel, of sunlight and crisp air and race hatred, of border checks and signs of moving bodies that make distance difficult. It is the knowledge that in all these memories, my whiteness matters, that changes history. Structures of racism exist because white supremacy makes white bodies superior to all bodies of color.[27] Race history, then, is the history of white bodies. Racial memory is one way into that history which acknowledges layered understandings of white bodies. I am white, and my history is racial.

Remembering my own growing up in light of race, thinking through the racial layers of my own choices, establishes a relationship between my white body and race matters. When I know race as a reality that lives under my skin, instead of only as a contrast to what I am not, a person of color, I situate myself as active in the daily negotiations of race privilege and race discrimination. Locating myself as a racial agent supports an understanding of history in which white people are racial agents. When I know the meaning of my own white skin, I use a different lens to view history. Locating my discomfort with Miguel in my white mother's car on my self, rather than on Miguel, opens up the possibility of viewing race history from the location of white privilege and white racial agency.

The thought of Miguel sitting in the car with my white mom scared me. That fear was rooted in race ideology that ascribes certain rules to raced bodies. Ida B. Wells-Barnett's investigation of the charges of lynching white people brought against African American men illuminates that ideology. While the white press reported rape as the most frequent cause of lynching, Wells-Barnett found that of 728 lynchings in a ten-year period, only one-third of the victims of mob violence had been charged with rape. Of this one-third, many of the so-called rapes 'had actually been affairs between consenting adults.'[28] White people understood African American men in white spaces as criminal, even as European Americans invited the presence of those African American men. Knowing my own racial marks offers me a different way to consider race matters, pushes forward a different set of questions. In the negotiation of power that is race privilege and race discrimination, I am willing to confront the patterns of being white, the ways in which I assume and act on a belief in my own white supremacy.

For example, when I consider southern white women's discomfort with black women's participation in and presence at women's rights meetings and conventions, how do I choose to enter this history? In 1919, the Northeastern Federation of Women's Clubs, a group of black women's organizations, applied to the National American Women Suffrage Association (NAWSA) for status as a cooperative member. Fearing the loss of the support of Southern Democratic congressmen, Carrie Chapman Catt immediately tried to 'persuade the black federation to withdraw its application.'[29] In 1894, Susan B. Anthony asked Frederick Douglass not to be present at the NAWSA meeting; 'Anthony claimed that Douglass' attendance would be an embarrassment for him as well as for the southern suffragists.'[30] What kinds of values and priorities fueled Catt's decision? How do remnants of Catt's practices continue to inform current European American feminist movement and thought?

These historical events, read with an awareness of race ideology, illustrate that white is a race, and that white people have always defined black/color/racial other in connection with white as racial norm. The existence of white as norm, and the power whites retain as definers, allows for the possibility of understanding white as universal and beyond race rather than as racially significant in itself. In other words, '[Whiteness] is a subject that asserts its centrality or dominance on social and cultural levels yet remains shrouded within a veil of transparency that ensures its absence, thus evading the subject of discourse.'[31] The cross-racial history of women in the United States can be read as realities shot through with racial dynamics, or not. European American scholars writing women's histories choose how to read race, and how to identify the racial layers of women's histories.

Remembering Miguel and my fear reminds me that I am white, and that white bodies are racial players. It is through my memory of Miguel and my fear that I remember I cannot understand the layers of race from a distance. Race is a construct inscribed on bodies. Knowing race as disembodied fact misses its materiality.

'What are all these people doing at my market?' The perceived and lived power of owning space, excluding people, and defining boundaries echoes in my head and I stand in that market still in my uncertainty, stopped by my knowledge that his words are not isolated. The perception of ownership, of the power to draw racial and racist lines, does not end at idea or notion. 'My market' assumptions are not far removed from European American women's assumption that we own feminism, that women of color must step into our constructions of feminism if we are to view their work as valid and as part of feminist theory.[32] The perception of ownership intrudes into present race relations; it is present in the assumption by a white woman that a Latin

American woman in her class will teach her, in the choice of a white student to talk to a white professor about academic concerns and to an African American professor about personal problems, in white scholars identifying any woman of color in ivory-towered halls as a cleaning woman and not a tenured professor.[33]

Such assumptions on the part of European Americans are common and they are always problematic. When white women do become interested in race, we often expect the nearest U.S. woman of color to educate us at our convenience. These expectations construct women of color as always available for the needs of white people and underestimate the difficulty of learning about race. Discussing academic concerns with white professors and saving personal problems for women of color emerges from and sustains the stereotype of all women of color as the caretakers of white women. Finally, the common identification by whites of U.S. people of color in academic hallways as custodians reveals a conceptual framework that has little space for U.S. people of color as scholars and knowers.

As I consider race history, puzzle through the politics of owning, excluding, and defining, my eyes crowd out color and business and difference and focus in on one white German man saying, 'What are all these people doing at my market?' I know I have a place in his question and beyond, know that I act on 'my market' assumptions. Memories of driving, of braking and accelerating, of ocean and beach and brown bodies, actively draw together history, memory, and the present. The contours of my memory trace along the crucial intersections of current immigration struggles, bring together pieces of lives that insistently overlap. Bringing together racial memory with racial present complicates race history. Remembering Miguel and my fear reveals 'my market' assumptions and my own enactment of racial borders.

Race history is not tidy, easy, or simple. Like memories of Miguel and fear, women's racial histories are often about white supremacy interrupting lives, moving through cars and borders and filling the intimacies and intricacies of human relationships. Remembering Miguel and my fear keeps racial history close. As my memory hangs suspended between braking and accelerating and certain of the need to make contact, remembering my own body as raced and my history as racial is one place to begin. Through the stories recounted below, I see myself inside race, remember myself as white and my history as racial, differently frame white women's histories, and consciously and critically understand race history through the intentional location of racial memory.

The Layered Memory of Minerva Blue

In Paulette Childress White's short story entitled 'Getting the Facts of Life,' twelve-year-old Minerva Blue, an African American girl, takes her first trip to the welfare office. On a sweltering summer morning, Minerva volunteers to accompany her mother when none of her other siblings seem eager to go. The walk there is hot and quiet, through racially segregated neighborhoods, past 'bad boys and drunks' and 'perfect-looking houses.'[34]

By the time of Minerva's first trip to the welfare office, the Blue family has been on welfare for one year. Minerva points out, 'I didn't have any strong feelings about it – my life went on pretty much the same.' Yet when they turn the corner and she sees the Department of Social Services, Minerva 'discovered some strong feelings. That fine name meant nothing. This was the welfare. The place for poor people. People who couldn't or wouldn't take care of themselves. Now I was going to face it ... I looked at Momma for comfort, but her face was closed and her mouth looked locked.[35] After three hours, during which 'White ladies dressed like secretaries kept coming out to call numbers,' Mrs. Blue's number is called. At the urging of the white woman employee, and to the disapproval of Mrs Blue, Minerva accompanies her mother through 'the maze' and into a room where 'the woman sat behind the desk and we before it.' Minerva waits through prying questions, watches her mother hold onto dignity, and witnesses a ritual of paternalism and attempted demoralizing. Her mother must fight for shoes and winter coats, must shop where the woman dictates, and must endure the white woman's lecture on family planning. Through all this, Minerva reflects, 'I felt bodyless – there was only my face, which wouldn't disappear, and behind it one word pinging against another in a buzz that made no sense.' When the white woman asks, '"This is Minerva?,"' the twelve-year-old girl-becoming-woman resists, 'No. I thought, no, this is not Minerva. You can write it down if you want to, but Minerva is not here.'[36]

On the walk home, Minerva 'wanted to cry or run or kiss the dusty ground' as they reach the black part of town. She asks for stories of when her mother grew up, a time of generous gardens and Alabama girlhood. As Minerva and Mrs Blue walk through the groups of men who often offer wisecracks and 'hollers,' Minerva thinks, 'I supposed they could see in the way we walked that we weren't afraid. We'd been to the welfare office and back again. And the facts of life, fixed in our minds like the sun in the sky, were no burning mysteries.'[37]

Minerva has learned about race and class, about girlhood and living as a woman. The insides of a welfare office and hard truths of segregated neighborhoods are 'no burning mysteries.' Minerva has taken in the power of a welfare system that holds the keys to school clothes, shoes, and winter coats. She sees that the employees are white, and that the people waiting are white and black and 'somehow they all looked familiar.'[38] On this particular August morning, Minerva learns about access and money, about prying questions and responses that preserve integrity.

Paulette Childress White constructs a girl whose memory is intensely aware of being black, poor, and a girl. Minerva understands that race, class, and gender matter in her life. She knows the realities of being black, poor, and a girl, and at the same time, she feels the crosscurrents of those who live life white, middle class, as boys, and later as men. Living with a changed memory, with close-up knowledge of welfare office truths, of white women who look like they 'never crack a smile,' of fear that in a room of poor people, she is noticed, Minerva is not afraid. She has 'been to the welfare office and back again.'

Minerva's memory is indelibly marked. Just as my memory could not reconcile the fact of Miguel in the car with my white mom, Minerva is shaping a way to navigate through her world, a way to understand past and present. The stories we carry from our past continue to shape us. I did not have to learn about welfare offices. I did not learn about race from the side of discrimination, like Minerva did. I grew up with different lessons than Minerva's.

Now, I choose how I know race. I choose to acknowledge what I never learned and do not know, choose to engage with the significance of a history of unquestioned white privilege, however uncomfortable that engagement may prove. I choose how I locate myself within the rhythms of race, how I tend to the lessons I never learned, how I confront my race and class assumptions. I choose, after reading about Minerva and her trip to the welfare office, how to know my own past, how to remember my history and feel my race and class marks. Antiracism requires a choice to work at knowing the inside of our race. I hold out my hands, grasping for pieces of history and memory and the lives that run throughout both.

Shifting Stories, Remaking Memories

Making connections between routine cross-racial interactions, memory, history, and cross-racial relationships between people in the academy is rarely simple. A privilege of whiteness is that inconsistent and even non-existent racial memory is not often experienced as immediate loss.[39] Understanding ourselves outside of race, as unraced, constructs a framework in which intentional distance from racial memory makes sense.[40] It is easy for white people to picture ourselves without race. But when European Americans seek to understand history about race without an intentional knowledge of racial memory, we approach history from a detached location. We seek to know race history with little or no conscious attention to our own racial memory.

This kind of knowledge-practice raises ethical and epistemological issues. If ethics is how we choose to be together, the we always variously constructed, knowing history is an ethical issue: we choose how we construct the together of past and present. Thinking through border battles, Latinos in the car with my white mom, and 'What are all these people doing at my market' ideologies, can be done from a variety of locations. White privilege immediately locates me inside race even if I do not notice that placement.[41] The ways in which I choose to be conscious of that privilege, to critically examine the meaning of my racial marks, and to carefully consider my own racial significance, is ethical. Anti-racism requires that we remember our race.

The following accounts of two parallel events at a predominantly female Saturday evening gathering in Chicago demonstrate the tangle of memory and history, the twin realities of race privilege and discrimination, and the difficulties of cross-racial relationships among women. An examination of the subtleties of in/separable stories, and of performances of women's agency, demonstrates that racial memory among whites is very often a denial of the ramifications of raciality. Racial memory and race history are connected, and anti-racist practice demands that we consider the complications of that connection.

A story, version number one:
I am in Chicago, the North Side, on a Saturday night in April 1995. A group of people, mostly white women, are relaxed, and socializing. A woman approaches a white friend and me; before we leave, she wants to talk to us about immigration issues. A few minutes later, she returns. A friend of a friend wants to immigrate to the United States. Her eyes

move back and forth between us; she wonders if either of us know anything about legal issues and procedures.

My roommate and I do know some things, and we are glad to offer what we can. Eva is German; she has had to negotiate her right to be in the United States. Visas do not last forever and the elusive green card has proven an ongoing and difficult project. We are eager to help, to offer information that was hard for us to find. We promise to send her more about ways to immigrate, and we say goodnight.

A story, version number two, told to me by a friend, the Monday following the Saturday night:

'Saturday night, Rhonda and I were standing there. Jan comes up to us – you know Jan, right? – and looking straight at me – the whole time – asks if we know anything about immigration. I couldn't believe it! – why did she have to look only at me?

'I told her no, and pointed her over to you and Eva. You know, at the time, Rhonda and I didn't immediately realize exactly what was going on. But when we started talking about it, it hit me: there's something wrong with this picture. She assumed that because I look Asian, I'm the one who must be immigrating! I'm still shocked at her assumption. Jennifer, some white people are so clueless. Even in Chicago in 1995.'

The second version of the stories happened first. In a gathering of about fifty people, a white woman, having been told that two people in the room had been dealing with immigration, approached another white woman and an Asian American woman. Looking only at the Asian American woman, she asked about immigration. The Asian American woman explained to the white woman that she did not know anything about immigration, and pointed her over to two white women. I was the second choice in that play solely because of my skin color. Until I heard the first part of the story at work, I had not conceived of how the situation might involve race.

I had no knowledge of the second story until Monday morning at work. In my memory, the first story that I experienced was self-contained, without extensions, bordered by a beginning and an end of which I was aware. When my Asian American friend came to work and told me her memory of that Saturday night, I remember the feeling of new knowledge, of a wider view of my friend's reality, and of what it had to do with my own. Positioned between two stories, feeling the fit of the first and surprise of the second, I began to consider the distance between our experiences of that evening. I realized I had easily assumed race was absent in a conversation I had with two other white women about immigration. In fact, race was always present in that conversation. How do I make room for memories and histories I have learned to leave out, exclude, and deny?

I have constructed my racial memory of Asian American lives out of concrete socio-historical realities, pressed on by uninterrupted stereotypes and assumptions, and at times my own choice of inattention to ongoing miseducation.[42] Understanding the connection between memory and history requires a knowledge of history, and attention to that which schools, the media, and our own learning misrepresent and ignore. In between those two stories are common representations of Asian Americans, immigration history concerning Asian Americans, and current immigration politics. In between those two stories are the differences in the life of my friend and my own life. In between those two stories are connections between memory and history, between my mind and body ignorance and her mind and body knowledge, and between the choice to ignore and the ethics of learning. In between those two stories is a lesson in race, memory, and women's histories.

Racism: Behind My Back, Outside of My Vision, Beyond My Memory

Racism.
Behind my back
outside of my vision
beyond my memory   racism.

Sitting between two stories, the
skin-quality of my whiteness
sticks me in the sides.

Behind my back/outside of my vision/beyond my memory
         racism
    slips by
    snickers behind my back
    snidely wraps around my body

My friend, forced to explain
My body, ignorant and undisturbed.
Behind my back
    outside of my vision
         beyond my memory

         racism   stares at me.

The racism behind my back, outside of my vision, beyond my memory: these three metaphors aptly demonstrate the location of race in my learning and socialization. As on that Saturday evening, racism in its most blatant forms is behind my back. I do not have sufficient skills to see race or to conceive of its varieties. Living life white encourages a racially unexamined life.[43] The Saturday night left me comfortable and unbothered. My whiteness resulted in assumptions that disturbed my friend but not me. Whiteness is the 'shape [of] white women's lives ... a location of structural advantage ... a "standpoint" ... [and] a set of cultural practices that are usually unmarked and unnamed.'[44] By the time a conversation between three white women played itself out, a white woman had already made 'unmarked and unnamed' cultural assumptions about my Asian American friend. My standpoint as a white person ensures that many racial situations play out literally and figuratively 'behind my back.' They play out in locations to which I, as a matter of course, do not have immediate access.

The racism behind white peoples' backs is a crucial element of whiteness and affects our knowledge of racial history. No matter how much white people learn about race and racism, we are not constantly faced with the possibility of 'in our face' race discrimination. Because whiteness continues to go 'unmarked and unnamed,' knowing the racial importance of white bodies is difficult. A limited understanding of current white bodies as racial leads to a similarly limited understanding of racial history. That Saturday night, I did not notice the racism that happened. My lack of awareness is a result of my racial history and affects my racial memory. Whiteness imposes limits on our knowledge that anti-racist scholarship must address.

Racism lives behind my back in part because my vision is inadequate. The history I have learned has not tended to the rhythms of race. My whiteness has not required careful attention to history, concerning matters racial, left out.[45] My whiteness enables a race/d history that practices 'selective hearing, creative interpreting, complicitous forgetting.'[46] The history I do not know allows me to ignore issues always present, including my whiteness. What I do not know does matter.

Unlearned or mislearned history results in an incomplete understanding of racial stories. That Saturday night, my racial memory ruled out the possibility of the story of my friend. I too quickly envisioned my history and memory as adequate preparation for understanding the stories and histories of race. On a Monday at work, I realized my limited racial memory was connected to my lack of knowledge concerning immigration history in this country. Questioning my whiteness means revisiting my history. Questioning my whiteness requires careful attention to which kind of memory I sustain on which subjects, and to how I remember. My own politics of memory did not make room for my Asian American friend.

The Chinese Exclusion Act, 1882; the Gentlemen's Agreement Act, 1907; the Asian-Indian Immigration Act, 1917; the Oriental Exclusion Act, 1924; the Tydings-McDuffie Act, 1934. United States government officials and legislators prohibited all Asian immigration to this country from 1924 through 1943. From 1943 to 1965, U.S. law based Asian immigration on a quota system. From 1956 to the present, the United States has dictated strict per-country limits.[47] All of this is women's history; all of this is history left out of my schooling, relegated to 'recommended reading.'

Public officials based immigration law on demand for cheap labor, and ensured that racism had strong links to particular bodies. European Americans targeted Asian women as sexually exotic and subservient and stereotyped Chinese women as prostitutes. Consequently, immigration officials assumed all Asian females came to the United States to engage in criminal behavior. This history persists, affecting not only Asian Americans but also ways in which European Americans view all people of Asian descent. Cheng Imm Tan writes,

> As Asian Americans and Asian immigrants, both our humanness and our oppression have been concealed. Our reality is rarely alluded to, let alone confirmed. We live in a country where the way we see ourselves and the way we experience the world is seldom reflected in images we see or the stories we read. We constantly have to translate information in order to have it make sense, or to apply it to our own experience. A big part of who we are is always being denied, because there is 'no space,' no understanding, no welcoming of our differences. We are then expected to conform to established norms and rules of being and behaving that do not include one that reflect who we really are.[48]

Given this history, a variety of myths likely visited my friend that night. My lack of historical awareness contributed to a memory that left absolutely no room for her reality. When I take stock of my own awareness of Asian American women, I know it is scattered, piecemeal, often shallow knowledge. White people commonly stereotype

Asian American women as immigrant, model minority, subservient, obedient, quiet, exotic, other. A white woman assumed my friend was necessarily immigrant and alien, stereotyped other. By not choosing to talk to me first about immigration, she assumed my white body belonged, was normal, fit in. Women's histories are complicated and full of conflict.

Specific memories and histories are in place when people, primarily European American, complain about immigration of people from Latin America, Asia, or Africa. The white woman choosing to approach an Asian American woman first when she had a question regarding immigration drew on certain memories and specific historical knowledge. I relied on selective memory and history when I concluded that a quick exchange about immigration between three white women was not racial. All memory and history are partial, selective, and limited.[49] U.S. women's cross-racial history can be read as realities shot through with racial dynamics, or not. White scholars writing women's history choose how to read race and how to identify women as different.[50]

Anti-racist scholarship requires shifting stories and remaking memories. Immigration law instructs race politics. Asia makes up 60 per cent of the world population and 39 per cent of immigrants to the United States. Africa constitutes 12 per cent of the world population and 3 per cent of immigrants to the United States. Europe is 9 per cent of the world population and 18 per cent of the immigrants to the United States. Statistics also demonstrate that for every two Asian immigrants to the United States, there is one immigrant from Europe, Canada, or Australia.[51] The ratio of Asian: European/Canadian/Australian immigrants is two to one. In a room of approximately fifty people, with two Asian Americans and forty European Americans, the odds are 10 to one that the immigrant will be *white*.

My history resulted in a memory that had no room for race. It took a second story to place race squarely in my line of sight. The connection of what I know about racism past, racism present, and racism in the making is crucial. What I cannot imagine, that to which I cannot make reference, inhibits my understanding of the racism around me and the whiteness I embody, relegates both to behind-my-back spaces.

Anti-racist scholarship requires white people to reshape their memories, to learn the makings of their whiteness. European American memories for realities racial, for race privilege and race discrimination, are often undeveloped, immature, and lack a required sophistication.

European American racial memories sustain 'sympathy yet distance.' Anti-racist scholarship requires a memory that knows how to read whiteness, that hears the racism snickering behind our backs, feels it sticking us in the sides, and sees racism where it tries to hide, unnoticed and unmarked in white vision.

In the context of cross-racial work among women in the academy, remembering and memory must be intentional acts of resistance. This kind of memory must be explicitly concerned with shifting stories.[52] To enable people to work together cross-racially, European Americans must begin to attend to their race history and racial memories. In the first story, my memory was inadequate to imagine the possibility of race. It was the memory of an Asian American friend that challenged my own, that stretched my images so that race was not relegated to 'other.' It was the memory of an Asian American friend that brought the story full circle.

A memory that tends to the intricacies and intractability of race does not happen by chance, especially if the shaper of that memory is white. Unlike Minerva Blue, I did not need race realities carved into my memory. 'Whiteness' needed no special instructions, no planned-out protection, no reservoir of refined responses to race discrimination. Because I have only recently regretted the turning of my back and the narrowness of my vision, my memory for racial realities is restricted. In order to shift our memory, we must carefully and critically acknowledge and assess a history of turned back and limited vision. Not only have many white people been intellectually miseducated, we have lived inattentive to the rhythms of race. We have not been trained to sense, perceive, feel the dynamics of race discrimination or the politics of privilege. I have never had to explain my whiteness, to clarify my raced condition. This makes my history and memory significantly different from that of my Asian American friend and other people of color.

A primary and unequivocal requirement for whites interested in anti-racist scholarship is that we actively work on learning race history. We cannot assume that any institution, educational, media, political or religious, will offer knowledge about historical racial dynamics that fairly or adequately represents the histories of the peoples involved in that history from their perspectives. Further, it is rare for European Americans to read history that fundamentally understands white people as racial agents. White people have written history, for the most part, as if European American choices are never racial. We can thus nearly always assume that the historical knowledge presented in most structured academic environments on race is insufficient. Most of my own learning on issues related to race and the histories of people of color and the racial history of European Americans has not taken place in traditional academic environments. Teachers rarely offer history written by people of color to support cross-racial dialogue, and almost never draw on history by whites that assumes that European Americans are always racial actors. Cross-racial feminism will move forward only when white feminists acknowledge their own lack of historical racial knowledge and choose to work at addressing that lack of information.

It is significant that my Asian American friend helped me to change my memory. Most women of color have no reason to tell us their stories. In an article about slave narratives, Melvina Johnson Young writes that a common feature of black life, especially in her growing-up years in the south, was that African Americans 'did not reveal [their] true self to white people because if [white people] did not like what they saw, they had a very real power to harm you.' Or as former slave Ishrael Massie told a black interviewer, 'Lord chile, if ya start me I kin tell ya a mess 'bout reb [rebel] [sic] times, but I ain't tellin white folks nuthin' 'cause I'm skeered to make enemies.'[53] Finally, in a conversation with a Latina, I heard, 'Women of color are privileged to information white women will never know. So white women must mark themselves ...'[54] Even though we are in a different 'day an' time,' white women have done little to earn the trust of women of color. Racism has paid so many visits to their bodies, there is too great a chance that my white body will continue the racist pattern.

'... and says she needs to talk to the two of us ... Looking straight at me – the whole time – says, "Aren't you the ones with immigration problems?" ... Why did she have to look only at me?' The risk taken by an Asian American friend became my learning. I could easily have responded, 'Are you sure she was really just looking at you? Maybe it just seemed that way. And, I mean, it makes sense that she thought you were immigrating ... Don't a lot of Asian Americans immigrate?' Such comments, perhaps defensive in tone, may have immediately brought an end to our conversation. My memory changed when an Asian American woman told me her memory of Saturday night. Entering the histories of women and the power of racial memory is difficult and complicated. Acting as moral agents in understanding women's cross-racial history requires active consideration of our racial memories and our scholarship. Moving beyond 'sympathy yet distance,' living with the relevance of the history of white women's racism to the present of women's cross-racial relationships in the academy, requires an ethics of remembering.

An Ethics of Remembering

Scholarship that chooses to remember race is profoundly and substantively different from that which does not.[55] Even as I did not know the existence of the second story, my Asian American friend will likely not forget the offense of one white woman's question. Behind my back, outside of my vision, and beyond my memory racism affects cross-racial relationships among women. Too-small memories exclude, ignore, and misrepresent women's lives. Racially unaware memories deny the complexities always present in white women's lives. White women's racial memories are intricately and intimately connected to their relationships with women of color, and to the quality and shape of their own scholarship.

Racial memory is important for white women because racism exists and because we routinely and regularly make racial choices. It is convenient for European American women to cite the growing body of scholarship by women of color, the increasing attention to women of color by white women, and the slight presence of women of color in the academy as students and teachers as evidence that 'things are getting better.' Very often, this kind of thinking carries an underlying hope that we can get beyond race, or more plainly, return to business as usual. Despite real and important changes, racism, specifically among feminists in the academy, persists. Further, a history of racism among women, over centuries and pressed into the bodies and psyches of all women, guarantees a depth to racism that is never simply or quickly solved. But changed scholarship by white women, when it pays more adequate attention to race, is a beginning.

Racial memory is necessary because racism persists. Manju S. Kurian recounts the following experience:

> In graduate school, it [the presence of racism] is no better; I am still holding control on the fringe. In one seminar, we were studying Harriet Beecher Stowe's *Uncle Tom's Cabin*. The white-haired, white-skinned male professor asked the white woman presenting on the book whether or not the character George should go back to Africa. She said she did not know,

maybe he should go back where he came from. To her, she said, it sounded 'kind of racist.'

'Kind of racist,' I thought, 'Kind of racist?' How can something be 'kind of racist?'[56]

'Kind of racist' points to a luxury of distance European Americans often choose when it comes to racism. 'Kind of racist' reduces the seriousness of the charge, lightens the burden of a word that threatens us with its weight. 'Kind of racist' results in a reality that does not stick, that rolls off our backs and leaves us feeling lighter and less confused. 'Kind of racist' supports a memory too small for people of color. Kurian continues, 'To deny the existence of racism is an evasive, self-protective action. We do not want to believe that such a hate-filled process exists. Racism exists. I know because I exist, and I have been its victim. To deny its presence is to deny what I have suffered.'[57] Ideologies embedded in the white woman's response are not only significant because they mark suffering. The flip side of Kurian's suffering is the white woman's privilege; the two, race discrimination and race privilege, are always connected. Knowing our own participation in racial matters and that racism exists moves white people inside of race, demands a racial memory that acknowledges the existence of racism and that white women's histories are racial.

Scholarship that aims to be anti-racist must acknowledge memory, must move through racial memory to race history. European Americans are white and our history is racial. Denying our own raciality results in shallow history and skewed scholarship. The ability of white feminist scholarship to be anti-racist depends in part on our ability to construct racial memory.

Remembering requires movement. It is 'potent; once its force is unleashed and the status quo named fetid and stagnant, the rememberer is implicitly charged to move forward in the bright light which says responsibility is yours now. Move.'[58] It requires movement away from harmonious ideas of women, away from apolitical border checks, away from fear of brown bodies in the car with my white mom, and away from 'my market' mentalities: '... responsibility is yours now. Move.'

Moving into racial memory encourages entering race dynamics from a position of racial agency. Race is never other. It is ourselves. Race history, then, is the negotiation of choices and relationships in which we always have a part. Racial agency builds on approaching racism with a sense of accountability and responsibility, and with knowledge of the white supremacy that continues to permeate our own choices, despite our best intentions.

A racial memory sufficient to sustain anti-racism on the part of white people requires at least three layers. All three layers call for intentionality, hard work, and long-term commitment. Shaping racial memory is an ongoing process, not a one-time event. White people interested in anti-racism must examine our knowledge of race history that is written down. We must think through the history we have learned and the limits of what we have not. A second layer of racial memory is critical awareness of our own racial past. Careful attention to the racial contours of the past supports a located understanding of race history, encourages connection rather than detachment. Finally, developing a racial memory that can sustain anti-racism requires listening to and reading the work by people of color in one's own context. These three layers, creatively and constructively working together and sustained over time, can support an ethics of remembering and anti-racist practice.

Attention to Knowledge of Race History

Knowers choose history; all history is selective.[59] The process by which historians and other scholars write the lives of people, and the choice of which and whose history to read, involves politics and preference. The academy has reluctantly acknowledged that historians have largely constructed written history according to the politics and preferences of a few European American men, and that the result has been a lack of representation or misrepresentation of women's histories and of men's histories as well. History has similarly been racially exclusive.[60] Scholars have often glossed over the struggles and resistance of the lives of people of color. Especially in recent years, scholars of history have begun to acknowledge that history is selective and that selection of what counts as history worth reproducing to a certain extent determines what teachers legitimize as knowledge.[61]

Scholars produce knowledge about history, and that production is selective and variable. Constructing racial memory requires an awareness that people produce specific histories and that history does not simply and purely exist. It demands attention to the ways in which knowers choose their own historical knowledge. In as much as professors assign readings, and students choose paper topics, bibliographic sources, and classes, people in the academy by and large determine whose history we read. Because histories are always racial, people in the academy choose racial knowledge.

Knowing race history is only a part of constructing racial memory. Especially for white feminists, a broad and in-depth understanding of cross-racial history among women may not yet be in place. Ignorance with respect to the racism of European American suffragists, the labor history of women of color and working-class white women, and the race discrimination people of color experience daily and as a matter of course and often in interactions with European Americans, is not necessarily an issue. The academy, and white feminists, continue to legitimize historical knowledge that is blatantly unaware of and inattentive to the lives and histories of women of color as well as working-class women. In many scholarly circles, this kind of ignorance does not matter and is not an issue.[62]

Ethical remembering, in the context of cross-racial work among women in the academy, requires acknowledging that the interconnections of women's lives do matter. Because history often emphasizes events over processes, and individuals over networks of people, identifying and understanding women's cross-racial historical connections is difficult. Learning the histories of women of color is one beginning. Reading books and articles by and about women of color expands the knowledge of white women, and can displace women's history with histories. Reading historical work by women of color can begin to fill in gaps in the knowledge of European American feminists, and can move us closer to the racial layers of women's histories. Cross-racial work among women in the academy requires at the least a recognition of the variety and depth of women's histories, and acknowledgment that knowledge of only white women's history leads to a shallow and skewed representation of women's lives.

Critical Awareness of Our Own Racial Pasts

A second crucial layer of remembering, of working at mutual relationships with people of color and attending to our own scholarship, is the development of ongoing critical awareness of our own lives. Knowing white as a race and European American history as racial supports a rethinking of our own past, a revisiting of memories that may have seemed outside of race. Remembering white lives as racial can gradually draw European Americans inside of race. When European Americans work at memory, we may pass through raced borders of which we have too long imagined ourselves outside.

A critical awareness of our own racial past encourages white people to understand their bodies as marked by race. For European American feminists, knowing our bodies as racial complicates acontextual theories and interrupts scholarship that is conscious of gender but not of race. Knowing our bodies as racial challenges simplistic representations of women, and makes difficult scholarship on women that ignores race.

When white people remember their race, they cease to perceive anti-racism as charity work. European Americans often approach cross-racial dialogue with people of color in order to better the lives of people of color. We rarely understand our own participation in these groups as a means to critiquing and examining our own lives and choices.[63] When I remember the fear I felt at the idea of Miguel in the car with my mom, I am more likely to know that racism is my problem and anti-racism my responsibility, and necessary for my own well-being.

Constructing racial memory requires an awareness of our past, of matter-of-course white privilege, and of the ways in which white lives are regularly and routinely raced. White is a race, and white history is racial. The ways in which we acquire an understanding of that statement affect our racial memory, our relationships with people of color, and our own work in the academy.

Recognition of People of Color in Local Contexts

A third prerequisite for cross-racial work is attention to and respect for people of color in our midst. If European Americans cannot communicate about racism with the people of color in our classrooms, across the lunch table, at conferences or as colleagues, there is little chance that we will feel any connection with the histories and scholarly work of people of color we do not know. Cross-racial work in particular academic settings continues to be rare and difficult, and it is not often a priority for white people.[64] White women often excuse their ignorance of and inattention to the lives and work of women of color in their midsts by citing a lack of time, different agendas, and plain and frequently open lack of interest. Further, because the work of women of color is often context-based, white women often view that scholarship as a subset of or secondary to their own frequently sweeping theories and generalizations which, although they may gain academic currency, are rarely relevant to the lives of actual women, whether white women or women of color. Not acknowledging and responding to the presence of women of color in our immediate contexts constitutes a deliberate choice not to work together.

It is often easier for white women to deal with people of color at a distance than to carefully consider the agendas and scholarship of people of color we see in academic settings every day. In a feminist theory course, Anna Julia Cooper, who wrote in the 1800s and is frequently critiqued for her classism, is assigned and not Patricia Hill Collins, a contemporary scholar difficult to dismiss once read. In doctoral programs, European American 'Africanists'[65] study women in Kenya and have no knowledge of or connection to black women in the United States. In classrooms, it is easy for white liberals to discuss the tragedy of Latinas and Asian Americans in clothing factories with dismal conditions and pay while they ignore the decreasing numbers of Latina and Asian American women at their own institutions and in their classrooms. Cross-racial work among women demands attention to a range of realities and issues, including those presented by women of color with whom white women come into contact daily.

Conclusion

This chapter has drawn connections between memory, history, and race, specifically in the context of white women and cross-racial work among women. As stated in the beginning of this chapter, women's histories are racial, and white women have a history of racism. White feminist scholarship that is anti-racist must understand white women as racially marked and recognize women's histories as racial. Sustained racial memory is one means for white people to move to the inside of race. Racial memory is one way to reframe racial knowledge and reinterpret racial history as written on white bodies. Finally, ethical remembering can lead to cross-racial relationships among people in higher education.

Reliance on my own racial memories, fiction, racial stories, and theoretical arguments allows me to transcend the position of 'sympathy and yet distance,' a position whites often choose when it comes to race. Embracing racial agency and responsibility in matters of race and history requires that we pry open racial assumptions and work through our own racial ignorance. Sustained racial memory, as described and modeled in this chapter, settles in the skin-quality of our whiteness, surfaces the racism in our bodies. Sustained racial memory knows white is a race and that all histories are racial. Sustained racial memory complicates passage through simplified lives and scholarship, and is necessary for European American scholarship that is anti-racist.

CHAPTER THREE

We Are Not Enough: Epistemology and the Production of Knowledge

How do those in higher education construct knowledge about gender and race? Most feminists consider that they know gender, but how do we know race, and how do we use that knowledge? Careful consideration of what knowledge consists of, who has access to its production, and how it is produced is critical to cross-racial work in higher education. Close examination of knowledge is also a necessary step toward answering the considerable critique from women of color of European American feminist theories and the knowledge we produce.

Feminists have worked hard to bring women's knowledge and priorities to the forefront of public discourse. In arenas as far reaching as education, business, health care, the media, and politics and government, women have struggled to gain control of policy and representation. We want our opinions and input to matter. Likewise, in the context of higher education, feminists have been concerned with who is able to control knowledge. When it comes to teaching, conferences, publications, and becoming an authority, those who control knowledge, who can claim, for example, that girls are not receiving enough attention in their science classes, or that places of employment continue to pay women at a rate lower than that of men, can affect policy and practice. Knowledge, and what it claims about specific groups of people, is a critical resource in higher education.

Feminist approaches to knowledge have emphasized the importance of women's experiences and women's lives. Feminists have long argued that academic analysis that ignores women is bad scholarship. To address the problem, many feminist scholars began to add research with and about women onto existing research. These scholars pointed out that, for example, a historian who wrote about men's roles during industrialization might consider women's significance to the same era. Similarly, scholarship in the area of interpersonal communication might choose to add gender differences onto existing theoretical frameworks.

In addition to emphasizing the importance of women's lives, feminist epistemologies have posited that the prevalence of gender oppression should change how and what people know. Thus, in historical scholarship, research must consider the relevance of women's lack of the right to vote to social life more generally; those in business and economics must address the relevance of the glass ceiling to all types of business interactions. Feminists have also argued that power matters to knowledge production. For example, men have had the ability to produce knowledge about women, while women traditionally lacked access to that production. This has meant that much of the knowledge produced by men about women is unfair or inaccurate. Feminists have argued that it is critical, for the content of knowledge and the process of knowledge production, to consider ways in which what passes as knowledge systematically marginalizes women. For example, economics studies that do not recognize work in the home as a form of labor and production discount the contributions of women to the national economy.

Knowledge is also critical to the practice of cross-racial feminism. In regard to knowing gender, white feminists have developed complex and often relevant epistemological approaches. We have worked out ways to combine theory with practice; to bring together our own experiences with more abstract knowledge; and to move from concrete, local experiences of gender to broader social dynamics. We have brought gender analyses into many disciplines and schools of thought – from anthropology to education to economics – that previously ignored gender. Further, European American feminists speak and write with assuredness about what it is to be a woman. We can usually identify and criticize sexism with ease. For example, most feminists can readily list the range of ways in which women are oppressed: through receiving less pay for performing the same work as men, through domestic and sexual violence, through our low numbers in high-ranking positions throughout the workforce, or through the abundance of images of women as unrealistically thin and thoroughly objectified bodies.

Yet our talk about race, and particularly about our own raciality, is often troubled and ambivalent. When it comes to race, we speak with less assurance, much less familiarity. For example, making a list of the ways in which white women routinely and systematically oppress women of color is rarely simple or straightforward for European American women. We often see women of color as women first, people of color second, and rarely as both. We might fail to see how oppression differs for women based on the interconnections of gender, race, and class. Often missing as well are the specifics of the men who have the power to oppress. How might we address the ways in which affirmative action has significantly aided white women, and offered very little to women of color? How do we begin to analyze the ways in which a lack of realistic media images affects women in relation to race, particularly in connection with who controls those images (primarily white men and women)?

Whites experience difficulty at a variety of levels when it comes to talking about race, particularly our own. If you ask white people what their race is, many will avoid or dodge the question. Some will talk at length about their ethnicity, identifying themselves as Italian or Irish, for example, without ever saying the word 'white.' Others will extoll the benefits of seeing 'beyond color,' conveniently ignoring the relevance of historical and current racism.

White feminists adept at analysis regarding gender-based oppression can easily falter if asked to provide an analysis of race-based oppression. Women who can quickly list the ways they know they are women on a daily basis, from the sexual comment at work to fear of being in a parking lot alone in the dark, might have little to say about the ways in which they know they are white. Rather than confront our own race privilege, it is easiest to pretend that we have graduated to a level of awareness in which we are beyond racism, or not to talk about race at all. For example, we might avoid discussing the fact that there are only three tenured women of color across the entire faculty at our university. We might choose not to explore what a range of people of color are saying in our field. We learn to ignore the absence of people of color at faculty meetings, or the abundance of people of color in service positions. Excuses are routine and familiar: 'At least there are now a few white women at those faculty meetings, and at least those people of color have work.' The question of race privilege and knowledge production is peripheral to most academic discourse. What is the connection between racial identity and racial location, and our scholarship?

Just as introducing gender within the context of traditional scholarship and knowledge radically altered existing theories and methods, differentiating between American Indian women, Asian American women, Latin American women, African American women, and European American women will also structurally change how knowers perceive reality and produce knowledge about that reality. White feminists understand that we owe at least part of our knowledge about gender to the fact that we occupy the location of the oppressed. The experience of being oppressed is part of what and how we know. We can speak with authority about being passed over for a raise, or about how it feels when others doubt our credentials because we are female. How does potentially occupying the role of oppressor affect our knowledge of race? If experience is part of what and how we know, how can white feminists be clear about the ways in which our experience of race privilege and white supremacy affects the knowledge we produce?

How do we know something? Who shapes our knowledge? What does it mean to claim authority? Of which elements, including experience, emotion, and rationality, does knowledge consist? How do we represent what we know? Who can represent whom? Who can speak for whom, and with what kind of authority? What do we choose to research, and why? To what ends do we produce knowledge, and for whom? How does experience affect what we know? What is the relationship between knowledge and one's location or standpoint? These questions have been particularly important for white women and women of color in questioning the production of knowledge so far. They run through nearly all of what happens in higher education: curricula, syllabi, reading lists, research, conferences, publications, and lectures; even our legitimacy as a knower or as an authority is linked to our views of knowledge production.

As teachers, when our research or experience has a direct connection to the material we teach, we frequently draw on that experience or research, bringing in examples and first-hand accounts of the subject matter. Likewise, students often view our presentation of this knowledge, and the knowledge itself, differently. Knowledge that derives from experience is more than a theory or idea; it comes from the inside of the subject at hand. One teacher might draw on his or her experience in the field in teaching a class on research methods; others might base their comments in a social work class on their experience with a particular social services organization. What teachers experience expands the knowledge they offer. Likewise, what we do not experience limits that knowledge, even as we are unaware of those limitations. To some extent, knowledge and authority are always connected to experience and one's location in different contexts.

Epistemologies consistently work to specific ends, and always serve particular interests. Knowledge is for something or someone. While one teacher may train future social service providers, another may gear his or her instruction toward areas in professional communication. Yet another teacher may be interested in giving students tools to work against specific institutional injustices, while her colleague might see his role as offering necessary information for students to succeed in an increasingly technological environment. At its best, knowledge is active and improves some facet of how people live.

In examining different epistemologies, it is helpful to consider which ends they serve, and whose interests they further. Particularly in the context of feminist critique of traditional epistemologies, and women of colors' critique of white feminist epistemologies, clarifying which knowledge is for whom, how it is active in affecting social relations, and who in particular benefits from the knowledge and who, in contrast, is hurt by it, can make scholarly work more transparent, and thus assist us in ensuring that our work accomplishes what we intend. For example, now that analyses of gender have some import in nearly all academic disciplines, feminist scholars familiar with anthropology might ask how those analyses have changed anthropological research at a general level.

Further, an anthropologist might consider how analyses of gender have altered research on groups that traditionally have not had the power to represent themselves. In the case of competing knowledges, in which different knowledges serve conflicting interests, epistemological transparency assists knowers in sorting through complicated agendas and priorities. In the example cited above, gender analyses may have carved out a space for more studies about women but not enabled women who have traditionally lacked power in academia, such as women of color, to write about themselves. In this case, gender analyses may have helped some women in anthropology and not others. Careful attention to epistemology can help scholars make thoughtful choices regarding their work and its purposes.

Epistemological choices run throughout white feminist scholarship, and white women interested in cross-racial work need to think carefully about their approaches to knowing gender and knowing race.

The examination provided in this chapter of three predominant European American feminist epistemologies reveals that white feminists have not developed consistent ways to analyze race.

Specific epistemological guidelines can be useful for white feminists committed to cross-racial work among women. In order for the arenas of knowledge production to become more cross-racial, and for the knowledge European American feminists produce to contribute to social change that benefits cross-racial groups of women, white feminists need to be committed to producing particular knowledge. As feminists we must be clear about the women to whom we direct our scholarship. We need to resist speaking for large groups of women. We must also acknowledge and act on the realization that we need people of color to create a knowledge base that will contribute to lasting social change. In a feminist context, white women's knowledge and practice will not, on its own, result in justice for all women. Finally, European American feminists will do well to practice a kind of epistemological humility: we do not know everything, and we have much to learn from women of color.

Feminist/Epistemology: An Overview

Epistemology is fundamentally about knowing and knowledge, is important to all disciplines, and has been active in nearly all feminist discourse. An epistemology '... is a framework or theory for specifying the constitution and generation of knowledge about the social world; that is, it concerns how to understand the nature of "reality." A given epistemological framework specifies not only what "knowledge" is and how to recognize it, but who are "knowers" and by what means someone becomes one, and also the means by which competing knowledge-claims are adjudicated and some rejected in favour of another/others.'[1] Epistemology operates on a variety of levels in the academy. Editors of academic journals decide which articles to publish and therefore what and whose knowledge to produce; curriculum committees require a certain make-up of course work and thereby set out which knowledge must be learned and taught for particular educational degrees; students choose courses with particular ideas about which professors are knowers and authorities in certain fields; graduate students opt for methods and approaches that validate one form of knowledge and challenge others; professors represent people as knowers in the shaping of syllabi and reading lists; and educators demonstrate their understanding of knowledge acquisition and of their students as knowers in the ways they conduct courses. Epistemology thus includes the 'standards used to assess what we know or why we believe what we believe.'[2] Escaping the significance of epistemology is difficult, if not impossible, in educational settings.

All epistemologies have practical consequences. They all move toward certain ends. People use knowledge in ways that both help and hurt. Feminist knowledge does not always help all women; in some cases, feminist knowledge has hurt certain groups of women. Consider Sara Ruddick's work on mothering. On the surface, Ruddick appears conscious of the limitations of her work. She writes, '[I] will be drawing upon my knowledge of the institutions of motherhood in middle-class, white, Protestant, capitalist, patriarchal America ... Although I have tried to compensate for the limits of my particular social and sexual history, I principally depend upon others to correct my interpretations and to translate across cultures.'[3] But at the very start of her article, she draws on ideas that apply only to specific women, and universalizes these ideas, writing as if they can apply to all women in the same way. 'We are familiar with Victorian renditions of Ideal Maternal Love ... Central to our experience of our mothers and our mothering is a poignant conjunction of power and powerlessness.'[4] Victorian notions of womanhood have always been most relevant to women who are European American and middle and upper class. Further, to assume that all mothers are powerless in the same way also discounts differences among women. Ruddick points to 'Nature's indifference – illness, death, and damage to the child' as a source of powerlessness. But powerlessness is never equal; it is always filtered through access to resources, such as safe housing, or lack of that access. Throughout her article, Ruddick employs terms like 'female traditions and practices,' 'maternal thinking,' and 'maternal nature.' She states that 'Maternal thought does ... exist for all women in a radically different way than for men.'[5] But she fails to acknowledge or address the varied experiences of women themselves. In addition to plainly disregarding large groups of women, she also leads the uncritical reader to assume the knowledge she does include is relevant to and representative of all women.

More recently, feminist writers tend to raise the issue of difference, yet neglect to specify any difference beyond that of gender differences. Sue Jackson's article on feminist theories of education and Susan Hekman's article on feminist standpoint theory, both published in 1997, provide two examples.[6] In both articles, the authors clearly acknowledge the existence of differences among women. Jackson frequently invokes the importance of 'crossing borders'; Hekman writes that 'subjects [are] constructed by relational forces.' But neither author concretely addresses differential power among women, and the knowledge produced tends to further theories that rely on notions of women as largely the same. Articles of this type usually do not serve well those groups of women whose lives and experiences break up those generalizations. Not only does such writing disregard large groups of women, it also sets up powerful norms against which white feminists often compare women of color.

For women of color to make use of Ruddick's writing, they must first discern if, in spite of their lack of affiliation with 'Victorian traditions of Ideal Maternal Love,' they still have a way into the knowledge Ruddick produces. In the case of Jackson's article, the author writes, 'Feminist theories of education centralise the experiential ... [they] examine oppression in educational institutions in terms of gender, clearly linked to other oppressions of class, race, sex and more.'[7] Unfortunately, we never learn how feminist theories of education respond when women's experiences are contradictory, such as when an Asian American woman finds no classes on Asian American feminist theory, or when all the theory courses assume a predominantly white perspective. Again, women of color must find a point of entry into Jackson's theory, assuming there is one. Hekman offers a detailed and useful analysis of standpoint epistemology, and asserts that feminists should adopt a theory that does not rely on a 'metanarrative, either normative or methodological, to which we can appeal.'[8] She reminds us, however, that 'this does not mean that the systemic analysis of the institution of patriarchy is necessarily precluded.'[9] Again, she leaves the reader wondering: is patriarchy the only discovery after analyzing differences among women? No tools, either theoretical or practical, are provided to address race and class. In all of these articles, in the end, women are women and men are men.

The history written about European American women suffragists is also instructive. Many of the histories produced by European American women repeatedly represent and praise the accomplishments of women such as Carrie Chapman Catt and Susan B. Anthony. Professors across the disciplines cite these two as leading women suffragists, and as playing a central role in winning women's right to vote. But both of these white women, at different times in their careers, also explicitly denied women of color entrance into the discourse and activist groups they controlled.[10] In particular, Catt 'displayed ugly racial attitudes toward Black women, excluding them from public parades and meetings and even supporting congressional provisions which would have barred Black women from suffrage.'[11]

In the late 1960s and early 1970s, feminists began significantly challenging the work produced by European American male scholars over the previous two centuries. They pointed out that existing academic knowledge had misrepresented or ignored women. They also asserted that acquiring knowledge is not an exclusively rational, detached endeavor, but is centrally about experience and emotion as well. In the process of challenging existing scholarship, the feminist scholars of the late sixties and early seventies produced knowledge that did pay attention to experience and that was about women. Allison Jaggar, for instance, wrote about the role of women's experience in philosophical knowledge, and the relevance of emotions to philosophical frameworks.

Gradually, feminist work began to make ignoring the realities of women's lives and insufficiently addressing the unequal status of men and women unacceptable. Gender and women's lives became additional criteria with which to evaluate research and scholarship. But while these white feminists discussed gender inequality at length, they did not say much about the equality of which women compared to which men.

This lack of attention to differences among women and among men has always been problematic for women of color. Women of color scholars have understandably challenged the notion that white women can speak for women generally. Further, whereas white women were and continue to be particularly eager to mark and theorize the significance of gender in all aspects of knowledge production, we have been profoundly reluctant to pay a corresponding attention to race, class, or nationality. We know we are always women; we do not consistently know or acknowledge that we are always white.

Traditional Epistemology

All epistemological discourse in the academy today occurs within the larger context of academic processes of legitimation. The ways in which people combine beliefs, experiences, learnings, and values to form knowledge, and the relationship of power to the ability to produce knowledge, have always been at issue in the broader arena of the development of ideas. For example, some people might value knowledge more if it has been tested on a significant number of people; others might be more compelled by a scholar who spends a considerable amount of time with a small group of people and then produces knowledge about this small group.

Different knowledges have never been accorded equal levels of importance or currency. In the example given above, larger numbers of subjects can mean better knowledge; in another example, students might be more likely to take knowledge seriously if they encounter the same theories in several books. Over the course of a semester, an article that offers a different theory from the one reproduced repeatedly in a textbook might have very little legitimacy. Knowledge production is also intimately connected to power. Those with economic privilege and those who have access to and/or control of resources, such as education, time, and publishing houses, have largely owned knowledge production and representation in the context of higher education. Further, knowledge producers are always aware that the legitimacy and success of emerging scholarship is in some part dependent on that scholarship's fit with existing knowledge.

Thus, new knowledge, whether developed by people from groups who have traditionally lacked access to the means of knowledge production, or by groups who have had long-standing connections to knowledge production in the academy, can never break entirely from existing knowledge, at least in the context of higher education. When Ruth Frankenberg engaged in her landmark research on the raciality of European American women, she used the tested method of oral history interviews.[12] In another example, sociologist Patricia Hill Collins carefully documents her knowledge of existing sociological assumptions in her writing.[13] Collins also points out that for African American, Latino, and American Indian women and men in the social sciences, as well as for individuals from 'other historically excluded groups, acquiring both the status and salaries enjoyed by their colleagues often require unquestioned acceptance of the dominant assumptions or guiding principles of psychology, political science, economics, and other social science fields.'[14]

It is necessary, to a certain extent, to play by the rules established by previous scholars. For example, early feminist scholarship, for the most part, wrote about the relevance of experience in the detached manner which remains the academic form of writing to which those in higher education grant the most legitimacy. Even as feminists paid attention to emotions, they rarely inserted those emotions directly into academic writing. It is also important to note that white feminist epistemologies have rarely fit quickly or easily into existing epistemological frameworks. All feminist epistemologies have had to be cognizant of, and to some extent, to employ, traditional epistemologies, which have in many respects disregarded all women and men of color. Scholars who write with no apparent knowledge of the other work and expectations in their field are unlikely to gain much respect from colleagues.

Feminist scholars have broadly critiqued what they have labeled traditional epistemologies.[15] The terms 'traditional epistemologies' and 'traditional theories of knowledge' as used by several feminist scholars refer to the main theories of knowledge production challenged by feminist and postmodern scholarship.[16] The most frequent feminist critique of traditional epistemologies is that 'scientific research has been deeply gender-biased.'[17] In other words, most academic theorists and researchers ignored, misrepresented, or devalued women in their work.[18] The resulting knowledge, which purported to be about people and humankind, in fact reflected only the realities of a small group of men. Traditional epistemologies often assert that knowledge is pure, abstract, rational, universal, dispassionate, and entirely disconnected from the knower;[19] feminists' engagement with experience and emotions has directly contradicted this premise.

In the United States, traditional epistemologies have shaped the predominant forms of knowledge production; these include positivism, most forms of empiricism, and other frameworks in which information becomes legitimate through norms modeled after scientific inquiry. These traditional epistemologies established a set of knowledge rules that those in higher education had to follow to ensure that others would take their work seriously. If the rules proved inadequate to their questions, the questions would often go unanswered. For example, in quantitative analysis, information must be discrete and easy to code to be considered relevant data for further study.

As the social science disciplines began to emerge, the processes of scholarly legitimation in the hard sciences forced scholars in other disciplines to adopt scientific means to establishing theories and truth. That is, the apparent clarity of certain biological and physical laws established a kind of measuring stick for truth. The words of an early twentieth-century social scientist demonstrate this: 'I want to prove things as nearly as may be and proof usually means an appeal to the facts – facts recorded in the best cases in statistical form.'[20] Even though challenges to traditional epistemological frameworks are now routine, quantifiable data continues to hold considerable sway with both academics and policy makers. Scholars continue to view qualitative data as less serious or somehow inferior to quantitative data.[21]

Traditional epistemologies have in most cases asserted the advantage and superiority of knowledge that is abstract, rationalistic, and universal.[22] Early anthropologists sought to discover and reaffirm the essentials of human nature and existence; sociologists looked for predictable phases of community development; and psychologists sought to establish stages of human development that could be applied across different cultures and groups.[23] In traditional epistemologies, information becomes knowledge when it can exist at an a contextual level. Knowledge derived from a particular context becomes accepted fact when it can transcend that context. Knowledge is real knowledge when it relies entirely or primarily on rational, logical thought and dismisses the relevance of emotions, and when it can be applied to all people in the same way. Thus in articulating stages of human developmental theory, researchers argued that these stages could be applied to everyone; they were only as legitimate as their supposed ability to transcend context. Traditional scholars did not integrate the possibility of different ideas of development, of different world-views, and of different ideas of what is good into their theories.

Philosophers saw epistemology as a 'normative enterprise'; their task was to 'evaluate methods of inquiry or strategies of reasoning; analyze what knowledge is and how it differs from mere opinion or false belief; and refute skeptical arguments that no knowledge of reality is possible.'[24] Thus, knowledge was clear cut, and there were firm rules for admission and exclusion. As with any rule-based endeavor, those who made the rules controlled them and could change them when useful.

Traditional epistemologies draw from Enlightenment thought and broadly assert that 'utilizing truthful knowledge in the service of legitimate power will assure both freedom and progress.' Knowledge will always do good, and that good applies to everyone. Scholars who rely on traditional epistemologies make two primary assumptions.[25] First, they assume that 'the social as well as the physical universe is governed by a uniform, benign, and harmonious set of laws.'[26] That is, social and physical relationships everywhere conform to the same principles, and these principles are universally good. Thus, in the

example that all people develop in exactly the same way, such principles are useful because they clearly show who is developing and who
is not. Different development becomes bad development. European
American men could then articulate stages of development and criticize white women or people of color for not conforming to these
stages.

The second assumption is that a 'homogenous form of reason exists
within all humans and that this reason is not determined or affected by
other (heterogeneous) factors such as desire or historical experience.'[27]
Knowers are able to separate reason from all other aspects of humanity
and social context, and humans move through developmental stages
regardless of social and environmental factors. Failure to move to a
certain stage is individual failure, rather than the consequence of different circumstances.

People in higher education have normalized these assumptions, and
in many cases, made them invisible. For example, most social scientists, whether they rely on quantitative or qualitative methods, believe
their work is both harmless and useful. It is doing good, and has no
'unjustifiable costs.'[28] Social scientists emphasize their ability to be sci-
entifically neutral, and to create more beneficial public policies. In reality, the ways in which people use knowledge is far more complex.
Knowledge often helps one cause while hurting another. A recent
study on child care, funded by a branch of the National Institutes on
Health, provides an example. This study 'found a direct correlation
between time spent in child care and traits like aggression, defiance
and disobedience.'[29] People might use this study in myriad ways: to
argue against funding for child care, to support additional training for
child care workers, or to criticize mothers and/or fathers who choose
to make use of child care.

Feminist epistemologists have argued that the purpose of traditional
theories of knowledge was to 'support a dominant elite.'[30] If there is
only one route to truth and to a moral life, it is convenient for the definers of that route to plot it so that it fits their experience and serves their
particular purposes. Upper-class European American men could create
knowledge that in turn became ideologies that served to dominate others, both in the United States and elsewhere.[31] Thus, specific ideas
about family life led Daniel Moynihan to declare African American
families dysfunctional and pathological in his 1965 report.[32] As one
researcher writes, those who labeled the African American family system 'as an organization inherently laden with problems and inadequa-

cies ... misdirect[ed] the blame for the concrete condition of African American family life' and ignored the structural disadvantages with which African American families lived.[33] Knowledge made by this elite few has also served to preserve unequal forms of social relations. In part because 'the university is a place that produces a particular selection and ordering of narratives and subjectivities,'[34] academics continue to legitimate knowledge that deems certain groups and individuals less worthy.

In the 1960s and the 1970s, it became particularly clear to feminist scholars that traditional theories of knowledge had under- or misrepresented women. Feminists also saw that in many cases, the knowers, mostly white, middle-class men, were not particularly interested in feminist knowledge. Theories that claimed universal knowledge about human nature and moral laws had had little input from anyone outside of the group which had created these theories. Thus, for example, until the late 1960s, European American men could argue that women's primary place was in the home. Even as women began to work in greater numbers than in the past, they did the work that assisted men.[35] Women wondered how their experiences challenged those theories. Where did emotion fit? Historically, women had primarily been the objects of men's knowledge. When did women become the subjects and knowledge makers in the academy?

Feminists pointed out that simply adding facts about women onto existing scholarship and theories that 'take men, their lives, and their beliefs as the human norm' was not enough.[36] Feminists sought to expose the 'distortions and perversions' in underlying theories of knowledge, and addressed fundamental issues across the disciplines. For example, Joan Kelly-Gadol examined methodological issues in women's history, Carolyn Wood Sherif analyzed the steps toward knowledge in the field of psychology, Dorothy E. Smith pointed out that traditional sociological knowledge hides the ways in which objects of knowing are situated in concrete social interactions, and Heidi L. Hartmann discussed how unequal labor relationships influence who performs housework. Such scholarship posed a significant critique to existing academic knowledge.[37]

Early work in the fields of Western science, medicine, anthropology, and history demonstrates the regularity of similar epistemological concerns. This work is also significant because it set the terms for later knowledge production, and because of the ways in which scholars in these fields represented white women and all people of color. In the field of Western science, feminists have 'rigorously question[ed] the exclusion of women, their interests, and visions of the good life' from scientific debates.[38] A bias against women in science leads to their underrepresentation in scientific institutions, as well as a 'lack of funding for women's expressed concerns.'[39] Racism in late nineteenth-century science can be connected to 'unabashed assertions of racial superiority.'[40] As one author states, 'scientific racist thought can explain how' ideas regarding evolution and the human race, human origins, and archaeology 'became entrenched within the scientific community, and in some cases, especially after World War I, came to have an influence on government policy in colonial administration, education, and social welfare.'[41] We can see a resurgence of scientific racism and biological determinism in books such as Richard Herrnstein and Charles Murray's *The Bell Curve*, which argues that 'intelligence is race-based,' and that social inequality reflects 'intrinsic biological inequalities.'[42] Such arguments continue to act as a powerful rationale for ignoring unjust social conditions.[43]

It is possible to see similar exclusions in the field of medicine. Those in the field have normalized definitions of health and well-being largely in accordance with European American male expectations and priorities. Medical research has, by and large, served and represented white men well. Medical textbooks continue to include paternalistic descriptions of women.[44] As recently as thirty years ago, physicians working for the United States Public Health Service denied treatment to nearly four hundred African American men who had syphilis, and did not tell these men that they had the disease.[45] The result is that white women and people of color have reason for significant skepticism of the medical profession. Even today, medical research is heavily weighted toward the concerns of middle- and upper-class white men. Further, a history of racism and sexism in medicine continues to limit significantly the access of all women and of men of color to health care.[46]

Early anthropological work often consisted of white European and European American men studying people in vastly different cultural contexts.[47] European American anthropologists frequently judged the worthiness of the communities they examined in the context of European and European American norms and expectations. Difference from these norms was usually viewed as an indication of inferiority. Similarly anthropologists 'have followed our own culture's ideological bias in treating women as relatively invisible and describing what are largely the activities and interests of men.'[48] In the field of history, in the 1970s and 1980s, feminist historians thoroughly criticized the 'inadequate integration of gender as a meaningful category of analysis in mainstream history.'[49] While adding women onto existing historical accounts was better than not addressing women at all, feminists had hoped for a more radical change.

The long-standing exclusion of women and people of color across the disciplines is extremely significant, as this exclusion prevailed at a time when most of these fields were developing as academic disciplines. The exclusions and attendant racism and sexism are thus built right into the disciplines themselves. Correction of the problem has been halting and difficult.

Since feminist scholars raised challenges to the exclusion of women and people of color in academic contexts, their work faced an immediate contradiction: feminist scholars sought legitimation, or at least acknowledgment from those whose theories they criticized. Feminist philosophers, for example, sought to establish that gender oppression mattered to concepts such as freedom, rights, and moral development, while much of their audience believed that these concepts existed outside of concrete human experience. This contradiction has had important results. First, feminists have rarely been able to work entirely on their own terms. Second, they have had to be cautious. Finally, feminists have had to be strategic, attentive to practical goals, theoretical ideals, and their audiences.

The existence of feminist knowledge and feminist epistemology in the academy indicates that feminist scholars have achieved a place in scholarly circles. At the same time, white feminists have had to make choices. A critical and ongoing choice relates to the ways in which feminists produce knowledge that resembles or has some fit with existing knowledge. How and when do we break with that knowledge? Who is our primary audience, and who are we seeking to convince?

Setting traditional epistemologies against feminist epistemologies as simply and always oppositional is too simplistic. Theories of knowing serve specific ends. Similar assumptions may be present in several different epistemologies. In as much as knowledge producers seek to change social practice, what epistemologies actually do, who they serve and how, who they leave out, and to whom they are loyal are critical issues. Likewise, it is important to examine the purpose and reach of early epistemologies – who they have served well and what they have accomplished in representational and meaning-making terms.

Feminist Empiricism, Feminist Standpoint, and Postmodern Feminism

Women's studies and feminist work challenge traditional scholarship by positing that women are scholars and knowers, and by asserting that knowledge must engage concrete social interactions and experience, including oppression.[50] Particularly in early feminist work in the academy, there were strong links between women's knowledge and improved conditions for women. The knowledge women brought into higher education 'turned into action [in the form of] self-help clinics, arts centers, rape crisis centers, abortion centers, [and] bookstores' and gave women's studies in the academy definition and meaning.[51] From the beginning of academic feminist thought, feminists considered how knowledge could help women.

Connections between academy and community, and between theoretical analysis and social change; critique of the separation between public and private spheres; the emphasis on developing a feminist consciousness; and the significance of the maxim that the personal is the political all had roots in the women's movement outside of the academy. They also found expression in early women's studies courses and programs. Feminists were engaged with changing curricular and disciplinary norms, as well as with altering theoretical and methodological paradigms. They were also committed to the women's movement outside the boundaries of academia, in regards to labor, efforts to combat domestic and sexual violence, politics, and health care. Feminists saw knowledge in higher education as one way to resist gender oppression, and for many feminists, that knowledge had to be based in women's lived experiences.

This mix of contexts and locations, including academy and community, academic and activist, coexisted to some extent in feminist circles, particularly in the early 1970s, and has continued in other ways through the 1990s and into the new century – witness the use of work by the Boston Women's Health Collective in many women's studies classrooms. Feminist knowledge that made direct links between the university and women's material conditions frequently bridged the academy and the community, and was both dynamic and effective. It was also threatening. In the 1970s, feminist faculty taught courses including women and their bodies and women's sexuality. In Long

Beach, California, community members responded to these classes, and to other actions of feminist faculty, by lodging a complaint with the then president of California State University Long Beach, arguing that courses in the Women's Studies Program 'were "not consistent with traditional family values."' Following this complaint, the dean took control of the program's hiring and fired a faculty person and the director of the CSULB Women's Center. Ultimately, in 1982, the American Civil Liberties Union represented the faculty and students in the department in a lawsuit against the state of California.[52]

In this case, epistemological questions such as who and what knowledge is for were at the forefront. Those who have traditionally held power in the academy were and are far more impressed by academic than by activist pursuits. Thus it is still rare for academics to value a list of a colleague's publications according to the variety of forums in which that person has published. As feminist thought reached for a place in the academy, theories that had some basis in traditional knowledge production, even as they challenged that knowledge, were necessary if scholars across the disciplines were going to allow feminist work any credibility.

Consideration of the ways in which feminist knowledge might lessen the existence and effects of gender inequality can be observed in white feminist thought over time. Mary Wollstonecraft and Simone de Beauvoir are two early authors of the widely accepted feminist belief that women are oppressed because of their gender. More than any other premise, belief in the centrality of gender-based oppression shaped feminist work in the early 1970s. At the same time, some feminists criticized knowledge that was based on this theoretical cornerstone. At a 1971 women's studies conference in Pittsburgh and a 1973 women's studies conference in Sacramento, participants challenged the 'white, middle-class, [and] heterosexual women's efforts to separate women's studies from the radical women's movement.' Seven hundred participants finally withdrew from the Sacramento conference because of conflict over this issue.[53] Writing by women of color in the early 1970s and into the 1980s also criticized white feminist theory and practice that ignored the realities of women outside the academy.[54]

Despite these tensions, academic European American feminists continued to define feminism as a body of thought that critiqued sexism and that addressed women's realities. In the 1960s, many feminists' experiences with left-wing politics led these women 'to believe that female subordination was more than just an effort of dominant political forces; it was endemic in all social relations with men.'[55] The feminist movement of the 1970s included consciousness raising, direct political action, and struggles for space in the academy. Even though white, second-wave feminists addressed a variety of subjects, there 'was generally substantial agreement between different feminists about the main issues for feminism.'[56] This agreement centered on the belief that women were oppressed primarily because of their gender.[57]

As feminists introduced new and often challenging knowledge into the academy, they realized that for that knowledge to have any weight or impact, they needed to formalize what they knew about gender oppression. It became useful to start articulating generalizations about gender oppression. Feminist scholars made broad assertions about, for example, women's wages, women in high-ranking positions, and the prevalence of domestic abuse, usually comparing large groups of women to large groups of men. Further, the more the forms of knowledge matched existing forms, the more legitimacy they received. Thus, even while feminists criticized knowledge that was generalizable to everyone because it often left out women, they themselves began to produce knowledge about all women, and in many cases, did not specify to which women they were referring.

When feminists wrote about women's roles in the home, or the split between public and private life for women, they were for the most part referring to middle- and upper-class white women. It was convenient to ignore the fact that most women of color and working-class women participated in both the public and private spheres. This willingness to mimic existing norms, at least to a certain extent, was paralleled by the ability of women to introduce and develop new theories. Thus, generalizations served white feminists well. In particular, feminists were able to bring concerns regarding the form and content of knowledge to the discussion. Feminists stressed that experience, emotions, and location affected knowledge production and developed theories to fit their experience and location.

Three theories central to white feminist challenges to traditional knowledge are feminist empiricism, feminist standpoint, and postmodern feminism. These three feminist epistemologies and theoretical frameworks have shifted, or at a minimum questioned, the way in which people in the academy know. They all contest traditional ways of knowing and raise important issues concerning who can know, the process of knowing, the components of knowledge, and the relationship of location to knowledge claims. All of these epistemologies have made contributions to feminist thought.

Because these three epistemologies are the most predominant theories of knowledge in white feminist thought, they also offer a way to consider how white women know gender and know race. As women of color continue to criticize white women for making overly broad generalizations regarding women, for misrepresenting the experience and scholarship of women of color, and for inadequately knowing race, addressing the contributions and weaknesses of these three epistemologies permits white women to reconsider how and what we know.

FEMINIST EMPIRICISM

Feminist empiricism emerged primarily in the latter half of the 1970s, largely in response to traditional empiricism and most traditional research methods, which presented themselves as 'value-neutral, dispassionate, disinterested ... protected from political interests, goals and desires by the norms of science.'[58] In a traditional empiricist model, knowledge is what researchers observe, and is pure, unmediated, and unitary. Women in biology and the social sciences began developing feminist empiricism as a way of articulating differences in their scholarship from more traditional forms of research in their fields. For example, a 1970 article by L.S. Fidell concludes that 'the hypothesis that academic departments of psychology discriminate in hiring on the basis of sex has received considerable support.'[59] This author's study assumed the possibility of gender discrimination in the field of psychology and used empirical methods to validate the study's hypothesis.

Early forms of feminist empiricism primarily argue that traditional empiricist researchers, who rarely addressed women as distinct and separate from men and almost never dealt with gender oppression, were not producing rigorous scholarship or science. In other words, psychologists who wrote about human development and ignored the effect of child-bearing and -rearing on women's development as compared to men's, were not good scholars. They were not doing empiricist research in a thorough manner. Empiricist researchers who failed to address the realities of sexism and androcentrism were insufficiently scholarly. More careful attention to the norms and biases of research would correct traditional empiricism. Recent articulations of feminist empiricism seek to revise empiricism itself, and carefully tend to social values and interests. One feminist scholar argues for an empiricism that 'detach[es] scientific knowledge from consensus ... [and] from an ideal of absolute and unitary truth.'[60] Thus there might be several frameworks for human development.

Scholars who address feminist empiricism distinguish between forms of traditional and positivist empiricism and contemporary empiricism. One advocate of contemporary empiricism asserts that 'social experience ... including the learning and use of public theories, practices, and standards of evidence are necessary and relevant to all of our theorizing.'[61] Science 'bears the signature' of those who articulate it. Contemporary feminist empiricists depart from traditional empiricists when they argue that 'sensory experiences are not, and cannot be, foundational.'[62] That is, all knowledge is articulated within a context. Knowledge does not exist apart from social discourse and interaction. Stages of human development are thus necessarily dependent on whether one lives as a man or woman. Further, they might be dependent in part on role expectations, which change over time.

Feminist empiricism responds to three issues related to gender and knowledge. First, in a traditional empiricist framework, gender has not been an epistemological variable. Contemporary feminist empiricists acknowledge that gender is a factor in knowledge; the question concerns the relevance of sex and gender to science. A feminist empiricist might ask how gender and the sociological experience of living as a woman are relevant to the process of aging. Feminist empiricists also address the relationship of political context to knowledge. At the very least, engagement with a particular political position or agenda infringes on traditional empiricism's allegiance to objectivity.

Contemporary empiricists also question the ability of empirical norms to adequately account for the existence of values. Finally, a third area of inquiry for contemporary feminist empiricists is how social arrangements in and outside of particular disciplinary communities have a bearing on the knowledge content within those communities.[63] In other words, how might theories about aging that ignore socio-environmental effects on the aging process limit the ability of feminists to construct different theories about aging?

Contemporary feminist empiricism raises useful questions. In addition to having a place within feminist epistemological discourse, it also 'fits within traditional accounts of science, thus paving the way for dialogue with nonfeminist philosophers and historians of science.'[64] At the same time, the central tenets of feminist empiricism, which are directly connected to the three issues addressed above, are inadequate to the critique from women of color. While contemporary feminist empiricists have responded to questions within the scientific community and within the discussion among white feminists, they have not responded to questions and critique raised outside of these two communities. For example, Nelson clearly asserts that *who* is theorizing matters.' But she does not address, in concrete or practical terms, how categories beyond gender affect the theorizing.[65] As she writes, the issue of who is theorizing 'as it emerges in feminist criticism clearly involves social and political experiences – including, fundamentally, experiences of sex/gender.'[66]

Feminist empiricists view gender as the central construct around which to theorize and criticize past research. Race, class, sexuality, and nationality may be part of the evidence the researcher observes, and are not necessarily integral to feminist empiricists' critique and analysis. Further, contemporary feminist empiricists do not address the issue of conflicting accounts of experience, or the issue of knowledge as partial, in as much as the experiences of individuals and communities are partial.

FEMINIST STANDPOINT EPISTEMOLOGY

Feminists began articulating standpoint epistemologies in the early 1980s and continue to analyze their usefulness and theoretical dimensions. Sandra Harding, Nancy C.M. Harstock, and Donna Haraway all address the relevance of one's standpoint to one's scholarship. Harding, for example, states that if experience is related to knowledge, then knowledge itself is not 'gender-free;' in other words, who we are has some connection to what we know.[67] As she points out, 'In the 1970s, several feminist thinkers independently began reflecting on how the marxist analysis could be transformed to explain how the structural relationship between women and men had consequences for the production of knowledge.'[68]

Standpoint theorists assume that individuals occupy various positions in stratified societies, and that these positions directly influence our particular vision of the world and of social relations. In one case, a feminist scholar articulates three ways of looking at the world that are particularly related to living as a lesbian: women's feelings for other women; the 'centrality of women's relations with other women; and the possibility that men are not essential to women.'[69] In another exam-ple, two authors assert that 'what we know or can imagine [ancient women] to have been' gives these authors special insight into their subject area of classical literature.[70] As one feminist standpoint theorist writes, 'the experience and lives of marginalized peoples ... provide particularly significant problems to be explained ...' In other words, 'one's social situation enables and sets limits on what one can know.'[71] Standpoint theorists challenge traditional epistemologies and their conclusions regarding who can know and what is worth knowing. Knowledge is never pure and unmediated but always 'socially situ-ated.'[72] Thus, knowledge about domestic work is in part related to whether the knower works as a domestic worker or hires one; knowl-edge about child-rearing is related to the stake one has in raising a child.

For feminist standpoint epistemologists, subjects of knowing are not simply 'interested position[s],' but engaged ones. These feminists reject simple dualism and view a connection to material reality as necessary for useful scholarship. Feminist standpoint theorists stress the impor-tance of social relations, paying particular attention to gender.[73] They begin with the assumption that politics dictates, or at least strongly influences, the production of knowledge.[74] That is, personal views about women's pay as compared to men's pay in similar positions, or a desire to retain or alter pay structures, would affect an economist's analysis of women's participation in the labor market. The attention paid by standpoint epistemologists to social relations, power, margin-alized existence, and positionality continues to interrupt traditional approaches to knowledge and claims to authority.

Standpoint theorists have also made claims that a variety of scholars find problematic. One primary point of conflict, for traditional scholars and feminists alike, is standpoint theorists' articulation of epistemic privilege. Feminist standpoint theorists argue that 'Women's experi-ences, informed by feminist theory, provide a potential grounding for more complete and less distorted knowledge claims than do men's.'[75] In this view, women who perform a great deal of household labor would have more insight into, and ask different questions regarding, this labor than men who rarely or never perform this labor. Additional-ly, the possibility of a standpoint and specific locations from which to make knowledge allows that 'there are some perspectives on society from which ... the real relations of humans with each other and with the natural world are not visible.'[76] In the above example, a man or woman who does not perform household labor might have little to contribute to the knowledge base regarding women and household labor.[77] In the field of psychology, a feminist standpoint theorist might assert that male psychologists do not have access to knowledge regarding the psychological effects of oppression on women's emotional and spiritual well-being.

The argument for better and less distorted knowledge is a brave claim in academic settings that retain positivist notions of solitary and unitary truth. Feminist standpoint theorists' assertion of the possibility of better knowledge has raised the issue of competing knowledges, and the possibility that not all knowledge is equal. For example, is knowledge about household labor better when a woman who engages in that labor constructs that knowledge? Feminist standpoint epistemologists' theoretical assertion of less distorted knowledge can be ineffective and misleading when used on its own, as an analytical tool isolated from additional critique. An important question is, for whom is this knowledge better? Is it always better for all women?

Harstock, for example, concludes that the tasks of child-rearing and housework are 'constructed in ways which systematically degrade and destroy the minds and bodies of those who perform them.' She also comments on 'the isolation of women from each other in domestic labor, [and] the female pathology of loss of self in service to others.'[78] Such knowledge might provide general insight into the situation of some women, and, in particular, those who lose their sense of self and who are isolated. At the same time, this knowledge, seemingly relevant to all women, obscures several angles of inquiry that are central to how women live. Does work at home result in pathology for all women? What about situations in which male and female members of an extended family share domestic responsibilities? Working-class women and immigrant women might obtain work more consistently than their male partners, in which case the male partner might have some role in child-rearing. Further, what about differences among women? How does the ability of an upper-class woman to hire and control the labor of a working-class domestic worker affect the pathology and sense of self of both women?

Finally, the concept that some knowledge is more real than other knowledge is uncomfortably close to traditional epistemologies' claim that certain knowledge claims are true/correct and others are false/ wrong. While knowledge equations are never simple, it is important to think through the possible implications of epistemological claims. In a sense, feminist standpoint epistemology moved the knowing subject from male to female, and did not significantly challenge the route to or ends of knowledge. Feminist standpoint epistemology's emphasis on location is extremely important to the study of knowledge production. But in moving toward an epistemology that is substantively and theoretically anti-racist and feminist, feminist standpoint epistemologies are pursuing the wrong ends.

Knowledge is never merely better or less distorted. Knowledge differently serves various groups of people. Feminist standpoint epistemologies do not offer an analytical model to understand who knowledge is serving and how that knowledge affects different groups. Feminist scholarship is not better in the same ways for all women. If knowledge serves particular ends, feminist knowledge serves particular women. White feminist standpoint epistemologies most immediately and directly serve women for whom gender is the primary category of analysis, women who do not choose to substantively address other issues, including class or race. Again, the unit of analysis falls short for many women. As one Latina writes, 'When I do not see plurality stressed in the very structure of a theory, I know that I will have to do lots of acrobatics – like a contortionist or tight-rope walker – to have this theory speak to me without allowing the theory to distort me in my complexity.'[79] A crucial component of white feminist work that is anti-racist and pluralist will be theoretical and material attention to the issue of whose interests such scholarship serves, and to whom it is accountable.[80]

POSTMODERN FEMINIST EPISTEMOLOGY

Postmodern feminist epistemologies make a decisive break with the notion of epistemic privilege, and in turn, with the idea of less distorted knowledge. As scholars have broadly articulated, postmodern theorists seek to expose representational and relational assumptions and shortcomings in Enlightenment thinking. Jane Flax, in her book *Thinking Fragments*, argues that postmodernists are especially interested in critiquing eight particular aspects of Enlightenment philosophy. Enlightenment theories assume a 'coherent, stable self'; articulate philosophy as the 'distinctive and privileged mode of storytelling'; assert that true knowledge is unchanging and independent of the knower; argue that pure reason eliminates conflicts between truth, knowledge, and power; claim that language exists outside of material reality; hold that history moves in a process of humans progressing toward perfections; believe that humans are intrinsically good and favorably control the natural world through science; and maintain that pure science, detached from the scientist of subject, is the best way of knowing.[81]

In other words, postmodernism shifted the Truth of Enlightenment thinking to truths. Knowledge is always changing, and reality depends largely if not entirely on the representation of that reality, which can of course itself be fluid. Postmodernists expose the contradictions within the eight assumptions listed above and assert ideas and theories that privilege de-essentialized and decentered concepts of truth and claims to authority. A postmodern analysis of child-rearing and housework would not aim for generalizations across large groups. Rather, it might try to demonstrate how a nearly unending list of factors affect women's psychological well-being. The focus of such a study may be to delineate the numerous factors and demonstrate that their relationship to each other is never predictable.

Postmodernists have in a sense displaced the 'Western sense of self-certainty,' especially in the academy.[82] For example, the idea that there is one exclusive and best account of history, of morality, or of human development, has far less currency now than it did twenty years ago. In another example, those in higher education do not so easily accept the early to mid-1900s idea that human relationships are set in stone and follow a linear path to the ideal stage of existence. Rather, distinct ideas about human and group development exist, and may in no way overlap. That is, at least in theory, European and European American notions of human development may be entirely separate from and not superior to Asian notions of human development.

In addition to social and political upheavals and Third World challenges to colonialism, particular academic movements, such as queer studies, ethnic studies, and women's studies, have interrupted 'Western intellectuals' sense of epistemological security.'[83] People in these various movements and fields have fundamentally challenged sweeping and long-standing knowledge claims that may have profoundly misrepresented a group or groups of people. Postmodernists seek to expose the role of power in the production of knowledge, the effect of discourse and representation on claims to truth and what is real, and the significance of multiple positionalities and subjects.[84] For example, how has a small locus of control in publishing in the area of philosophy affected the standard philosophical textbooks? How does one's position in relationship to racial profiling affect knowledge about racial profiling?

Because many white feminists have claimed the fact of women's oppression as a unitary and cohesive reality, postmodernists, including postmodernist feminists, have been critical of their work. As one author writes, 'No matter how enchanted one might be by the postmodernist redefinition of the categories masculine/feminine, and even male/female, feminists need to be able "crudely" to assert that woman as category, encompassing the action and reaction of "difference," in its many semantic layers, remains the subject and Subject of its political discourses.'[85] In other words, white feminists have needed to locate a subject – woman – in general ways. Postmodernists question the need for and reliance on general truths about women. In an epistemological sense, postmodernism asks white feminists to know the category of woman as fundamentally shifting and decentered. That is, woman is always women, and generalities about women are impossible and unnecessary.

In as much as postmodernism rejects binary oppositions, it displaces gender as a primary marker of difference. As one scholar writes, 'if feminism presupposes that "women" designates an undesignatable field of differences, one that cannot be totalized or summarized by a descriptive identity category, then the very term becomes a site of permanent openness and resignifiability. I would argue that the rifts among women over the content of the term ought to be safeguarded and prized, indeed, that this constant rifting ought to be affirmed as the ungrounded ground of feminist theory.'[86] 'Constant rifting' may appear to many white feminists as theoretical chaos. The focus on women as a generalizable category, is, indeed, for many European American feminists the core of feminism. Postmodern feminists assert that 'postmodern-feminist theory would ... [treat] gender as one relevant strand among others.' In other words, for postmodern feminists, gender is no longer the primary category of analysis.[87] It is unfortunate that most white postmodern feminists fail to acknowledge that U.S. women of color have never represented gender as the only 'relevant strand.' In fact, women of color have been advocating 'gender as one relevant strand among others' for at least a hundred years.

Postmodernism undoubtedly upsets the certainty with which traditional epistemologies have arrived at knowledge and truth. It further supports and expands certain aspects of feminist work by white women and by U.S. women of color. For example, its recognition of multiple subjects and competing interests runs parallel to similar ideas among feminist thinkers. At the same time, postmodernism contains its own problematic inconsistencies, especially in relation to feminist scholarship. Most postmodernist discourse does not engage feminist scholarship, even when the parallels are clear.[88] Further, for feminists, postmodernism's denial of any possibility of a concrete self or subjectivity makes support of postmodern theories difficult. As one feminist writes, 'Postmodernist rhetoric about "the self" is simultaneously one of its most intriguing and disappointing features. Like feminist theorists, postmodernists intend to particularize and historicize all notions of "self." However, unlike feminist or psychoanalytic theorists, postmodernist deconstructers of the self empty subjectivity of any possible meaning or content.'[89] Feminists have long asserted the central importance of women as subjects and agents, and thus are 'suspicious of theories that require denying the centrality of human relatedness.'[90] The insistent focus on decentering in most of postmodern thought leaves its theorists, in a sense, with nowhere to land. For feminists interested in changing social relations and in resisting various forms of oppression, a place to land is necessary. If we ask hard questions of postmodern theorists, inconsistencies quickly become apparent. For example, what is postmodernism trying to do? What are its desired practical ends? Does decentering in itself offer anything to anti-racist practice?

Further, critics of postmodernism have pointed out that postmodernism emerged at a time when communities long excluded from nearly all levels of higher education by dominant groups began to gain an initial grasp on power in higher education. Postmodernism's lack of attention to practice and its largely theoretical expressions tend to ensure that those who have always had power, primarily European American men and some European American women, simply keep it, even if they are advocating ways of thinking that, on the surface, are different from positivist and Enlightenment thinking. For example, many white feminists now acknowledge that class and race are relevant categories for analysis. But little white feminist work offers concrete insight into how feminists might address differences among women. Most white feminists continue to give the most substantial and theoretical attention to gender.

The notions of decentered subjects and multiple positionalities have existed outside of academia in complex ways for years. It is particularly disturbing that European and European American scholars want to take credit for inventing knowledge that working-class communities and communities of color in and outside of the United States have been practicing and articulating for at least a century. Finally, in a cross-racial context, while feminist postmodernism has brought a number of important questions to the forefront of knowledge production, it has not consistently resulted in increased attention to anti-racist practice.

Postmodern feminist epistemology is potentially responsive to multiple layers of identity and social organization, including the category of race. It is in tension with feminist empiricism and white feminist standpoint epistemology because it does not prioritize gender theoretically. While postmodernism arguably encourages consideration of race and anti-racism, it does not require it. White postmodern feminists do not consistently and substantively address the category of race or the reality of racism. And European American postmodern feminists most often engage the work of white women and men; they do this with a seriousness and depth they rarely afford to people of color.

Theoretical understandings and material expressions of the self and of human relations are at the center of all epistemologies. How white feminists know our gender and our race, in addition to how we articulate gendered and raced social relations, is fundamentally epistemological. Although postmodern feminists such as Flax construct theoretical frames that leave room for race, few have articulated ways in which epistemology might address the raced identity of its subjects.

This lack of attention to race, and a parallel disregard for the lives and scholarship of U.S. women of color, is particularly problematic in that U.S. women of color have for decades articulated theories that de-essentialize gender while simultaneously accounting for the materiality of the subject and of social relations. The work of Ida B. Wells Barnett, an anti-lynching activist in the late 1800s and early 1900s, and of the Combahee River Collective, a collective of black feminists that formed in the 1970s, are only two examples.[91] Postmodern feminist epistemologies may decenter gender as the primary category of white feminist analysis, but they do little to provide theories of knowledge that account for layers of identity and differences among women. Further, none of the three feminist epistemologies identified above consistently ask the question of what epistemologies do, who they help and hurt, and whose ends they serve. As stated at the beginning of this chapter, if knowledge exists to change some aspect of how people live, all epistemologies ought to have ethical guidelines as theoretical cornerstones. As knowledge producers, what do we seek to change? To whom are we loyal? In working toward cross-racial feminism, such questions demand clear responses.

Feminist empiricists, feminist standpoint theorists, and postmodern feminists all contest traditional routes to the production of knowledge in significant ways. All three epistemologies have informed the development of white feminism, and they have challenged research methods in a variety of disciplines. The next section addresses epistemological practices. How do the choices of those in higher education assume and express specific epistemological frameworks? How do knowledge producers act on epistemological frameworks, and how do our choices support and prohibit cross-racial dialogue?

Epistemological Practices

All European Americans, regardless of subject matter, employ particular epistemologies. In a broad sense, epistemologies are fundamental to routine choices we make in higher education. For example, the way people approach a research project immediately raises epistemological issues. It is often our beliefs regarding who knows what that inform methodological and theoretical choices. In approaching a subject such as the effectiveness of a social service agency, or an oral history project, the researcher makes choices about the format of his or her research, deciding whether to accord the subjects of that research a role of great authority, limited authority, or no authority at all.

In a classroom context, how teachers respond to knowledge from a student that contradicts their own, or that is entirely outside of their scope of expertise, is connected to epistemological issues. For example, how might a white professor respond when a Latin American man raises his hand and comments on his experience of racial profiling? Or when an Asian American woman points out that many of her peers and professors assume she is an immigrant and not a third-generation resident of the United States? In discussing race issues, students' questions are challenging. As one African American woman asked, 'What is the significance of white privilege to all African American neighborhoods?' The ways in which we claim authority, particularly in regard to race and cultural areas, are epistemological issues that are directly connected to the possibility of cross-racial work and dialogue. As stated earlier, all epistemologies serve specific ends, and the operative assumptions regarding what we want our knowledge to do, stated or not, are also centrally about epistemology. Epistemologies can support or hinder cross-cultural interaction and change.

Epistemological Barriers to Cross-Racial Feminism

For white people, routine choices have often become so normalized that we may not recognize their epistemological or cross-racial significance. Epistemological assumptions that whites make as a matter of course can significantly work against the possibility of cross-racial dialogue. Consider three of these assumptions and their implications.

The first assumption that hinders cross-racial work is that book learning can offer the entirety of knowledge on any given subject. When we encounter a topic with which we have little experience, we tend to think that if we simply read enough, we can conclusively fill in the gaps in our knowledge. For example, a white woman studying to be a teacher in an urban neighborhood might read up on the economic and housing conditions of children in that neighborhood. A social worker might seek out articles on Asian American understandings of mental health. Teachers might research the learning styles of Latin American students. While this kind of study can be useful and important, it may also lead to the assumption that book learning is all that is required. Indeed, this idea is certainly an easy one to adhere to in higher education, where people often succeed, in the institutional sense, on the strength of how much knowledge they have accumulated. Particularly in higher education, the authority accorded to books and articles contributes to the idea that an understanding of what is in them can confer expert status.

However, knowledge is far more than book learning. While this may be easy to acknowledge at a superficial level, individuals and structures in higher education still struggle to recognize the breadth of what knowledge includes. When constructing knowledge that leads to cross-racial dialogue and interaction, several components of knowledge are operative. Knowledge always includes an active combination of book learning, experience, values, and location. Book learning is acquired through reading. Experience is that which we live through, a more all-encompassing category than book learning; it adds to and shapes what we know. Values are part of what we know. What we care about and where we invest our energies, to whom and what we are loyal, not only shapes what we know but seeps through our knowledge. Finally, our personal social location, in relation to structures of power, privilege, and discrimination, is a factor in what we claim as knowledge. Where we stand affects what we know.

Therefore, even when white teachers read about Latin American learning styles, we might easily compare them to our own European American learning styles. It is likely that we are more conversant with our own, which have been abundantly affirmed through our experiences in the classroom. Our values might intervene: if our goal is to serve the majority well, why should we try to learn new skills that will serve only a few students and exclude others? On the other hand, a person who believes that educational systems have unfairly privileged white students might choose to value educational opportunities for a few Latin American students whom the system has not served well rather than continued privileges for the European American students and continued disadvantages for the Latin American students. Values are crucial to many of our decisions in higher education.

Knowledge is never made up solely of book learning. It is a complex and developing mixture of book learning, experience, values, and location. In this framework, one person cannot know everything. Instead, an individual will be better able to contribute to the production of knowledge that is directed toward any kind of social change when he or she is aware of how the four components of knowledge are working together. Further, an understanding of these four components of knowledge in our work will help us to recognize what we do not know, and where we do not have authority. In the example provided above, clarity about how any teacher wishes to serve different groups of students is critical. In acting on these values when constructing syllabi and her approach to teaching that class, a teacher will also draw heavily on the other elements of knowledge.

A second assumption, directly linked to the first, is that if one can accumulate the entirety of knowledge about any given subject, an organization, department, or university can be cross-racial or cross-cultural if members of that organization simply learn enough. Although we do not often say it in plain language, white people, particularly in higher education, are extremely reluctant to admit that we are not enough. When it comes down to discussing the rationale for efforts at diversifying student bodies or faculties, it is extremely difficult for many whites to fully support the idea that that diversity will result in a richer knowledge base.

Simply put, it is difficult for white people to acknowledge that we are not more or less than a part of the picture, rather than the center, or the most important part. We also are reluctant to agree that democratic education would be better served if there were a range of people at the table. In other words, we are comfortable working toward diversity as long as that work does not require us to think about how we might change so that a different picture can be created. Organizations cannot be cross-racial or cross-cultural simply by virtue of the book learning of a few individuals. In the interests of cross-racial dialogue, knowledge will best serve particular ends when people share similar values, and bring together a diverse array of the other components of knowledge, including experience, book learning, and location.

A third and final assumption regarding epistemology in higher education is that knowledge operates in a neutral space. Particularly in efforts toward any kind of social change, the production of knowledge is always political and full of power relations. Hiring efforts, grant distribution, curricular decisions, and distribution of funds within a university are always related to power, and to the people who hold it. In this sense, knowledge is never an independent entity. Those who hold power usually endorse knowledge that in some sense parallels their own, while simultaneously asserting that their knowledge is neutral. The result of this has been that white norms and expectations hold sway in higher education settings.

When those with power produce knowledge that addresses difference, they often do so from an additive or single-issue approach. That is, a chapter addressing listening strategies in a text on basic communication skills might include two or three pages on how listening practices differ across cultures, without ever acknowledging that the rest of the chapter is based on a particular set of norms, usually white and middle class.

In moving toward change, those interested in cross-racial dialogue must recognize and learn to articulate that the realities that knowledge seeks to represent are always multi-layered and complex. In higher education, often for the purpose of theoretical simplicity and ease, thinkers continue to reach for large, generalizable categories and ideas. It is useful, for example, to espouse broad truths about listening. They are easy to teach, should last over time, and can supposedly apply to everyone. Those who advocate broad truths about listening might argue that cultural differences are essentially an appendix to the general truths about listening. This striving for and insistence on manageable truths rarely fully reflects life as we live it. Knowledge that supports cross-racial change must be as intricate, as attentive to power, and as untidy as life itself.

Knowledge that encompasses book learning, experience, values, and location; that builds from a cross-section of people who differ in all four of those components; and that engages in an open and consistent conversation about power, and about norms, privilege, and discrimination does not yet enjoy a reserved seat within higher education. In educational contexts, such knowledge still speaks from the periphery. It rarely displaces the clean, packaged, and polite knowledge that continues to set the standards, particularly at the levels of publication and formal knowledge production. For cross-racial dialogue to be a possibility in the academy in sustained and effective ways, those of us committed to that practice must make, represent, and leave space for knowledge that challenges those standards. One step in this process is recognizing the ways in which seemingly routine, and sometimes, apparently innovative, epistemological choices result in very little actual change.

Cultural Competence and Epistemological Issues

People in education, activist, social service, and business professions routinely use the expression 'cultural competence.' Over the last few decades, the increasing presence of people of color in these professions, as well as lingering attitudes and behaviors on the part of white people that leave little room for cultural values and practices other than our own, have led to a new consideration of how groups and organizations might achieve and practice behaviors that are respectful toward all people. Definitions of cultural competence rely heavily on the context in which the definers of the term work. In the field of social work, scholars define cultural competence as 'an ability to provide services that are perceived as legitimate for problems experienced by culturally diverse persons.'[92] Most definitions point to the importance of the ability of a professional to recognize, understand, and change their practice in relationship to various cultural norms and values. Definitions may also stress knowledge regarding a client's potential 'history and experiences with prejudice, discrimination, and racism, as well as cultural specific beliefs' related to the specified context. In health care, this might mean attention to the beliefs related to health, illness, and well-being in a particular culture.[93] Organizations devote varying levels of time and resources, financial and otherwise, to achieving cultural competence.

Even as efforts toward cultural competence have increased over the last decade or so, critics point out that it has become a profit-making industry in its own right, with attendant training, consultation, and technical assistance. Often, people pay lip service to cultural competence but refuse to change organizations and structures in any significant way. Some businesses institute Martin Luther King day as a paid holiday, or sponsor company meals that feature ethnic food and music, but do nothing to give people of color more power within the organization. Cultural competence can consist of nice-sounding words with little substance. The result is that people of color 'are invited to keep their culture but enjoy no greater access to power and resources.'[94]

In organizations and fields that white people have traditionally dominated, whites may be divided on the issue of cultural competence. Employees may argue that anti-discrimination training may take too much time out of their day. Jokes such as 'I have to go learn about what's wrong with being white,' or thinly disguised impatience with any attention paid to cultural difference, be it via an ethnic meal, holiday, or discussion of racism or homophobia in the workplace, also reveal an intolerance of cultural competence. Other white people may genuinely hope that their workplace is culturally competent, and believe that time and energy should be invested to meet the goals and ideas that the theories of cultural competence espouse. They may participate in a task force devoted to changing the workplace, or agree to read articles relevant to cultural competence.

Whatever its expressions and meanings, cultural competence continues to be a contentious topic. People bring a range of definitions and understandings to the term, and there may well be disagreement within one organization regarding what cultural competence will look like in that specific context, and what kind of investment and extent of change are necessary. Some may see holidays and celebrations with ethnic food and music as sufficient; others may ask why there are not more people of color in management positions. Further, white people often see cultural competence as a series of bounded events, rather than an ongoing process to which people within an organization commit. Even when people agree on cultural competence as a goal, there may be few structures in place to facilitate it.

In the context of higher education, cultural competence is often a topic white people approach reluctantly. There is a strong tendency to believe that racism or cultural inappropriateness is nearly impossible in higher education, or at least that it occurs in isolated circumstances.

We are educated, thoughtful, fair people. There is often an implicit assumption that these qualities will guarantee the practice of cultural competence. This assumption persists even as we criticize the lack of cultural competence elsewhere. For example, we may condemn the lack of people of color in power in the organizations on which we do research, yet remain conspicuously silent on the same situation in our own context.

Unfortunately, those in higher education have, in a sense, the privilege of maintaining that silence. Many white people, however liberal and fair-minded, are content to leave the work of cultural competence to others. We are busy enough with teaching, grading, preparing course material, writing, and attending meetings. Actively promoting cultural competence would take considerable time and effort, of which we have little enough already. Further, practicing cultural competence and actually bringing more people to locations of power in the academy will be most successful when these efforts are broadly supported. Within an organizational or educational setting, it is nearly impossible for one or two people to make significant changes in the span of a few years.

When the subject of cultural competence is first raised, European Americans typically offer a quickly spoken commitment to and interest in it. Cultural diversity and cultural competence are obvious goals to which we must be committed. But when asked to consider what that means in practical terms, there is often a noticeable pause, as if someone has asked an impolite or inappropriate question. The pause, and the conversations that follow, reveal a link that is critical when considering epistemology and cross-racial dialogue in higher education.

Does cultural competence require a racially and otherwise diverse group of people? Particularly in the academy, many white people, directly or indirectly, act as if it does not. There is often an unspoken yet powerful belief that whites and the organizations in which we work can be sufficiently culturally competent if we learn enough about the lives and experiences of those with different backgrounds than our own. In other words, although bringing a diverse group of people to the table is ideal and of course desireable, it is not, in fact, necessary to achieve cultural competence. In an epistemological sense, then, cultural competence is a commodity that can be achieved through acquisition of book knowledge. Rather than change our workplaces or admit the existence of racism, we simply move beyond the problem.

The epistemological assumptions and consequences of such beliefs and practices are significant. First and foremost, the idea that white people can achieve cultural competence in any given organization simply by learning enough means that diversity and just power relations are not necessary or even important. It flatly contradicts the idea of education as a democratic, participatory endeavor, and it makes it possible for whites to speak, act, and bear moral responsibility for everyone. Diversity and sensitivity to cultural difference become an outfit we put on and take off at will, rather than a reflection of individual and institutional choices. Power within organizations remains in the hands of a few who have the right, and paternalistic responsibility, to speak and think for others.

Cultural competence based on how much whites gain from reading books and articles is a thinly disguised form of cultural imperialism. But the assumption is not particularly rare, or even often regarded by European Americans as problematic. As long as white people believe they can know everything about, and know the best interests of, all people of color, without ever having frank conversations with people of color about race privilege and discrimination, knowledge that supports cross-racial dialogue will be particularly unlikely. Cross-racial dialogue and work will be supported when we can talk plainly about what we know and do not know, what our knowledge supports and furthers, who it harms and who it leaves out. We must firmly reject the illusion that book learning alone is sufficient to support cross-racial dialogue, and renounce the arrogance and privilege that convince us it is perfectly appropriate to speak for others' interests.

Angela Harris and Catharine A. MacKinnon: Perspectives on Race and Gender in Feminist Theory

How feminists theorize race and gender to represent the practices and lives of any one woman or a group of women continues to be a contentious issue that crosses political and theoretical lines. White feminists have long held that asserting women's oppression as women has been critical to social change. Women of color have pointed out that conceiving of women as a unified group has excluded many women, and has not resulted in change that benefits all women equally.

Legal scholars Catharine A. MacKinnon and Angela Harris address this issue directly. MacKinnon is known for her work on gender equality in the legal arena, and has taken up issues including sexual harassment, pornography, and feminist theory and the state. Harris writes widely in the areas of feminist legal theory and critical race theory.[95] The differences in the writings of Harris and MacKinnon point to issues central to feminist epistemology, and to the debate on the theoretical relationship of race and gender.[96]

MacKinnon's work clearly expresses her theoretical belief in the primacy of gender-based oppression in all women's lives. She advocates building theory out of practice, and recognizes skin privilege. For MacKinnon, 'specificity makes up what gender *is*.'[97] But although she recognizes race and class, '"sex" is made up of the reality of the experiences of all women.'[98] MacKinnon argues that good feminist theory 'makes gender out of actual social practices distinctively directed against women as women identify them.'[99] However, she does not speak in detail about when women disagree about the representation of those social practices, nor does she address the issue of women with power and privilege, in institutional, racial, and class-based terms.

When MacKinnon does raise the issue of white women's privilege, she is unwilling to examine the issues central to women of color's treatment of women's lives. MacKinnon does not take on the theme of intersectionality, the ways in which all women's lives are cross-cut with multiple layers of identity, or the ways in which white women live simultaneously with privilege and discrimination. Further, in 'From Practice to Theory,' her references to those who critique gender essentialism are vague, and they do not always squarely confront the arguments. For example, her sources do not reflect feminist theorists of color. Neither does she indicate which theorists of color, as she writes, claim that white women do not experience gender oppression.[100] MacKinnon points out that white women are poor, raped, coerced into pornography, and economically exploited. Feminists would be hard pressed to find any feminist theory, by any feminist, a white woman or a woman of color, that disputes this, or that tries to lessen the impact of the oppression that European American women experience. MacKinnon's critics have never opposed her view that all women suffer gender-based oppression. But MacKinnon fails to consider the ways in which race and class privilege and discrimination change gender oppression.

MacKinnon asks, 'What is a white woman anyway?', and it is useful to answer her query. Consider my own case. Some may question my credibility and authority as a teacher because I am a woman, but no one has ever challenged it because of my color, or because of an accent. I have no trouble finding housing or securing a loan; I am never suspected of shoplifting or of being the custodial staff in the institutions where I work; I always heard from guidance counselors that I should go to college and study whatever I chose.[101] I am a white woman, who, even as I experience challenges because of my gender, routinely benefit from profound institutional privileges that come with being white. I am rarely out of place because of my skin color at faculty meetings, at professional conferences, or in the classroom. I live in a comfortable home in a safe neighborhood, where I am not challenged or disregarded because of my skin color, and I can easily access health care resources or other social services that fit my needs. I am well-represented in politics, media, and high-ranking positions. I see my image reflected everywhere, and I have never received the message that the racial group to which I belong is worthless, insufficient, dysfunctional, or pathological. I will not directly suffer if I ignore race all the time. I am one of the white women, privileged by race, that MacKinnon does not address. As a white woman, I would not say that the discrimination I suffer because of my gender supersedes or outweighs the privilege I experience because of my race. However, I am not any more or less marked by race than I am by gender. Both categories are always real and under my skin.

Angela P. Harris takes a markedly different approach to the issue of race and its connection to gender. In her article, 'Race and Essentialism in Feminist Legal Theory,' Harris directly addresses MacKinnon's work and the dangers of gender essentialism: 'The result of this tendency toward gender essentialism ... is not only that some voices are silenced in order to privilege others (for this is an inevitable result of categorization, which is necessary both for human communication and political movements), but that the voices that are silenced turn out to be the same voices silenced by the mainstream legal voice ...'[102] Harris goes on to say that feminist theory and legal theory too often ignore the experience of black women, and that 'gender essentialism in feminist legal theory does nothing to address this problem.' She further argues that feminist legal theory would do well to move away from privileging the abstract and unitary, which can be a significant consequence of gender essentialism in feminist theory.

The final two sections of Harris's *Stanford Legal Review* article shed considerable light on the attractiveness of gender essentialism. Harris points out that there are good reasons for the success of feminist theories that continue to leave certain women out. First, 'essentialism is easy.'[103] It relieves white women of the task of learning about the lives of women we know little about, and in particular, the lives of women of color. Further, as a theoretical approach essentialism fits with the dominant cultural and academic expectations, where speaking for large groups of people and in highly generalizable terms is desirable. Gender essentialism also 'represents emotional safety.'[104] For many white women, the feminist movement represents a comfortable space and one that accommodates our experience. We have worked hard to achieve that space, and feel we deserve that comfort. Conflict, disagreement, and fundamental challenges to our images and experiences of feminism and the feminist movement are simply out of place. Gender essentialism also allows white women to stay in control in ways that make sense in a highly competitive and rank-friendly academic environment. Our own suffering as European American women confers on us a right to define women's experience. Against this, women of color must assert the particularity of their experience. Confronted with multiple and perhaps conflicting representations of experience, it is acceptable and usual in academic contexts for white women to return to the safety of 'women are women and we are all oppressed by men.'[105]

Finally, Harris addresses what black women bring to the argument about gender essentialism, and how their contributions might help feminists move toward a different kind of feminist theory. Black women often know what it means to live with multiple selves, to want a place in institutions that have historically excluded them. To understand and analyze their own lives, African American women have had to construct theories that can hold 'selves that contain the oppressor as well as the oppressed.'[106] As Harris says, this encourages an abandonment of innocence, and draws attention to women's agency. This willingness to let go of the idea of a unitary self leads to a second step in movement away from gender essentialism: the recognition that difference and identity are always relational. Harris argues that feminist theories about women must 'be strategic and contingent, focusing on relationships, not essences.'[107] In this framework, men can be allies, and 'women will be able to acknowledge their differences without threatening feminism itself.'[108]

Another contribution black women can make in challenging essentialism is a focus on women as agents rather than as victims. White women have been particularly eager to represent women as so victimized that we are hardly able to act. In fact, we have never stopped acting, and in many cases, have never stopped resisting. As bell hooks has also pointed out, the 'women as victims' framework directly feeds into male supremacy.[109] Highlighting agency need not discount oppression. Rather, it can accurately identify when women do have power, how we use it, and in whose interests.

The difference between Harris and MacKinnon's approaches to feminist theory and the relevance of race reveal some of the long-standing differences between white women and women of color. Their work also points to a few of the primary criticisms women of color have made of European American feminist theory. White women can be profoundly reluctant to relinquish gender essentialism. We struggle with additive approaches, and hope that adding on the experiences of women of color will be enough. We argue that asserting the category of women as a unified block has been and is necessary for any real social change. We quickly accuse women of color of causing dissension within the feminist movement, of wanting too much, or of not seeing the wisdom in the theory that exists.

Rarely do we stop, pause, and consider the meaning and direction of their words. We want to move on, keep all our theories tidy and tightly knit, and dread looking back. 'Did we make a mistake?' and 'Have we left someone out?' are questions we push firmly out of our minds, reassuring ourselves that we did our best. White women would do well to loosen their hold on gender essentialism. We might recognize that the construction of theories that espouse gender essentialism has not been democratic or involved a cross-section of women. We might also acknowledge that the criticisms of gender essentialism are long-standing and widespread, and that a sincere willingness to shift the focus of white feminist thought would be a responsible and constructive choice. Finally, we might admit that in our real fear of what we would lose by giving up gender essentialism, we have perhaps failed to consider what we would gain.

As MacKinnon demonstrates, defenses of gender essentialism, or of theories that centralize gender and make other markers of difference secondary, can make sense, particularly for white feminists. When faced with critiques of these theories, it is usually more convenient to rush to a defense of gender essentialism than to consider the processes by which such theories were constructed. A move away from arguments that focus on the rightness or wrongness of gender essentialism and other feminist theories is necessary in the context of cross-racial feminism. European American feminists might consider who these theories have served well, and who has been involved in their construction.

Do white feminists really want to support so thoroughly theories constructed by one group of women? In many respects, the emergence of feminist theory has been undemocratic and unfair, and European American feminists interested in cross-racial feminism have good reason to call for reflection and analysis before we so quickly move to defend, and in many cases, continue writing and relying on, theories based on gender essentialism. Feminist theories that support cross-racial feminism must be built on theories constructed by a cross-racial group of women. Theories that have been articulated primarily by European American women are not best suited to lead us to cross-racial feminism.

A second point MacKinnon and Harris's differences raise is related to white feminists' response to the long-standing critique of our theories. Women of color have been arguing against gender essentialism and in support of more multi-layered theories across the disciplines, in large numbers, and for a long time – arguably, two hundred years. The critique of gender essentialism is not isolated or occasional. The history and breadth of this critique offers white feminists an opportunity. We might respond by offering to let go of gender essentialism not because we suddenly believe it is wrong, but because we are willing to acknowledge the potential value in another theory, and to make a sincere effort to learn and practice more multi-layered theories.

The near-exclusive focus on gender as the primary category of analysis has resulted in white feminists ignoring many of the concerns that are central to women of color. Asian American feminists have drawn attention to some of the primary issues for Asian Americans, including immigration, stereotypes of Asians and Asian Americans, cultural identity issues, the relationship of Asian Americans to Asian history and culture, Asian American sexuality, and gender issues in Asian American families.[110] American Indian women have emphasized the importance of language and cultural issues, of the effects of boarding schools, of land and environmental concerns, of American Indians' well-being in social and economic terms, and of representational issues related to research and scholarship by European Americans on American Indians as topics that are central to American Indian tribes and communities.[111] For Latin American women, issues including immigration; the large number of Latina women in the garment industry, computer assembly, and domestic work; sexuality; the dominant culture's homogenization of Latinas; and the particular consciousness that comes out of the concrete, historical experiences of Latinas are all important.[112] Finally, African American feminists urge consideration of African American women in the labor force; of African American media images, particularly the portrayal of African American women as hypersexual women; of the role of church and community work in social change; of class differences among African Americans; and of the historical and current implications of African American women's political activism.[113] One potential area for study is the connection of white women with each of these issues. For example, how do European American women further stereotypical notions of Asian Americans? How were they active in ensuring that most African American women in the early part of the century worked as domestic servants?

Such a response would indicate to women of color that we take them seriously, that we can set aside our agendas and theories, and that we can act in the spirit of collaboration. If white feminists are interested in learning from and working with women of color, we would do well to loosen our grip on our priorities, particularly when women of color criticize those priorities as exclusive and simplistic. A willingness to shift our framework, to 'pivot the center,'[114] would be a particularly constructive move for white feminists interested in cross-racial dialogue.

Finally, it is critical to ask what white women are so afraid of losing when we cling to theories of gender essentialism, and what, in our unwillingness to pick up and apply other theories to our own research areas, we are missing. Such questions are not inconsequential. Indeed, it is possible to charge white feminists with a reluctance and inability to share power and work across differences. Has our refusal to engage work by women of color been an insidious attempt to maintain control of and power over feminist discourse?

The availability of scholarly work by women of color across the disciplines makes it difficult for European American feminists to claim that we were simply unaware of this body of work. Yet we have in large part ignored that work, even as we claim to be interested in women's well-being. In this case, white feminists have decided to retain the power we enjoy, rather than to shift the balance, in terms of both our research areas and representational issues in our departments and universities. This is a profoundly elitist and exclusionary choice. It may be impossible for European American feminists to fully comprehend the ways in and the extent to which such choices have damaged existing cross-racial interactions among women. At the very least, they demonstrate a profound disrespect for the lives and work of women of color.

White feminists have worked hard to generate theories that have legitimacy in scholarly circles. Working with different theories to understand gender and women's oppression may feel like or appear as an admission of failure. In some cases, we may prefer to proceed with imperfect theories that have some credibility than to embrace new theories whose future acceptance we cannot predict. But when our imperfect theories leave some women out, it is critical to ask which women these theories are serving. Further, a reluctance to learn and practice new theories profoundly limits our ability to expand our knowledge base, as well as the practical applications of feminism, particularly in cross-racial contexts. European American feminists who refuse to let go of gender essentialism, are, to a large extent, missing the benefits and knowledge different theories offer.

Categorization and Epistemology

White women's attempts to reject gender essentialism are often intertwined with the act of leaving white women in the center, even if in apparently subtle ways. While white women have made methodological and content-related shifts in their scholarship, these shifts frequently fall short of understanding all women as marked by race and gender. Two books shed light on the paradox of addressing race and prioritizing gender and white women. These books also provide insight into the difficulty of achieving feminist scholarship that is pluralist and cross-racial.

Imelda Whelehan's *Modern Feminist Thought: From the Second Wave to 'Post-Feminism'* offers a useful overview of particular strands of (and problems with) white feminist thought. Addressing issues, thinkers, and tensions central to second-wave feminism, Whelehan's text both summarizes past feminist work and takes up current topics in feminism, including postmodernism and feminism, men and feminism, and identity and feminism. Whelehan is interested in 'the main features of major strands in contemporary second wave thought,' and she addresses liberal Marxist/socialist, radical, lesbian, and black feminisms (the term 'black' is used to refer to all women of color).[115] But apart from briefly historicizing these strands and acknowledging that 'it is not always easy or desirable to divide up feminism into discrete strands,' Whelehan does not discuss her method or rationale for organization. And the organization chosen has two particularly damaging results: Whelehan underrepresents the historical aspects of the work of feminists of color and racially essentializes the theories of women of color.

Whelehan begins by placing European American feminism in an historical context. She makes reference to Mary Wollstonecraft and Simone de Beauvoir, and white feminism thus takes on a history of two hundred years. In the introduction, Whelehan mentions bell hooks and her work in the late 1980s, but she does not cite any earlier feminist work by women of color. Yet African American feminism has roots in the work of Maria Stewart and Anna Julia Cooper. Readers unfamiliar with the origins of feminism will finish Whelehan's book aware that white feminist thought can be traced back to the late eighteenth century; they will also leave this book thinking that feminist work by U.S. women of color dates from the late 1970s.

Whelehan's misleading representation of feminism is directly connected to her choice to address liberal, Marxist/socialist, and radical feminism topically and to confine a range of feminisms by U.S. women of color to an essentialized space of blackness. Whelehan's first four chapters consist entirely of white women. U.S. women of color and black women in other countries are simply black. They have no place or agency in liberal feminism, Marxist/socialist feminism, radical feminism, or lesbian feminism. Her organization further suggests that lesbians of color do not exist, since one must be either a woman of color or a lesbian. In her chapter on black feminism, moreover, Whelehan refers to bell hooks, Angela Davis, Michelle Wallace, Kum-Kum Bhavnani, Pratihba Parmar, Stanlie James, Abena Busia, and several white European and European American feminists. But she makes no reference to Latin American feminism, or to American Indian or indigenous feminisms. Whelehan's organizational choice to confine feminisms by women of color to a single chapter imposes a variety of limits on her text, the most simple of which is that feminists of color do not receive attention proportionate to their work.

Whelehan's text offers little to feminist academics working at antiracist and pluralist feminist scholarship. While she briefly notices that feminism exists beyond the world of white women, she also furthers racist constructions of feminism by deracing white women and by confining U.S. women of color to racially essentialized categories. All women are complex and have identities that extend beyond gender. U.S. women of color address a range of subjects, and disagree with and challenge each other. They have done feminist work within the categories of liberal feminism, Marxist/socialist feminism, radical feminism, and lesbian feminism, and have worked outside of these categories as well. Feminist work written by white women is racially marked. Modern feminist thought is not as simple, unitary, and cohesive as Whelehan would have us believe.

Whelehan's organizational and theoretical choices in *Modern Feminist Thought* evolve out of particular epistemological assumptions although these assumptions are not explicitly addressed. Whelehan represents feminism to be most centrally the work of white European and European American women, and she posits gender as the primary category of analysis while subordinating sexuality and race. Whelehan in fact completely ignores issues of class and nation. Thus she knows feminism as primarily white, and women as primarily gendered. White, middle-class, heterosexual women from the United States and Europe are the norm in this text. Whelehan's book also indicates ignorance of or inability to engage the critique offered by women of color, and thus furthers European and European American women's ongoing devaluation of women of color's scholarship. Organizing the chapters by strands of feminism relevant to a racial cross-section of women would have represented an attempt to treat all feminisms as relevant, and none as central or most important. This organizational format would also have allowed for engaging discussions within each strand regarding how different feminists approach similar issues.

The Problems with Our Theories: Robyn Wiegman and American Anatomies

Robyn Wiegman's book, *American Anatomies: Theorizing Race and Gender*, 'looks to various aspects of Western knowledge regimes since the late Renaissance as they have contributed to the articulation of race and gender differences.'[116] It is part of the growing discourse addressing the construct of race and particularly the saliency of white bodies and theories to these constructs. It also parallels a growing body of white feminist work that is either increasingly abstract and distant from daily practice, or which interrogates racial dynamics without addressing how a critique might contribute to change among actual cross-racial groups of women in or outside of the academy. In its 'rarefied style that seems reserved for a very select group,'[117] as well as in its attention to recent postmodernist discourse, *American Anatomies* is unfortunately removed from material practice and from the concerns raised by women of color.

Through a sophisticated analysis of the visibility of bodily markers,

Wiegman addresses the overlapping nature of patriarchy and white supremacy. As one reviewer comments, 'The book vigilantly analyzes the violence enacted in easy equations of blacks with women and reveals how gendered constructions of whiteness, blackness, and sexuality are crucial to the unequal distribution of American bodies.'[118]

Wiegman writes early on in her text that she 'hopes to contribute to an anti-racist and anti-sexist critique,'[119] and she pursues these issues by analyzing the identity categories of 'blacks and women.' She criticizes the 'homogenization of identities into singular figurations,' and aims to present a careful and thorough approach to multiplicity, 'what we might understand as the central issue in contemporary cultural politics.'[120] She briefly alludes to the oversights of the phrase 'blacks and women': 'Lost in the systematic reduction is the black woman, whose historical and theoretical presence has quite rightly been pursued in recent years as a way of rethinking the inherently compounded nature of social identity.' But Wiegman leaves this insightful statement out of focus as she systematically and thoroughly examines the theories, novels, and films of mostly white men. In a book devoted to 'situating the black woman at the center of investigative study,'[121] that Wiegman chooses to center neither the lives nor the work of African American women is problematic.[122]

American Anatomies will certainly convince some readers that whiteness and racial constructs are academic topics with relevancy to current discourse on cultural pluralism. Wiegman's stated intention was to question modernist constructions of race, sexuality, and gender, and she offers a helpful analysis of these constructions, 'provocatively ... pushing the envelope of current theoretical debates about race, gender, and sexuality.'[123] But white feminists must continue to ask ourselves hard questions about our work, particularly when our aim is to contribute to an anti-racist and anti-sexist critique. Anti-racist feminist work must be in substantive theoretical dialogue with a range of feminist work, and clearly relevant to anti-racist practice. Wiegman's text meets neither of these expectations. Wiegman refers fleetingly to the invisibility of African American women in her introduction. Throughout the rest of the text, she rarely treats African American women as agents. Although she makes reference to Patricia Hill Collins, Hazel Carby, Jacquelyn Dowd Hall, Paula Giddings, and bell hooks, she does not deal with the work of any African American feminist scholar in depth. Further, although Wiegman's book at times addresses race beyond the black-white binary, references to and reliance on work by

Latin American, Asian American, and American Indian feminist theorists are practically non-existent.

Wiegman's lack of attention to theoretical work by African American women is particularly unfortunate in that she misreads African American women's lives and work. Further, when she speaks of feminism, she appears to be referring to white feminism, as her comments do not reflect the work of U.S. women of color. She states,

> Feminists who have sought to answer these questions [the multiple identity of black and female] have recently turned to a methodological refashioning, countering the paradigmatic negation of 'blacks and women' by situating the black woman at the center of the investigative study ... In the context of the visible economies of race and gender in which she is entrapped, the movement from margin to center may in fact replicate the kind of commodification that has recently captured other identity-based political retrievals ... For while the contours of contemporary feminist politics suggest that the only means for tracing and specifying the conjunctive body underlying 'blacks and women' is a methodological recentering, it is not clear that only in this way can the cultural modes and disciplines that define and perpetuate her historic absence can be explained.[124]

U.S. feminists of color have historically and consistently theorized race and gender as intertwined. 'Recent turns' are the reluctant and hesitant realizations of white feminists. 'Visible economies' do trap and misrepresent African American women. In this section, Wiegman erases the particularity of the authors of these tropes, who are often white women. She also ignores discourse in which black women are agents and refuse to represent themselves as trapped. Finally, the 'methodological recentering' she refers to is most applicable to European American feminist theory.

As mentioned above, Wiegman employs theoretical language that is frequently detached from practice and context. Her theories, often related to literary and epistemological critiques, may establish a particular starting point, but they rarely result in levels of practice relevant to the present. For cross-racial work to occur among women in the academy, white feminist work must be meaningful to daily and routine interactions.

Wiegman's conclusion highlights the shortcomings of her text. She is aware of several of the mistakes of white feminism: she criticizes the hope for a 'transcendent sisterhood,' notes the problematic exclusion of issues of race and class in most white feminist scholarship, and agrees that there has been little substantive change in white feminist theories in response to the challenges of U.S. women of color. But, in the last section of her book, she seems to be totally unaware of the historical, in-depth, and broad variety of work by U.S. women of color. Rather than examining the potential dynamics and contours of the type of feminism she proposes, Wiegman writes in her last sentence, 'To take refuge here where answers are always most incomplete – in the how that can never reveal the why it methodologically seeks – means, in the context of this study, suspending any gesture of arrival at its end.'[125] Despite its resonance with some postmodern theorists, in a context of working toward white feminist scholarship that is anti-racist and pluralist, Wiegman's final statement is inadequate.

Racism is rife in the academy and in cross-racial relationships among women. Achieving anti-racism in white feminist theory will be an ongoing struggle. 'Suspending any gesture of arrival at its end' directly contradicts the aims of anti-racist feminism, which does specify an end, even as the movement toward that end is a process. In her last chapter, Wiegman sits in the privilege of extreme and ineffective postmodernism, choosing to indulge in 'knowledge for knowledge's sake.'[126] In proposing that feminism be disloyal to itself (and I assume Wiegman is referring to white feminism), Wiegman avoids a crucial epistemological issue: to whom, then, should white feminists be loyal?

In the context of white feminist work that seeks to offer an 'antiracist and anti-sexist' critique, our scholarship must explicitly attend to two issues. First, it must begin to deal with changed practice and social justice in ways that make sense and are accessible to a substantive group of people in the academy. Those of us who claim to produce anti-racist scholarship can ill afford to ignore or downplay theory that does not tend to practice, especially in light of the critique of women of color and the persistence of racism in higher education. Second, white feminists interested in anti-racist scholarship must make choices, draw conclusions, and take sides. We must choose our loyalties clearly and well. For white feminists committed to anti-racist scholarship, those loyalties should at a minimum relate to the critique women of color have offered and to practical goals in our immediate university and disciplinary contexts. These goals should also have indisputable ties to changed practice among cross-racial groups of people, and they should enable a wider range of people to come to decision-making tables at all levels of higher education.

Conclusion

Who is an authority; issues of identity and representation; and the connections between knowledge, practice, and social change are not amenable to straightforward, simplistic guidelines. The distinctions between traditional epistemology, feminist empiricism, feminist stand-point, and feminist postmodernism draw on assumptions regarding how people construct particular knowledges, and the ways in which these theories incorporate the realities of race and gender. The links between the production of knowledge and race matters in the academy have meaning at a variety of levels. Who is able to speak for, represent, and make decisions about whom; who has the power to create knowl-edge about, and therefore, to a certain extent, to control the images of, particular groups of people; and the social relationships and structures that knowledge producers seek to change are a few critical areas. For example, in a class on American Indians, is it appropriate to rely exclu-sively on texts by European Americans? Is it fair for a faculty with no Asian American representation to decide what the significant number of Asian American students in that department should learn? As teachers, do we educate our students to fit into existing structures, or to challenge those structures, and how do our syllabi and teaching phi-losophies and actions meet those ends?

Knowledge production in the academy can further cross-racial inter-action and change. That is, engaging in cross-racial dialogue with a few colleagues over several years may change the curricular structure and faculty make-up in a department, which may in turn affect what students learn and what they do with that knowledge. White people interested in producing knowledge that supports a wider variety of people at decision-making tables, as well as knowledge that does not normalize and implicitly privilege white and middle-class behaviors, beliefs, and practices, will need to be thoughtful and clear about the knowledge we produce, represent, and claim as authoritative. Do we continue to rely on texts that retain an unmarked affirmation of European American norms? In our own research, do we seek out knowledge by people of color that challenges and upsets our own knowledge?

First, in working toward a more shared endeavor of knowledge pro-duction, we must remember that knowledge is particular, emerging out of specific values, location, and experience. One person cannot know everything about a given topic, nor does he or she need to. Second, cross-racial knowledge will require a range of people at the table. Whites must stop acting as if our presence is enough. European Americans interested in cross-racial knowledge will do well to adopt a kind of epistemological humility. We do not know everything and never have. Our ways of knowing have done and continue to do harm.

Particular Knowledge

In part due to race-related structures and realities, one's location affects what one knows. Many of us live with white privilege every day and in every situation. Even if we reject or interrupt this privilege, it is still offered to and experienced by us. Likewise, we know racism from a different angle than an African American or Latin American. Our knowledge is partial, bounded by experience and values, and by how we attach meaning to any given interaction. How we make meaning is connected to our relationship to power: the ways in which we have power, and the ways in which we do not.

Consider a story that I often tell in class. It is the lesson of not being followed. Employees in stores that sell any kind of product, from books to music to clothes, often follow people of color around the store. Whatever the given reason for this choice, it is nearly always connected to the assumption that an African American, Asian American, American Indian, or a Latin American is more likely to steal merchandise than a white person. No employee has ever followed me in any store. What I know – about myself, about my race, about shopping in general – is shaped by not being followed, particularly when I am not attentive to the absence of being followed.

In part because of the result of not being followed, I may not be immediately suspicious of store employees; I may intuitively believe that merchants, and perhaps others who work for social institutions, trust my intentions and will not do anything to harm me. Likewise, this knowledge stays with me when I do my research: my analysis may be to a certain extent dependent on my experience that social institutions serve me well, and an extension of that experience to the belief that they serve everyone well. Similarly, the power to follow constructs a certain kind of knowledge. In as much as an employee chooses to follow an African American, he or she chooses not to follow a white person. Thus, for every European American who enters a particular store, that employee reconstructs white people as a group, as people who do not steal.

Of course, depending on the location, it may be an African American employee who chooses to follow another African American, and not to follow a European American. Likewise, an employee of any race may choose to follow any person who appears to be poorly dressed, including a white person. However, the range of possibilities is not the point. Rather, structures of power related to race, together with long-standing assumptions and practices, offer a level of consistency to cross-racial interactions that deserves analysis.

Location, and in particular, one's relationship to power, matters. It informs how we look at the world, how we make sense of our surroundings, and how we approach our professional goals and personal relationships. In this framework, in as much as my location and experience in that location affect what I know, my knowledge is particular. Further, my absolute inexperience in being followed affects my values and ethics, how I view injustice and what I seek to change. Knowledge is thus far more than what I read or acquire through mental exertion; it is constantly informed by my daily mix of experiences and interactions. The relevance of experience and location to knowledge should make plain what is still difficult for many European Americans to admit and confront. For knowledge to be democratic and complete, there must be a range of people at the table.

Cross-Racial Knowledge

As pointed out in the earlier discussion of cultural competence, it is convenient for white people to view knowledge as an individual enterprise. However, in the context of higher education, the production of knowledge is always a group endeavor. Even when the work of an individual becomes widely known, it is nearly always the case that other thinkers have validated that person's knowledge. In higher education, thinkers critique, promote, and build on others' knowledge. In the interests of creating a cross-racial knowledge base, then, many will be involved. When pressed, whites often assert that they can be cross-racial simply by learning enough. However, if knowledge is far more than book learning, the production of cross-racial knowledge will require a cross-racial group of people, who bring a range of experiences to any given context. European Americans need to resist the choice to simply add on the lives and realities of people of color to our research and scholarship.

Imelda Whelehan's *Modern Feminist Thought* exemplifies knowledge that represents itself as valid and inclusive while favoring and normalizing white European and European American feminists. As discussed earlier, the author's choice to give white European and European American feminists the privilege of topical areas and assign the feminisms of all women of color to a nondifferentiated space of blackness is a particularly monocultural and monoracial choice. Books like Whelehan's that seek to represent broad strains of knowledge will continue to be monocultural and monoracial until they find a way to methodologically displace white knowledge as the norm, and to clearly identify that displacement. In textbooks across the disciplines, white European and European American values and theories predominate. Chapters or sections on racial-ethnic differences are usually a small part of the book. Rarely is an organizational structure or methodology changed so that the frame is shifted.

While people of color have produced and continue to produce cross-racial knowledge, and while a few fields such as critical studies, cultural studies, and critical pedagogy may bring a racial cross-section of people to the table, cross-racial knowledge, particularly in fields that white people have historically dominated and controlled, is rare. In most cases, European Americans are not willing to share control of the process of producing knowledge. White people are particularly eager to move to celebrating differences before we have learned to absorb the depth and complexity of those differences, or how to work through the distrust those differences have engendered. Further, cross-racial knowledge production rarely happens. A history of exclusion exercised by European Americans, and the resulting distrust of people of color toward white people, means that sustained cross-racial work in higher education is particularly elusive. Whites can take steps to chip away at that lack of trust, the first of which may be to admit that we cannot know everything, and that we need the expertise and experience of people of color to create a useful knowledge base that will contribute to democratic education and social change.

CHAPTER FOUR

The Challenges and Possibilities of Cross-Racial Dialogue

Cross-racial dialogue is one way of negotiating the difficult topics of race and racism. Particularly in the interests of different practice, the ability of cross-racial groups of people to talk to each other is a fundamental necessity. Dialogue can also be a critical component of the development of knowledge at all levels of higher education. Dialogue encourages a useful exchange of ideas. People involved in dialogue routinely assert, question, wonder, offer, challenge, doubt, disbelieve, disagree, and begin again. Dialogue among groups of people, however focused or broad the group might be, is certainly a cornerstone of social change.

At the same time, cross-racial dialogue can be particularly daunting. Race is not a topic that moves easily or often through routine conversations among whites and people of color. While Europeans Americans may frequently interact with people of color at work or in other settings, discussions of race that last longer than five minutes and that are more than a one-time event are particularly unusual. Race, and especially racism and white supremacy, constitute dangerous territory; when white people move up close against these topics in public spaces, the air changes. The inclination for most whites is to register their concern and leave.

'I hang out with people of color all the time. They've never talked about racism as a problem,' white students say. 'Everywhere you look, things are getting better,' white students and some students of color say. Yet when we talk about racism and white supremacy in class, conversation stalls. Students are at first hesitant. When they do voice their ideas freely, sharp differences usually surface. At this point, conversation often shuts down. Talking in meaningful ways about race in public settings is an undeveloped skill; for the most part, even the hint of practicing that skill makes white people nervous.

While racism may not be as blatant or overt as it was thirty or fifty years ago, it is still present. It is possible to think of a range of examples of white supremacy: three European American men dragging James Byrd to death in Texas on 9 June 1998; the lack of accountability on the part of city government and institutions designed to serve the people when four white policemen killed Amadou Diallo on 4 February 1999, as he stood in the doorway of his apartment building; or the fact that Richard Quinn, former presidential candidate John McCain's chief political strategist in South Carolina, is the editor of a newspaper that denounces Dr Martin Luther King and Abraham Lincoln.[1] Kweisi Mfume, the president of the National Association for the Advancement of Colored People, recently brought the lack of media images of people of color to public attention when he criticized the major networks for their choice of nearly all white characters in major roles for the 1999 television line-up.

European Americans are usually hard pressed to agree on the existence and extent of damage of more subtle forms of racism. Indeed, racism in higher education is often less obvious and rarely as clean cut as it is in the situations described above. In hiring processes, whites may profess a desire to diversify their workplaces, then excuse their inability to hire people of color with familiar rationales: not enough people of color have the right credentials; she did not have exactly the right background; or his working style is not the best fit for our department. White teachers continue to allot race at most a one-day or one-week insertion into the term, rather than grappling with how a recognition of race and racism might transform all course material. European Americans are reluctant to look for assumptions and norms in the texts they use, the majority of which have an unmarked bias toward white sensibilities and ways of thinking. Similarly, white people readily make decisions about the use of funds and resources, programmatic priorities in curriculum, university policy, research agendas, and publications, in the absence of people of color, even when those decisions directly affect people of color. Whites do not hesitate to decide for others, even when their authority has little or no connection to those affected by the decisions made.

European Americans are currently somewhat more attentive than they were in the past to the possibility of problems involving race, if unaware of the actuality, variety, and depth of those problems. But the good intentions of those in power may not be sufficient to challenge the seriousness and difficulty of racism in different settings. In feminist contexts, white women believe they are doing more to confront racism than in the past, yet many women of color are convinced they are not doing enough. Racism, in obvious forms or hovering just under the surface of everyday exchanges, is both nuisance and hurdle, especially for white people. We would like it to be gone, sometimes believe that it is, and are often quietly afraid that it is still a problem.

This chapter examines dialogue as one way to confront these realities, to move into the space between 'We're doing all we can' and 'It's not enough' impasses. Dialogue is subject-to-subject interaction committed to critical transformation,[2] and it can provide a place to begin. It allows participants to come to the table as agents interested in changed practice and offers the possibility of directly addressing issues of power and injustice. The history of cross-racial dialogue in the context of white feminism is instructive to dialogue in other contexts.

Dialogue: Subject-to-Subject Interaction

This chapter asserts that cross-racial dialogue is the centerpiece of cross-racial change and anti-racist practice. Most simply, dialogue is respectful conversation. It can happen in classrooms and conferences, in hallways and over coffee. It is possible to view dialogue as a routine and frequent occurrence in our everyday lives. After all, we talk to each other often and easily: in neighborhoods, classrooms, meeting rooms, hallways, and offices.

At a different level, dialogue requires subject-to-subject interaction. Dialogue is built on interactions in which people participate as agents, and not, from anyone's perspective, as victims; where the participants have a stake in the outcomes; and where they come with the desire to confront injustice, and not out of a sense of defensiveness or guilt, or for reasons of charity. Dialogue does not happen in a hurry, or in brief amounts of time. A ten-minute conversation at the end of class about the lack of American Indian images in the media is not dialogue. Dialogue requires attention to changed practice in local and broader locations.

Subject-to-subject interaction most often occurs in the context of working relationships that have developed over time. An Asian American who is in her fourth year at a university may speak about her experience of race and racism to a white student she has known for two years. An African American community organizer may engage in dialogue with a white colleague when the African American has observed that colleague persistently and strategically advocating for people of color over the course of a year. Dialogue may occur when a group of students and faculty work at changing media representation of people of color with a local news station. Dialogue is not easy or routine; it is earned and difficult.

In addition to subject-to-subject interaction, dialogue is mutual inter-action committed to critical transformation. That is, dialogue occurs when people engage in a process that challenges the status quo, and works for power to be shared more widely. Dialogue is not a neutral process that occurs by chance; it is intentional rejection of white supremacy and racist practice. Mutual interaction requires that those committed to anti-racist work attend to history; structures of socio-economic power; issues of access, privilege, and resources; and accountability. Critical transformation is based on choices and practices, individual and institutional, that undo racist realities, that bring a wider variety of people to the locations of decision making, and that transfer power from the hands of a few to those who are most directly affected by the choices made in any given context.

Thus, in a higher education setting, dialogue might lead to a women's studies department examining their curricular and departmental goals. It would require that people in that department consider who the department has served well over time, and whom it has not served well; who has power in the department and the university as a whole, and who does not; to whom departmental resources are available; and to whom the department feels accountable. Dialogue might raise such questions as: Does the department have strong ties with ethnic studies departments in that university? Why, or why not? Does the department, in its courses and programming, offer courses and events that meet a range of students' priorities? Do faculty teaching in the department agree on the department goals and vision, and are a wide range of people, such as students and community members, involved in articulating those goals and that vision?

Dialogue is intentional and value-laden, and it carries an agenda. Mutual interaction committed to critical transformation may occur when a group of faculty, or employees at a non-profit organization, over the course of a few years takes the steps needed to hire and retain faculty or staff of color; when a curriculum committee within a department explicitly addresses how to change curricular models to ensure that culture and social inequality are discussed throughout the term instead of for one week; when a community group working on environmental issues begins to listen to people of color within their local communities defining environment and pollution's effects rather than focusing on national or statewide concerns; or when a day-long workshop on the issue of difference in women's studies is organized around a panel of Latin American women, and the white women present value their contributions instead of feeling marginalized or left out. Mutual interaction committed to critical transformation does not occur on the run, within a single exchange, or simply because a group of people talk about race or diversity.

Dialogue and European American Feminism

In educational and community contexts, knowledge is worked out within groups. People assert knowledge within certain settings and others challenge the assertions made. Thus women of color have challenged the feminism of white women. Lorraine Bethel's 'What Chou Mean We, White Girl?', and Audre Lorde's 'An Open Letter to Mary Daly' are two examples.[3] Knowledge that intentionally privileges dialogue and explicitly articulates context is immediately ethical: such knowledge urges reflection on the ways in which particular people choose to be together.

White feminists who participate in cross-racial dialogue must openly acknowledge long-standing assumptions on the part of European American women which often excluded and continue to exclude women of color. As argued in the previous chapter, white feminist work has not thoroughly and consistently engaged the work of women of color. Further, 'before coalitions [between white women and women of color] can exist on an equal level, much of what women of Color have produced theoretically has to be addressed in the spirit in which is was produced. There are not many examples of white feminists embracing women of Color's writing without cannibalizing them.'[4]

White women often stumble when it comes to understanding the work of women of color 'in the spirit in which it was produced.' Too often, we are unwilling to give up our own norms; we resist learning new frameworks for defining reality, particularly when those new frameworks challenge our own; or we choose to not invest the time, labor, and self-reflection this kind of process demands. Undergraduate students may have come to view Susan B. Anthony as a feminist leader without flaws, and they may strongly resist learning about her racist and exclusionary practices. A faculty member may have drawn heavily on the work of Carol Gilligan, whose commonly cited earlier work is about the psychology of girls, primarily white, middle- and upper-class girls. She may have developed a course largely based on Gilligan's and a few others' work, with little regard for what that work has left out; she may equally be reluctant to redesign that course. Indeed, learning about the scholarship of women of color in the spirit in which it was produced often interrupts our own work. Such learning is inconvenient, brings few rewards in an academic sense, and is often disturbing to white women. Such learning is fundamentally about relinquishing assumptions and revisiting what we know in the context of new knowledge.

One of the most central assumptions this learning challenges is white women's belief in sisterhood. It has been useful for white women to assume and then act as if a common bond exists among all women. Claiming sisterhood quickly establishes the illusory notion that all women can and will come together in resisting gender-based oppression. In the absence of concrete and earned relationships with women of color, holding onto the notion of sisterhood often wrongly reassures white women that they have an ideological bond with women of color, even when material bonds do not exist. Belief in a universal sisterhood also implies that racism is a thing of the past, particularly among liberal, educated, European American women. The claim of sisterhood, or of a fundamental connectedness among women, continues to contribute to tensions between white women and women of color. For example, in women's studies classes, middle-class, white, female students often assume a closeness or affinity with the women of color in the class, simply because they are all women. Likewise, a white faculty member may have one Asian American woman colleague, while the remainder of the department is male. The white woman may act as if she and the Asian American woman colleague share similar priorities and struggles, when in fact, this may not be true.

Particularly in epistemological and ethical discourse, white feminists have frequently drawn on the idea of an overarching feminist consciousness. Such general conceptual frameworks lead to broad notions of 'a previously untapped store of knowledge about what it is to be a woman, what the social world looks like to women, how it is constructed and negotiated by women.'[5] In the 1970s, the idea of a unified 'woman's culture' was common among white women, and again, this notion was primarily based on European American women's interactions with other white women. While some white feminists acknowledge the existence of several expressions of feminist consciousness, they rarely examine the relevance of different, and possibly competing, consciousnesses among women theoretically.

White feminists often act on the unarticulated assumption that feminist consciousnesses exist without rupture or unevenness; apparently differentials of power and access matter in the context of men and women, but not among women. The notion of a fundamental connectedness among women arrogantly assumes that all women desire such a connection. In the example given above, the Asian American woman cannot assume that the white woman is aware of her reality or experience. There is even the risk that the European American woman may make public her assumed affinity with the Asian American woman to other colleagues, entirely without the knowledge of the Asian American woman. The European American woman might joke to her male colleagues, 'We women need to stick together.' In the absence of a genuine mutual relationship, such a comment is inappropriate. Finally, while white feminist work topically addresses specific groups of women, the notion of sisterhood often remains subtly embedded in our work. A reluctance to abandon the idea of sisterhood makes it difficult for white women to engage the existence of difference, conflict, and competing priorities among women. Cross-racial work will not begin with ideas of a fundamental connectedness, or with notions of feminist consciousness that do not significantly address concrete racial variations and tensions among women.

Many women of color have argued that the assertion of a connection, or an overarching and often extremely general claim to living as women, actively prevents cross-racial dialogue. Glossing over or ignoring differences strips women of particular histories and material conditions that are directly related to negotiations of power, and to race privilege and race discrimination. Ignoring difference simplifies women's lives. Often, what really separates women is 'our refusal to recognize ... differences, and to examine the distortions which result from our misnaming them and their effects upon human behavior and expectation.'[6] Cross-racial dialogue among women might most appropriately begin from a recognition of and engagement with our differences. Notions of connectedness and feminist consciousness have not been shaped in cross-racial frameworks and thus have meaning primarily for white women. In the earlier example, the white woman would do well to be open to learning about her Asian American colleague, and particularly about the differences between the Asian American woman's experience and priorities and her own.

White feminists interested in cross-racial dialogue do not walk into cross-racial contexts unburdened or dislocated from the past. Regardless of our individual behavior and practice, cross-racial dialogue among women is problematic. European American women's insistence on sisterhood, on commonalities, and on gender as the primary marker of difference continues to characterize white feminism. Many women of color have experienced white women's arrogance and assumptions. These experiences are not quickly overcome, and European Americans' reluctance to thoroughly examine white privilege as a condition and practice that marks white bodies is similarly problematic. We are still learning how to approach the work of women of color 'in the spirit in which it was produced.' In light of this, a necessary part of cross-racial dialogue for white feminists will be tending to the damage that has resulted from such assumptions, as well as critiquing the exclusionary practices that appear normal to white women. As demonstrated in the next section, looking at racism plainly in a feminist context is made even more difficult by the normalcy of white supremacy in higher education more generally.

'It's All a Setup':[7] Cross-Racial Dialogue and Higher Education

My insistent hope in the possibility of cross-racial dialogue at times borders on the naïve. While in graduate school writing my dissertation, I attended a day-long workshop on cross-cultural feminism. I was particularly excited because the workshop would be led by three Chicana feminists. I had read and appreciated the work of two of these women, and one of the speakers, Cherríe Moraga, was not only or primarily located in the academy, and identified as an activist. I looked forward to a workshop led entirely by Latin American women, and to the possibility of seeing a different way of doing things.

About halfway through the morning, a white professor talked about a class she was teaching on the bonds between white and African American women. Moraga's response to this professor's comments was brief. 'I am not sure what the white women in this class can offer the African American women,' she said. Her point was not hard for me to accept. I realized that I had vast gaps in my learning when it comes to the lives and experiences of women of color; I could also agree with the viewpoint that I was short on resources and perspectives that might offer something of unique value to African American women. But during my doctoral program, I had developed what I knew as constructive working relationships with a few women of color. Those relationships were important to me; our conversations and their knowledge were a significant part of my education in graduate school. My research also assumed the possibility of mutually beneficial relationships among white women and women of color. I was immediately aware that Moraga's comment on the white woman's class was possibly a comment on my own work as well.

'I see that in such a class white women have little to offer women of color,' I said in that workshop. 'We still want the connections to be cheap and easy. But what about when a cross-racial group of women really work at it, when they struggle with race and what it means in immediate ways, in the academy,' I asked. 'Isn't dialogue sometimes possible?' One of the presenters was smiling. Even before Moraga's response, I sensed that my genuine earnestness was both amusing and foolish.

'I don't think so. Not in the university. It's all a set-up. Dialogue in university settings rarely happens.' The conversation quickly moved on and away from my question. But I was and am glad for Moraga's plainly spoken and honest answer. 'It's all a set-up.' I continue to reflect on that comment, to weigh it against my hope for change, to juxtapose it with my desire to move forward too quickly. In many ways, Moraga is right. The academy was set up by a very small group of people compared to the people it now serves. A small group of economically privileged European American men have made decisions about much of what we experience in the academy. The ways in which knowledge is represented; the process by which student-learners become professional academics; how students are taught and evaluated; and the existence and structural configuration of separate academic disciplines are all profoundly relevant to higher education today. All of these processes were largely put in place by this small group of white men. While challenges have always existed, the structures, as well as those who control them, have been firmly in place for years. Any subject-to-subject interaction that occurs in higher education, including the few working relationships I had developed with women of color, is framed and limited by the norms of the academy.

In the context of cross-racial dialogue, Moraga's comment is particularly significant. Given its history the set-up privileges European and European American norms and sensibilities. Thus even when changes are made, the structure usually remains the same. Addressing culture or race for one week in a course for instance, usually does very little to challenge the material presented in the other ten or twelve weeks, all of which may be based on white norms and thus be subtly culturally exclusive. A set-up occurs in the absence of rigorous critical assessment of the norms and assumptions present in academic contexts.

This set-up is especially difficult to alter for three interrelated reasons. First, power in the academy is still in mostly European American hands. Until access to decision-making processes and to resources is made available to a wider racial cross-section of people, there is little likelihood that large groups of people in the academy will seriously question its foundations and structures. A second reason that a set-up prevails in the academy is related to white liberals' belief in the possibility of neutrality when it comes to race and racism in local contexts. Most white liberals choose to believe that racism and exclusionary practices in the academy are the exception rather than the rule. White liberals hope that the elitism of the academy's founders did not infiltrate the system as a whole. Many white people believe that good intentions and a fair system are sufficient to prevent racism and encourage dialogue. They are not. Finally, a third reason for the difficulty of dialogue in the academy is the widespread and frequent lack of awareness among most European Americans regarding the experiences of people of color, in higher education and in other contexts, related to racism and white supremacy. Put simply, most whites are oblivious to the range and depth of ways in which people of color live with racism on a daily basis.

Many scholars can agree, at least verbally if not with our actions, that there is value to diversifying the academy at all levels. 'The general goal is to achieve diversity in all rooms, decision-making rooms, classrooms, faculty rooms, rooms of all kinds, shapes, and sizes.'[8] Unfortunately, this kind of diversity is far from being realized. In 1995, women of color held 2.1 per cent, men of color held 7.6 per cent, European American women held 15.8 per cent, and European American men held 74.6 per cent of full professor positions in the United States.[9] Whites held 85.9 per cent of full-time administrative positions in higher education in 1995, and people of color held 14.1 per cent. It is also clear that for people of color to be present in more rooms in higher education, they will need to continue earning doctoral degrees. Of the

27,000 U.S. citizens who earned doctoral degrees in 1996, white people constituted 23,856, or 87 per cent, and people of color made up 3,542, or 13 per cent of the total.[10] It is not merely the presence of whites in the academy that is the problem. It is the disproportionate presence in relationship to the general population, and in part, their disproportionate presence in higher ranking positions.

Power also resides primarily in white peoples' hands in the academy by virtue of their near-exclusive control over the course of the academy's existence in the United States. The earliest institutions of higher education in the United States were founded in the 1600s, and they were shaped primarily by middle- and upper-class European American men. People of color did not begin to enter institutions of higher education as faculty in significant numbers until the late 1960s and early 1970s, a mere thirty years ago. By that time, the terms and structures of academia, such as curricular norms, disciplines and their organization, hiring and promotion processes, and the representation and legitimation of knowledge, had long been in place.

When white women and men and women of color came to the table of higher education, it had already been thoroughly set. Their choice was to work with what was there, or not to be present at all. Change, especially change that requires an examination of fundamental assumptions and working structures, is particularly difficult when the foundation has been in place for more than a century. European American norms, ideas, and theories about education are deeply embedded in most educational institutions. We do not know what higher education would look like if the process of its development had been democratic.

The continued hope among white liberals that neutrality is possible poses another significant barrier to dialogue. In my experience, most white people in the academy will address and act on issues of race and culture as long as the process is easy, smooth, and within their expectations of what is enough. A monthly meeting about race issues as they relate to pedagogy may be a commitment we are able to make; we may equally decide that restructuring our syllabi in light of what we have learned is not possible. We continue to believe that if we act fairly, we will be working against racism and white supremacy. For example, in a hiring process, European Americans might choose to advertise for the position in a variety of publications that reach racial-ethnic populations. When the applications come in, and there are very few from people of color, we feel that we have done our best. As the hiring process continues, it might become clear that of the one or two candidates of color among fifteen applicants, one, in our minds, lacks the requisite experience for the position. At the end of the process, when a white person is hired, the comments are by now nearly routine: 'The candidates simply aren't out there.' 'Unfortunately, there aren't yet enough people of color in doctoral programs.' 'Her research interests were really too specialized for this position.' 'Hopefully, next time the pool will be a little better.'

Once the process is finished, there may be no follow-up or attention to how the search process might be altered or what universities or organizations can do to ensure that the pool will be more diverse in the future. Further, white people often believe that if they acted fairly and did their best, they are excused from any responsibility regarding who and how they hire. In situations such as the one described above, whites easily draw on sympathy – 'we would truly like to hire a person of color' – and on professed intentions to hire a person of color. Yet when we do not, and when the diversity of our staff does not change, there is little examination of the reasons, or how structures might change, or of the issue of responsibility. The result is that systems and institutions do not look significantly different.

Within contexts that routinely privilege white people, 'fair' is a relative and selective concept. If we can acknowledge that racism has been a problem in the past, and that it is, at least to some extent, systemic, 'fair' means little to those whom people in power have systematically excluded. Further, serious change requires those who hold power to go beyond the usual expectations or norms concerning hiring. Effecting a change in the results of a faculty hiring process or other academic endeavors will require significant changes in the process itself. Because institutions of higher education have been and are systems that exclude certain groups, business as usual, or business as usual with easy and superficial changes, such as advertising in racial-ethnic publications, will simply sustain the exclusion. Neutrality usually means supporting the status quo. Racism in the academy persists because very few white people are willing to offer the energy, time, and commitment to alter the norm.

Finally, most white people are largely unaware of the racial experiences of people of color in the academy. When these experiences do come to public attention, white people frequently deny them, often with a high level of defensiveness; diminish the extent of the damage; and significantly limit the time and attention devoted to listening and responding to those experiences. For dialogue to occur, all participants must know that their knowledge will be respected and validated. If there is a history of denial or of simply ignoring experiences of racism, people of color will be understandably reluctant to bring similar experiences to the table. This denial on the part of white people, and the accompanying reluctance to raise racial issues on the part of people of color, further contributes to a set-up in which located knowledge is not relevant or legitimate.

People of color in the classes I teach have commented to me on statements they hear routinely from professors. 'Your last paper was terrific. I didn't expect that from someone coming from your background.' White students, for their part, often have a hard time accepting the racial profiling that many men of color regularly experience. There is usually an awkward silence when the subject comes up, and white students rarely pursue the discussion. Discussion of such topics among faculty also seems to be firmly off limits, at least in formal settings. There is general and unspoken acknowledgment among most faculty that thoroughly discussing local racisms in any setting is inappropriate. In the minds of white people, it is not our fault; the faculty of color must be glad to have a position here – aren't we doing enough? Again, the set-up limits the conversations we are able to have.

I am convinced of the possibility of dialogue. I also know it is always difficult. The next section articulates four components of dialogue. These four components offer points of entry into cross-racial conversations, a way in which to begin to address the legacy of the set-up that permeates higher education.

Avenues to Dialogue

When white people participate in dialogue, four components are minimally necessary for subject-to-subject interaction to occur. First, whites need to know themselves as subjects within the context of race. We must be aware of and able to grapple with our own socialization, experiences, assumptions, choices, priorities, and agendas when it comes to talking about race. We must know why we are at the table, we must be able to claim what is ours, and we must let be what is not. Second, subject-to-subject interaction requires that white people know people of color as subjects. European Americans must know what people of color are writing and saying, and that people of color are unique individuals with histories and experiences that overlap. Whites must also accept the reality that people of color live outside of our notions of their lives. Third, white people must learn to share space rather than control it. We must learn how to give up the center, to listen, and to pay attention to what people of color offer. Finally, white people must enter the conversation knowing that change is necessary. Cross-racial dialogue will not occur when European Americans are in a hurry; when we are not willing, in practical terms, to act differently; and when we are not ready to work at race, racism, and white supremacy.

White People as Subjects

Talking about race over time is difficult for European Americans, particularly when the conversation is even loosely connected to our own racial identity and white bodies. In most settings, European Americans are accustomed to being in the center. It is difficult for us to sit for an extended period in groups of people without being the main characters. If we consider feminist settings in which women of color occupy more than a token space – one week in an introduction to women's studies course, or one panel on women of color in a two-day conference on women's issues – white women often quickly feel unimportant and peripheral.

For example, in the day-long workshop I mentioned earlier, white women's discomfort with an all-Latina leadership emerged an hour or so before lunch. There was a clear attempt to move the center of conversation from the large group to a smaller group of white women and their concerns. Afterwards, one of the white women organizers of the workshop told me that she had received several complaints from the white women. There was a perception among the European American women participants that the concerns of women of color were not relevant and had nothing to do with the European American women's concerns, and that they were only marginally women's issues.

White people have not learned to be subjects in ways that support cross-racial dialogue. Our patience in regard to learning about and hearing from people of color is limited; we yearn for the process to be neatly bounded and brief. When it is not, we rarely openly profess our discomfort or impatience. Instead of clarifying, 'I misunderstood what this [any cross-racial dialogue] would entail. I am no longer interested,' we usually indicate our lack of interest by trying to shift the agenda to our concerns, or by simply distancing ourselves from the process.

My experience in courses on African American women's lives and scholarship is instructive to white women's ability – or lack thereof – to locate themselves as subjects within the context of race. These courses provide one way into the difficulty of cross-racial dialogue. Four classes in particular, all on womanist ethics, exemplify what I know about cross-racial dialogue. They offer one window onto the tangle of priorities and challenges encountered when white women are not the subjects.

Womanist ethics derive directly from African American women's activism over the last two hundred years. It is a field of thought that explicitly emerges from and speaks to the lives, struggles, and resistance of African American women in the United States. As I consider dialogues in which I have participated about womanist ethics, one question keeps rising, pushing through the memory that is those four classes. It is asked in all of the courses, and repeatedly unsettles, disturbs, interrupts.

'Can white women be womanists?' Women of color in the course look down, look up, clear their throats, look at the white woman who asked the question – it is always a white woman who asks that question – and settle in their chairs. Just when the course was finally moving ahead, finally feeling like everyone realized that African American women are subjects in this course, just when we thought white women could stay out of the center for a few more weeks. Just when ...

'Can white women be womanists?' The white women look up, wait expectantly, widen their eyes in gratitude. After a few weeks in a course about African American women, the word 'feminist' has acquired ugly undertones. I can feel the white women shedding their feminist layers, trying on new womanist clothes, prancing around in an outfit not of their making. We hang on the question mark, waiting for one of the women of color to celebrate, even bless, our conversion. But the blessing we expected is not forthcoming, and our conversion stalls. In the silence, the women of color wait, patient and at ease with the knowledge that 'this is not our mess.' The white women settle in their chairs, give up on the blessing, and hope for some kind of redemption.

'Can white women be womanists?' After four courses, I am learning not to take or lay claim to things that are not mine. After four courses, I know my answer to that question is, 'What about being good feminists?' I know that I need to work with what I have; need to shape my knowing and theories from my own body; need to address the flaws in white feminism, acknowledge my part in the mess, and act differently.

Cross-racial dialogue among women will occur when white women know who we are, when we know what is ours, and what is not. That is, we must not quickly move to appropriate and use for our own purposes that to which we have no claim, such as an ethical framework developed by African American women based on African American women's activism. At the same time, we must acknowledge our historical connection to white supremacy, raised earlier in the example of racism in the suffrage movement. An awareness of who we are in the context of race requires thoughtful attention to our interest in and connection to race and racism, from a position of agency rather than defensiveness or guilt.

Entering the conversation as subjects also requires white women to think through the ways in which they own and represent knowledge and experience. How easily do we speak with authority about experiences that are not our own, and to which we have no ethical claim? How readily do we engage that with which we are uncomfortable that is actually ours, such as racism among white women leaders of the suffrage movement? Finally, when we have not addressed the issues of who we are and what is ours in the context of race in an in-depth manner, do we acknowledge this, pause, and listen hard to what women of color are saying? Entering into cross-racial dialogue with women of color as subjects may require a serious shift for white women.

In the womanist ethics classes, white women were eager to distance themselves from a category – feminism – linked to racist actions. As we began discussing the relationship of European American women and African American women historically, distance from the general category of feminist became desirable. It became difficult and in some cases impossible for the white women in those courses to constructively link themselves to other European American women and white women's histories within feminism. Once we knew some of those European American women were racists, we wanted nothing to do with them.

Such distancing not only signals our reluctance to undertake necessary hard work but also indicates a lack of racial understanding on the part of white women. The struggle for women's suffrage is partly about white women's racist choices. Addressing this complexity, rather than denying or ignoring it, must be part of European American women's anti-racist movement. To enter as subjects into cross-racial dialogue, we must be able to know that we live with white privilege and act within the context of white supremacy. White people must know where they have been in terms of their own socialization and history, where they are now, with a clear grasp of their assumptions, knowledge and lack of it, ethics, loyalties, and reasons for being at the table, and, in the context of race, they must know where they want to go and how their priorities and agendas will support that movement.

Knowing ourselves as subjects within the context of race requires a clear sense of our own socialization and history, at both individual and broader levels. Have we thought long and hard about the lessons we have learned about race? Have we read any book by a person of color with significantly different ideas than our own? When our defensiveness surfaces, do we put down the book, leave the conversation, and/or decide to stop thinking about race? I regularly see students read an article about race with which they disagree, then complain about one sentence or one idea in the article, without considering the overall content and contributions that article makes.

Questions such as 'Can white women be womanists?' are in part the result of being taken by surprise in a public setting. Learning racist history and the disrespectful choices of European American women may be new for white women. When we feel guilty or ashamed, it is easiest to simply leave that history and those choices behind. Defensiveness and guilt often act as stop signs for white people, and prevent us from grappling with what we might learn. While guilt and shame may be part of the process when white people learn about racism and white supremacy, neither feeling is useful for cross-racial work.

Socialization is a powerful and pervasive teacher, and acts on us regardless of our good intentions to refrain from racist behavior, our interaction with people of color, and our knowledge of people of color. For most white people in the United States, media-based images provide the most frequent and ongoing knowledge we have of people of color. Even as we interact with and read work by people of color, these media images leave their imprint. Long-standing images of women of color have origins in historical events.[11] Further, while many of these images may seem obvious to most white feminists in the academy, the social construction of images is far too complex for us to quickly dismiss their relevance.

In the context of race, each of us carries assumptions, knowledge, and ethics. Coming to the table of cross-racial dialogue to ease guilt, to fulfill a one-time commitment we made to ourselves or to a colleague, or simply out of the desire to be seen at a meeting about race are usually entirely self-serving and counterproductive reasons. Cross-racial dialogue occurs when people come to the table interested in changing a certain situation or context to which they have a connection, and when those people are interested in a long-term process.

In addition to knowing why we are at the table, we must have some idea of where we hope to go in the context of particular dialogues. What is the work leading toward? Often, relationships among cross-racial groups of people can begin to form when there is a task at hand to which that group is committed. Commitment to and accomplishment of particular tasks, such as learning about African American women's realities and experiences in the courses mentioned earlier, can offer a basis from which cross-racial groups of people might together articulate similar or parallel agendas regarding anti-racist work.

'Can white women be womanists?' In a rush to distance themselves from white feminism, the white women in that class felt they had the privilege to simply appropriate and employ a way of thinking and living to which whites have no claim. Such impulses are arrogant and shallow. In moving to take what is not ours, in the context of cross-racial dialogue, whites signal both profound disrespect for and ignorance of the work of people of color and a lack of understanding with respect to the difficulty of the process of dialogue. The ability to claim what is ours and to respect what is not occurs when we acknowledge our relationship to white supremacy; when we locate ourselves in our own contexts; and when we speak specifically about our experience and knowledge and resist broad generalizations.

Whites signify a commitment or lack of commitment to cross-racial dialogue in the ways in which we articulate our relationship to white supremacy. Statements that establish our self-perceived racial awareness or rejection of racism and white supremacy roll off our tongues effortlessly. 'I have lots of Asian American friends,' 'I signed up for the diversity committee at work,' 'I have read all of Alice Walker's books,' or 'I've learned so much from Native American spirituality' are a few of the comments whites make in an attempt to separate themselves from other, less aware white people.

At an immediate level, such statements are disturbingly problematic. First of all, none of them insure change, or guarantee justice. 'Lots of [any group of people of color] friends' is a worn-out expression that whites most often raise out of a conscious or unconscious defensiveness and as an attempt to establish diversity credentials. Further, we may never have talked about race or racism in any significant way with those friends. 'Serving on the diversity committee at work,' or 'reading all of Alice Walker's books,' again indicate little if anything about a commitment to anti-racist practice. Finally, European American misrepresentation of, packaging of, and profiting from American Indian spirituality, nearly always severely out of context, is a particularly offensive and damaging practice.

Cross-racial dialogue is built on actions that support anti-racist movement and change, and not on claims or beliefs that fail to translate into changed practice. White people must understand that they engage in white supremacist behavior and live with white privilege. We are always and everywhere white. Separating our bodies from an intimate connection with white supremacy is materially impossible. Further, such professed separation immediately signals our reluctance to claim what is ours, and demonstrates an inability to grapple with race as it is written on our bodies. Comments such as 'I'm not racist but ...,' or 'Racism is so terrible. I'm really glad that I'm not racist ...' immediately signal to others that the speaker is unaware of the pervasiveness of racism and its presence in our lives. Discussions of whiteness and white privilege in class often prompt white students to ask me if I think all white people are racist, a question which usually immediately reveals the hope that they are not. Such comments, and an accompanying reluctance to acknowledge the intractability of racism, make dialogue difficult.

In contrast, considering the ways in which we live with white privilege can indicate our willingness to accept what is ours and acknowledge the mess that is racism and white supremacy. For white people interested in cross-racial dialogue, it is critical to understand that even as we work at anti-racism, we will continue to make racist choices. Dialogue is far more likely to occur when we are able to mark our complicity in racist structures than when we distance ourselves from the problem and reach for badges.

Finally, in the process of claiming what is ours and letting be what is not, white people must learn to speak specifically and resist broad, general statements. As demonstrated in the previous chapter, white feminist discourse that aims to speak for all women usually leaves large groups of women out; such work indicates we are not ready for or interested in dialogue. Learning to speak out of our own particular experience and knowledge, and resisting speaking for others, will increase the chances of dialogue.

The question of who can speak for whom is a difficult issue. In the context of dialogue, paying careful attention to who speaks about whose lives is important. When we read scholarly work about specific groups of people, are we aware of who has produced that scholarship? Determination of the standpoint of the author can help scholars discern the role of values and priorities in a particular article or chapter. Certainly, one's stake in an issue, or lack of stake, affects the ways in which one views, researches, and writes about an issue. White feminist work emerged in part because white women became tired of European American men speaking and writing about women's experiences.

A willingness to speak specifically also encourages white people to stick to the topic at hand. In conversations of which I have been a part, white people move quickly away from local racisms. One tactic I see used repeatedly, and which immediately stops dialogue, is a diversion away from local white supremacy to the potential for similar behavior in all people on the planet. 'I know it is human nature for people to compare themselves and try to find out who is better. It is natural to create and use stereotypes, for example.' The attempt to confine every single human being within an overarching comment is a particular feature of white supremacy. It also provides an escape route for white people and dulls the sharp edges of racism closer to home.

European Americans often choose to discuss race relations in another country, particularly a country in which they have spent only two or three days, or about which they have read a single article or book. Often, this limited exposure gives us the feeling that we are instant experts. 'I know in Brazil racism is a big problem. The indigenous Brazilians really have a lot of oppression to deal with.' This external focus indicates that white people in the United States are not ready to discuss racism in their own contexts. It is also often easier for European Americans in the United States to move to an international context, or to talk with people of color who are not from the United States, than to deal with U.S. cross-racial relationships, or learn to speak to a U.S. person of color in their own department about racist practice.

Knowing what is ours and what is not requires us to limit our speech to our own knowledge and experience, and to practice caution when we claim authority beyond our location or outside of where we stand. Once racism is the subject at hand, white people must be able to stay with the topic, no matter how difficult. Participating in dialogue as a located subject calls for whites to practice humility, rather than moving out of subject status to an expert level in which we assume the right to make sweeping generalizations.

Knowing People of Color as Subjects

The second component of cross-racial dialogue is knowing people of color as subjects. Recognizing our own raciality and location in cross-racial dialogues is only a first step and on its own is not sufficient for cross-racial dialogue to occur. White people must learn to interact with people of color in ways that move beyond stereotypes and too-small ideas of what people of color have to offer cross-racial dialogue.

The ways in which European American women talk about women of color in routine interactions offer insights into the potential for cross-racial dialogue. Whether we recognize it or not, white women regularly signify a level of interest in and commitment to cross-racial dialogue. The following brief conversation provides an example of how white women mark themselves as uninterested in cross-racial dialogue.

'bell hooks and Patricia Hill Collins – they got all their history wrong.' In a narrow hallway in the comfortable setting of a social science department, I am caught short by these words. That hallway is filled with two white women's bodies, my own and that of the professor, a prominent and well-published feminist scholar, and her smile and dismissal take up any leftover space. I feel no way out, no unburdened emptiness to which to flee.

'bell hooks and Patricia Hill Collins – they got all their history wrong.' The statement is made during a break in a course that includes attention to feminist theory, and the professor has initiated our interaction. I am still learning the suddenness of racism, how it sweeps into common space, seemingly without roots or context. '... all their history wrong' is tagged onto quick 'hellos' and 'how are yous.' In that narrow hallway, commentary on the weather would have been more suitable than her smile and dismissal. I search for a mask that discredits that dismissal. I hope the silence that now cuts the space between us tells her that although we may be standing in the same hallway, we are not on the same side.

Then she is gone. I am alone in the hallway, relieved and disturbed, glad at her going. I quickly step back into the classroom, where voices and faces and bodies push out her smile and put her dismissal on hold.

'... they got all their history wrong.' In six words, the professor opened and closed the file on both scholars. A couple weeks later, when the same class is in small groups and we are discussing feminist theories, I ask the women in my group: 'What about Patricia Hill Collins's work? How does her scholarship fit here?' The conversation is brief. Although the one African American woman in the group knows Collins's work, none of the white women do. Although I was able to press the issue in the small group, I chose not to do so with the professor herself. As a doctoral student, I knew I might choose to ask for her professional support, even as I disagreed with her comment. I did not find a way to balance, for myself, the importance of challenging her comment and the possible risk of losing her potential assistance.

These two exchanges, one in a shrinking hallway and the other in a small group, are part of the larger conversation white feminists are having about the work of women of color. In a narrow hallway, quick dismissal between two white women ended any conversation before it began; in a small group, what we did not know prevented discussion. Quick dismissal and ignorance have no place in cross-racial feminism. It is obvious that working knowledge of and critical interaction with the work of Collins and other women of color are minimally necessary for white feminism that is cross-racial.

Patricia Hill Collins is well aware of the dynamics that encourage situations such as the one described above. She writes, 'This dialectic of oppression and activism, the tension between the suppression of Black women's ideas and our intellectual activism in the face of that suppression, comprises the politics of Black feminist thought. More important, understanding this dialectical relationship is critical in assessing how Black feminist thought – its definitions, core themes, epistemological significance – is fundamentally embedded in a political context that has challenged its very right to exist.'[12] White feminist scholarship that is cross-racial will question our own contribution to denying work such as that by Collins its right to exist in our local contexts. Through our engagement of the scholarship by women of color, in what we read, learn, teach, assign, write, and represent, we actively position ourselves in concrete relation to scholars of color.

We cannot talk in meaningful ways about that which we do not know, or about that which we choose to dismiss with little explanation or apparent rationale. It is critical for white women to know what women of color are writing and saying, in our respective fields and in our local communities. But when we do begin to take an interest in the lives and work of women of color, we often expect those women to educate us at our convenience and on our terms. We might ask to go to lunch to talk about their experience of 'being Asian in [any given city],' or communicate to a colleague or an acquaintance our excitement about our new interest in diversity. Such requests and comments assume women of color have the time we are demanding; we insist on their attention, often on the strength of an interest that may fade, and on few, if any, actions. We may also neglect to consider if, why, and to what extent women of color are invested in our new interest.

White women committed to cross-racial dialogue will be able to do much of the work of anti-racism on their own and with other white women. We will also recognize that meaningful cross-racial relationships are usually based on changing unjust situations. Such change will only occur when white women have educated themselves about women of color in their local communities. Are we paying attention to what is going on in their communities? Are we thinking about how the local news media portrays and represents people of color? Are we seeking out their local newspapers? In an educational context, have we carefully read what people of color are saying in our field? If, in our particular area of research or teaching, we do not easily find the work of people of color, do we consider the reasons for this? Does our particular field offer anything to people of color, other than a purely theoretical and academic exercise? Are we talking with other white people about racism in constructive ways that are aimed at change?

White people committed to anti-racism will begin to take the time to learn what they do not know about people of color in their local communities and contexts. We can listen to what people of color are saying, rather than suddenly presenting them with a series of questions that imposes our own agenda and assumes our right to know. We can read, watch, listen, and drop any defensiveness or arrogance we may have around our own racism or race awareness. We can consider what we learn, and its significance for our commitment to anti-racist practice.

Part of this learning process requires us to recognize that people of color are at once unique individuals and members of racial and ethnic groups with histories and relationships to structural power that overlap. All people of color experience a different relationship to white supremacy and institutional racism than white people because of their race. As discussed in chapter 2, whites brought African Americans, Latin Americans, and Asian Americans to the United States, or permitted their entry, for economic gain. White people committed genocide and forced assimilation on American Indians. This overlap of history is significant and must be recognized.

At the same time, people of color are individuals with a variety of experiences, values, and priorities. Further, they may experience significant differences in an ethnic and/or tribal sense among the larger racial group. For example, Asian American women have connections to China, Vietnam, Japan, India, and Thailand. African Americans may have strong regional differences. Latin American women come from Chile, Nicaragua, Venezuela, and Puerto Rico. American Indians are Navajo, Mi'kmaq, Tlingit, Lakota, Spokane, and Menominee. These countries and tribes have unique histories and specific experiences of colonialism, autonomy, and resistance. Class, language, and sexuality also mark women of color.

White people must recognize and appreciate the diversity among people of color. Particularly when we begin learning about race, we may want that learning to be simple and quick. It may be challenging enough to have a conversation with one person of color about race, and we may hope that a single conversation can illuminate the issue. After building a relationship with a Latin American woman at our workplace, we may be surprised when another Latin American woman colleague has very different opinions and experiences. We must also resist expecting a single person of color to speak for everyone in their group – 'What is the American Indian perspective on this issue?' 'What do your people really want?' – or that reading a single article by a person of color is sufficient to inform us of the views of all people of color.

White people must resist making assumptions about people of color in general based on what one person of color says or does. If we work with several people of color, it is inappropriate to talk to one and then speak to a supervisor as if we have knowledge about all of the women in our department. Hearing from one person of color in a classroom means that the ideas of one person of color have been brought into that classroom. Knowing people of color as subjects requires that white people commit to reading and listening to a range of people of color.

A final component of knowing women of color as subjects is accepting that people of color live beyond white peoples' notions of their lives. No matter how well I know or how much I talk to a person of color, I never grasp the entirety of his or her reality. This idea may be perfectly clear to us in regard to other whites, particularly when they hold authority over us. We understand that even after working with a white colleague for ten or twenty years, they are larger or more than our notion of them. However, in a racist society, in which white people and institutions persistently represent people of color as less than and as subsets of the norms whites have created, knowing that people of color exist beyond our conceptions of them is a significant challenge. For example, after a brief exchange with a colleague of color about the class she is teaching this term, we may think we know her research interests. Living in a racist society that presents whites as more accomplished and better than all people of color enables this kind of jump, which may from the outside appear illogical.

When white people begin thinking about the lives and work of people of color, it is easy to impose the 'newness' of the topic onto those lives or work. That is, if I only recently began seriously considering people of color with whom I come into contact everyday, then they only recently began to exist in that framework as well. I may share my surprise at a student's experience of racism with a colleague of color, expecting that colleague to be surprised as well. I may see that colleague as owing me a solution, and not consider what I hope to achieve by telling him of the incident. It is similarly easy to assume the universality or exclusivity of our frameworks for understanding race relationships and racism. That is, we act as if our assumption that racism only occurs in isolated ways in our department is universally accepted and true, and we may be taken aback when we hear it is routine. White people rarely have to question the legitimacy of their world-view in a racial sense. But we often apply that world-view to other lives without a second thought, even when the fit, or the desire of people of color to live within that white frame, may not exist.

An example of this tendency in a classroom context occurred when a women's studies class I taught read Jewell Parker Rhode's book, *Magic City.* The book is a historical novel about white people burning to the ground an African American community in Oklahoma in the 1920s, in the process killing hundreds of African Americans. In this book, African American men and women have concrete and specific roles within the community. When the crisis begins, these roles become sharper and more clearly defined. In class discussion, the students, twelve white women, one African American woman, and one Asian American woman, were eager to talk about these roles and the gender issues attached to them.

Shortly into the conversation, I asked the students if they had studied gender roles and relationships from an African American perspective. Apart from the one African American student, none had had close or ongoing experience with African American understandings of gender. When I asked which knowledge and theories they were using to approach gender in this book, the white women acknowledged they were relying on white experiences and scholarship. Relationships among women and men in African American contexts developed under different historical conditions, and continue to exist in a context in which white people have far more control over images that represent how people live. In this class, I felt it was inappropriate for us to analyze African American gender roles with little or no knowledge of how African Americans have conceptualized and constructed gender.[13]

Knowing people of color as subjects means that white people must accept the possibility of not knowing. In the situation described above, most of the class had no in-depth knowledge of African American gender roles. We must learn to pause before we move forward with the kind of shallow authority demonstrated in this example. The extent of misrepresentation and lack of representation of the lives of people of color, and particularly the lack of representation of people of color by people of color in academic contexts, is vast. Simply not knowing, not having the tools, framework, or knowledge with which to approach a topic involving people of color, is common among white people. Cross-racial dialogue will be more likely to occur when whites can acknowledge that people of color are subjects who occupy and enjoy entire worlds with their own norms, values, belief systems, and ethical and relational frameworks, which have been and remain outside of white vision and knowledge.

Subject-to-Subject Interaction: Negotiating Cross-Racial Spaces

Once whites have begun the process of understanding themselves and people of color as subjects in the context of cross-racial dialogue, we have reached the point where dialogue is possible. At the same time, the actual practice and experience of dialogue can be taxing, difficult, and frustrating. Even when white people are clear about their own racial identity, know their reasons for being at the table, and have some knowledge of the concerns and work of people of color in local contexts, dialogue may prove elusive and unattainable. In the example used above, the white women in the class may decide that they have done enough, that reading about African American gender roles in addition to the text is simply beyond their level of commitment. Similarly, a faculty member on a diversity committee at his university may be reluctant to invest beyond the time required by the meetings themselves. We may realize that we do not know enough about the situation of people of color in a given context, or that we underestimated the energy we would need for the process of cross-racial dialogue. Once at the table, moreover, we may also experience different styles of communication. Finally, once we begin to actively pursue cross-racial dialogue, we may realize that even though we believed we had some understanding of what the process of dialogue would look like and involve, it is in fact entirely new, and suddenly feels awkward and overly difficult.

How whites practice cross-racial dialogue is critically important to subject-to-subject interaction. For the most part, popular culture and the majority of social and academic institutions do not offer a range of models for cross-racial dialogue. Cross-racial interaction that addresses racism and white supremacy in an ongoing, in-depth manner is rare. Even students taking classes specifically on race issues comment that it is difficult to engage in discussions. For most white people, and perhaps for some people of color, concrete talk about race in cross-racial groups that lasts more than thirty minutes and that leads to changed practice at any level is nearly non-existent. For most of us, awareness of race is not present in our lives in routine and meaningful ways. Most whites have not learned the practice of dialogue in cross-racial spaces, and unquestioned and unexamined white supremacy leads white people to make assumptions and assertions that shut down dialogue before it can even begin.

The moment white people enter a cross-racial context, they, intentionally or not, begin indicating to those who are watching their interest in and ability for cross-racial dialogue. Our conversation patterns, communication choices, and interactive tendencies mark us. For example, are we able to listen, which requires us to cease talking? Are we able to stay out of the center, as subjects and as participants? Do we quickly publicize our high level of race awareness by listing our anti-racist accomplishments? Do we insist on our own terms and agendas, or are we able to let others set the terms of discussion and action? Do we pause before asking questions, giving others a chance before claiming the space for ourselves? Particularly for white people who are used to some level of authority in public spaces – for example, that enjoyed by teachers – it can be difficult to resist the impulse to 'get things moving,' to simply stay out of the center and wait. Whites interested in cross-racial dialogue will need to consider the advantages of watching, listening, and sharing control in cross-racial spaces. Given the systematic exclusion of people of color from nearly all areas of public life and institutional control, whites will need to sit down – the process will take time – and be willing to work with different frameworks and approaches.

In a class I taught addressing topics including race, class, and gender, I met with a group of fifteen students twice a week to examine how women and men live race, gender, and socio-economic class. I designed the class explicitly to pay attention to values, as well as to questions of power and access. Likewise, I encouraged students to think about the issues at immediate and material levels.

Students brought in case studies based on their own experiences to learn how to analyze the intersections of race, gender, and class at routine and practical levels. These case studies, along with the topic matter, quickly brought sensitive issues, and our relationships to them, to the surface. In this context, subject-to-subject interaction became a central challenge, and a primary way for students to learn from each other.

About halfway through the term, students raised the issue of how racial diversity plays out in a city that is 90 per cent white. The white students commented on this. 'It is hard to find people of color to hang out with.' 'Yeah, at work we are mostly all white ... neighborhoods are pretty segregated ...' The Asian American and African American women chose not to comment. Suddenly – I did not expect the swiftness and intensity of the question – a white woman asked the African American student in the class, 'What do you think about this issue? How do you experience the lack of racial diversity in Portland?'

The African American woman did not answer. Another white student made a related comment, and then the white woman who asked the first question returned to her urgency to know. Addressing the African American student again directly, she pressed for an answer. The African American student clarified she did not want to answer that question, and that she did not have to respond. She also wondered 'what was behind the question.' At this point, the other students were waiting, uneasy. 'Will this pass without doing damage?' was a question, hanging.

The white woman who asked the question was angry. In her mind, she had a right to ask, and the other student should answer. 'What do you mean, "What is behind the question?" I just want your opinion.

How else am I going to learn?' Her voice is hard, demanding, impatient. The African American student is quiet, finished with the issue.

I answered the white woman, and stated that the African American woman was not required to answer. 'Nothing is "just a question,"' I said. 'Questions carry assumptions and values. They carry reasons for wanting to know. Trying to force an answer is not appropriate here.' At this, the white woman quickly gathered her books. 'I'm getting out of here. I have had enough of this shit' were her parting words. She was gone. We were all left, sitting in the ripple of her anger, and in the tension resulting from the exchange.

Cross-racial subject-to-subject interaction will not consistently proceed in ways that are always and entirely comfortable for white women. The format of question-answer is a way of gaining information that most whites understand and regularly exercise. It is never the only way to learn, nor is it always respectful and mutual. When white people begin to act on an interest in race, and not necessarily on a commitment to anti-racism, they often turn to a form of interaction that is comfortable, easy, and familiar. We start asking questions, and assume the person of color we have asked is ready to answer, in our framework and on our terms. We assume their readiness to answer regardless of how long we have known the person, our relationship to that person – teacher-student, student-teacher, supervisor-employee, neighbor-neighbor, or grocery shopper-checker – or that person's interest in or connection to our perhaps recent (and possibly fleeting) interest in learning about race.

The white student in the situation described above assumed that she had a right to know, and that forcing an answer was appropriate behavior. Particularly in learning contexts, the often-repeated 'no question is stupid' fuels the assumption that 'all questions are welcome.' If people of color do not answer questions when asked nicely, whites have a right to demand an answer. Even had the white student acted in a more civil manner and not pressed for a response, other white students in the class might easily feel frustrated with the African American woman's decision not to respond, rather than wonder at or identify the assumptions embedded in the white woman's question. Once a question is asked, the burden falls on the person asked to answer. The very right of asking itself is rarely challenged.

Subject-to-subject interaction requires European Americans be thoughtful about the ways in which they move through cross-racial contexts. Do we, out of habit, assume our centrality, our right to know, the appropriateness and perhaps superiority of our way of communicating and learning? Do we assert our terms without taking the time to notice and honor other terms, different ways of communicating, learning, interacting, and talking? How do we leave or make space for other realities and norms? In the example above, if the European American woman had waited with her question, and the rest of us had likewise put aside our agendas and waited, the entire class may have learned from what the African American woman chose to offer to the learning process, on her terms and in her own time.

Once white people force an issue, people of color may understandably feel differently about their potential contribution to a group. Cross-racial dialogue requires European Americans to consider the nature of their participation in cross-racial groups. Choosing to listen, rather than always to talk and question; to watch, rather than to decide; and to share space, rather than to assert our own norms and thus control the space, are useful guidelines for whites interested in pursuing cross-racial dialogue.

As I began intentionally paying attention to how I interacted in cross-racial contexts, I realized that my habitual insertions and practiced norms were both awkward and disruptive of cross-racial dialogue. Persistent questions, attempts to hone in on what I decided I needed to know, occasional references to my high level of awareness of white privilege, especially in comparison to other European Americans, and quick sprints away from any shimmer of guilt – 'I don't/ never [insert any racist act or choice]' – do far more to maintain my own position within the status quo than to further any possible dialogue. White people typically move into common space and assert norms and ways of interacting which then set a context for exchange that can be difficult to shift.

Choosing to watch, to observe, to pay attention to the norms of interacting and behavior of people of color, even if there are twelve whites and only two or three people of color, will support cross-racial dialogue. Space in which white people dominate the communication patterns and norms is so prevalent, particularly in academic contexts, that people construct and maintain this space with profound ease and regularity. European Americans ask, assume, choose, decide, tell, proclaim, and conclude, and in so doing, make clear to people of color an inability to negotiate and share those processes. Watching in an engaged manner, rather than in an aloof and detached way, signals that we are willing to learn, that we recognize the existence of multiple realities and norms. It marks the possibility that white people are ready to share space instead of grabbing it whole. A sincere humility, and one that does not turn into an inability to work at change, also lends itself well to cross-racial dialogue. Reminding myself that there are entire worlds of which I know little or nothing helps me watch, wait, and acknowledge that I am ready to learn.

'Pivoting the center' can be a particularly useful concept for white people interested in cross-racial dialogue. Pivoting the center, the ability to 'center in another experience, validate it, and judge it by its own standards without need of comparison or need to adopt [one's own] framework' as normal or primary, enables the recognition of different realities and experiences.[14] It does not require whites to 'walk in another person's shoes.' But it does challenge us to resist judgment, evaluation, or assumptions as we interact with people of color. In the example cited previously, where students were ready to analyze African American gender relations in *Magic City* from a European American perspective, it allows whites to acknowledge that African American gender relations are independent of, rather than embedded within or a subset of, white notions of gender roles. Pivoting the center can help European Americans learn different ways of interacting. It can assist us in accepting that which is different on its own terms, instead of persistently measuring differences against the 'norm' of white sensibilities and frameworks.

As I teach about race and culture in my classes, one of the most challenging ideas to communicate is that the question-answer format is only one way of gaining information. I am particularly aware of how my increasing ability to practice not asking has contributed to my own learning about racism and white supremacy. Listening rather than asking requires white people to relinquish control, to trust that people of color will offer what they want whites to know, and to exercise a patience and trust in the process that may feel impossible, and at times useless.

The decision to listen rather than to ask is neither simple nor straightforward. I do not wish to be prescriptive. In many situations, people of color may be pleased that white people do ask, rather than simply making assumptions or moving forward without consideration of different ideas. In contexts in which white people often choose ignorance when it comes to the lives and realities of people of color, European Americans' questions can be welcome relief. Particularly when a working relationship has been established between a white person and a person of color and has a history of at least one year, asking can be appropriate and can encourage dialogue.

In the absence of such a relationship, asking, and the unspoken yet present assumption that the person one asks will/should respond, can be invasive, arrogant, and an obstacle to cross-racial dialogue. In many cross-racial situations, questions roll off European American tongues easily, with little or no thought to the assumptions inherent in them.

Questions impose a set of terms, privilege the asker's right to know, may demand private information in public settings, assume the person asking the question should have access to a piece or pieces of someone's life, and in many cases, place the asker and the person asked in an unequal relationship. For example, in the classroom situation described above, the white woman's question assumed that her way of framing the issue – in terms of the absence of racial diversity in the city – was relevant for the African American woman. As the white student pressed her question, the burden of answering fell on the African American student. The intrusiveness of the question, and the arrogance behind it, faded as the center shifted: all eyes moved to the African American student. How would she respond? Would she answer? A lack of response, despite the African American student's ease in her choice, would indicate a refusal to participate or to act constructively. White supremacy ensures that European Americans can ask intrusive questions of nearly any person of color in a public setting and expect a response.

White students, following a presentation on racial profiling, newly aware of the seriousness of this issue, may turn to students of color in the class and press them for their experiences of racial profiling. While knowledge of students of color may be relevant to the topic at hand, it should be shared on their own initiative. In plain terms, that information is not, as a matter of course, other students' or the teacher's business. 'I am just trying to learn ...' a white student may object after asking such a question. But such questions demand that students of color discuss personal, perhaps painful issues. It is wrong for whites to assume that they can demand that information.

At the conclusion of a colloquium on the challenges faculty of color face in obtaining senior scholar status, faculty members may newly wonder about the reality of this situation in their departments. Suddenly faced with the possibility of discrimination in their own department, they may seek quick absolution. If, in the public setting of the colloquium, a white faculty member asks a faculty member of color,

'Have you experienced those discriminatory practices here?' it may be extremely risky for that faculty member of color to offer a response. Pleasing the chair of the department may require him or her to deny the existence of discrimination in a cursory manner, when the situation is likely far more complex, regardless of whether that individual faculty member has experienced discrimination. If the white faculty member who asked the question is sincerely interested in the possibility of discrimination in his or her department, it may be most appropriate to begin an investigation with European American colleagues, and to carefully examine practices and structures within the department to see how they fit with the presenter's description of discrimination. Unfortunately, many European Americans believe they have a right to ask. Asking is a privilege we easily assume. In asking, we rest on our norms, assert them above all others, and overlook entirely the presence of alternative ways of interacting and learning.

The practice of listening offers a way into dialogue for white people that asking regularly shuts down. Listening on the part of European Americans allows for other norms to be present, makes space for different realities and experiences, and allows several agendas to come to the surface of the interaction. Listening in cross-racial contexts acknowledges that we do not know everything, that we have the desire and ability to learn, and that we recognize the attendant racism when we enter center stage.

As a researcher and ethnographer, I have learned to ask questions. Indeed, faculty and researchers often establish and maintain their scholarly identities by the variety and complexity of questions they ask in routine interactions. But I continue to learn the value of becoming familiar with other ways of interacting. Work with an American Indian tribe, and one woman from that tribe, whom I will refer to as Kathy, clarified, for me, the concrete benefits of listening in cross-racial contexts.

I came into contact with this American Indian community when working on a paper on how communities can support children's mental health. In an initial, two-day site visit to this tribal community, I spent much of my time with different groups of people. I knew I had much to learn; it was my first visit and I realized the depth of my ignorance regarding the issues I would address in the paper. I had searched local libraries and bookstores where I lived for work by tribal people on issues of health and well-being, but most of the work available was by European Americans. I arrived with little knowledge, and made a decision to watch and listen rather than to ask questions.

Following this first visit, and the resultant paper, the woman with whom I had worked invited me back for the specific purpose of writing a second paper. She explained to me what she was looking for in the paper, where the information might come from, the audience for the paper, and what the paper should do. For this visit, I requested back copies of the tribal newspaper, as well as reports from local health agencies. From these sources, as well as from additional conversations with the woman who invited me, I developed an extensive set of questions. I had specific areas in which I decided I needed information, and I worked at questions which I believed would elicit this information. Again, in my mind, I was doing my job well. As a researcher, carefully thought through questions were a minimum requirement, in light of my training, for the task at hand.

When I arrived at the first of the meetings that would take place during my visit, I pulled out my list of questions, glanced over them, looked at Kathy, and at my blank pad of paper. Particularly because during my first visit, questions had seemed out of place, I realized in asking questions now, I would be trying to enter through the wrong door. I suddenly felt foolish and inexperienced. Kathy glanced at my questions, but as she waited for me to begin, I realized that once again, the best choice I could make was to listen. Kathy started to speak. Thankful for her beginning, for her grace in helping me move out of an awkward situation without openly marking the near-interruption of my questions, I listened. I listened and wrote, and after half an hour, I put away my questions. I listened, and after three hours that day, two the next, and some research in the tribal library, I went home with my notes.

Although it was at times difficult to set aside my questions, I began to see that Kathy knew what she wanted in that paper about her community. Even though I had come with what I believed was a framework for our work together in the interests of the paper, I realized that Kathy knew best about where we needed to go with our conversations. Following her lead, I listened and wrote and then went home. I left my questions out of our work. In writing the paper, it was inevitable that Kathy's knowledge set the terms. I worked with her insights and comments to structure and then to write the paper. It was critical that she set the reality. Had I asked my questions, her input may well have become secondary to the framework I had established in my mind.

In cross-racial work, people of color know who they are and what they need to say to white people. In turn, whites need to listen to what people of color offer. If people of color do not say what we want or expect to hear, are we able to listen to what they *are* saying? In conferences and meetings, if what people of color are saying does not seem to fit the topic or the issue at hand, do we consider why they leave out certain things, and bring up others? Are European Americans paying attention to people of color: to how they define the issues, to their agendas, issues, priorities, and realities? Can we suppress our questions and listen? Asking first and listening later signals to people of color that white people believe in the primacy of their own agendas and have little patience. Asking first often precludes listening later.

Such practices of interaction require whites to share the space they occupy rather than control it. It is easy for European Americans to assume their goals, interests, and realities are primary and the most deserving of attention. Particularly in academic contexts, in classes and meetings, there are usually more whites present than African Americans, American Indians, Latin Americans, or Asian Americans. It is profoundly easy and acceptable to assume European American norms and communication patterns. But in cross-racial contexts, when we speak first and the most often, or use up the most air time, we are already to some extent setting the terms. Additionally, we are marking ourselves in many ways, some of which clearly indicate our disinterest in and reluctance to combat racism and white supremacy.

Subject-to-Subject Interaction: The Challenges of Change

The fourth requirement for subject-to-subject interaction is accepting that, in the context of cross-racial dialogue, change is necessary and difficult. Working at anti-racism is always a labor. It is hard, wearing, and upsetting. It is not a project we apply ourselves to and then finish. It is a process that demands critical self-reflection and changed practice.

White people often voice a commitment to anti-racist work, unaware of the demands of that commitment. It is common for whites to profess an interest in anti-racism, or to attend a conversation or meeting about diversity or anti-racism, and never return. It is easy to remain committed as long as there is no work involved. When there is conflict or disagreement, or when we reveal our own racism, which will happen, do we come back to the table, not to be excused for our mistake or praised for coming back, but to continue working? Cross-racial dialogue is not about friendship or comfort. It requires that whites take risks, invest in a process, and commit to changed practice.

Anti-racist practice occurs most often when there are contexts of support for change. These contexts of support are in part built on relationships. Cross-racial relationships may take at least a year or more to develop. Trust may be uneven and not necessarily even present. In my work with the American Indian woman, it took several months after I had met her for us to agree that we would together work on the first report. This was only a beginning; nothing about our working relationship was sealed or finished. Cross-racial relationships are most often built on a commitment to change within a certain context. It is also critical for whites to develop and sustain relationships with other white people working at anti-racist practice. For example, meeting regularly with a group of four or six European Americans committed to anti-racism in their work and lives is often an essential component of anti-racist change for white people.

Because anti-racist work requires long-term commitment, it may interrupt other research, scholarship, or community work. Adding a commitment to anti-racist practice onto already busy schedules may require us to choose among priorities. Time-based expectations are not useful. That is, ideas such as 'in another six months, maybe this committee won't take up so much time'; 'one meeting should be enough to get things going'; or 'Do you think we can get through this in forty-five minutes' are usually problematic. I routinely see whites make an initial commitment to anti-racist learning or practice – a six-week class on white supremacy, or a one-day training on anti-racism – and decide not to continue that work in an intentional or consistent manner. As long as we are comfortable turning our back on anti-racist work in favor of other projects or responsibilities, cross-racial dialogue is not likely to occur. A commitment to addressing white supremacy and racism demands that white people create a space in their lives for that work. It cannot be an afterthought, a 'when I have the time' concern.

The process of dialogue is also difficult for white people because it requires risk-taking and vulnerability. In my own work in cross-racial contexts, I continue to make embarrassing and sometimes ugly mistakes, and I do feel inadequate. One response to these realities is for whites to choose to risk absolutely nothing. In groups of European Americans formed to address race and white supremacy, I have seen white people choose never to talk or reveal their thoughts and feelings in the group. In cross-racial groups, a quick 'I am not a racist, but white people can be so terrible' kind of statement from a white person quickly and falsely removes that person from any racist practice. It creates a location that, however artificial, is often more comfortable for many white people.

Finally, cross-racial dialogue committed to critical transformation is difficult because change is necessary. Cross-racial work involves beginning again, rethinking fundamental values, and challenging core assumptions that white people habitually make. Anti-racist work requires more than a commitment to be present. It requires a pledge for white people to be present in different ways than in the past. It is a commitment to listen, watch, learn, take risks, mark white supremacist behavior in public settings, and act on a loyalty to often unpopular work.

Conclusion

Structural and institutional change, including increasing the diversity of people of color at decision-making tables in higher education, is made possible in part by the ability to communicate across differences and work together at a process. White people have had a disproportionate amount of power and access in shaping the norms and processes of legitimation in higher education. This long-term and near-exclusive control of resources means that achieving a system of higher education that involves a wide cross-section of people at all levels will be difficult. In this setting, dialogue can be a useful tool in effecting change. In the practice of feminism more specifically, cross-racial dialogue allows cross-racial groups of women to begin reaching across the gaps and impasses that often exist between them. As outlined in this chapter, four components of cross-racial dialogue are particularly important: white people must know themselves as subjects in a racial sense; we must know people of color as subjects; we must learn how to listen, watch, and share space; and we must be prepared to work at change.

'It's all a set-up.' Cherríe Moraga's dismissal of the possibility of dialogue in the academy was hard-edged. But I know the practice of dialogue is in between knowing the extent of the 'set-up' and the importance of undoing the way things are. Even as cross-racial dialogue happens slowly and in rare instances, those who participate in that dialogue may be able to chip away at the set-up, to offer a different picture of talking and acting across difference.

CHAPTER FIVE

'Racism Is Not a Theory':
Race Matters in the Classroom

This book has firmly located the practice of cross-racial dialogue in higher educational settings. Classrooms, publications, university administrations, and the production of knowledge are all arenas in which people make choices that are connected to race. Which texts a teacher includes as required reading, the material and assignments included in a course syllabus, the objectives of our writing, who universities hire, and the assumptions present in our theorizing are all connected to specific ideas about race.

Often, standard university textbooks contain one or two chapters or as little as a few pages on cultural issues, such as gender, race, and class. The other ten or twelve chapters usually include knowledge that is mostly produced by white people and that adopts a white framework, without explicitly acknowledging this bias. In the classroom, white students may have a particularly low level of awareness about racism in relation to the subject at hand, while several students of color may have first-hand experience of that racism. This difference in racial knowledge can pose difficulties for the teacher. To continue to address race even when the classroom becomes uncomfortable is a related challenge.[1]

In addition, the number of white students in a particular classroom might be significantly higher than the number of students of color. In this situation, it may be difficult to make sure all students have equal air time. Likewise, a few white students, usually mostly European American men and a few European American women, may speak often and easily, consistently inserting their opinions and experiences. If not decentered, these opinions and experiences can quickly set the norm in a classroom. After only two or three weeks, students of color may decide to keep their ideas to themselves.

There can be several reasons for this situation to prevail: a white instructor may offer a limited range of cultural referents, frameworks, and realities, and fail to affirm the cultural norms of students in the class; the students of color may not see their role as educators of the white students;[2] students of color may see little gain in arguing with white students, when protection or even validation of their ideas and lives is not guaranteed; or professors may have indicated a lack of knowledge about race or an absence of the capacity for understanding experiences that may differ greatly from their own. In any case, the results can be frustrating for professors, students of color, and perhaps for white students who are not among the few who speak regularly in class discussion.

By mid-term, those who do speak up regularly feel important and central to the classroom experience, and they may not even notice the difference in air time. The class validates white peoples' knowledge in every meeting, and students of color may conclude that the professor and some students do not value their opinions and knowledge in the learning process. The professor may feel frustrated that more students of color are not speaking up, may be thankful for the white men and women who do speak, and may be unaware of how such routine inter-actions have profound implications.

This chapter explores ways in which educators in college and university contexts can become more sensitive to race in the classroom. Cross-racial dialogue and change requires that teachers be committed to creating classrooms that are open to knowledge about race, that can accommodate conflicting experiences and emotions, and that do not consistently normalize European American realities. In the classroom, opinions, ideas, experiences, and communication patterns may diverge sharply in connection with race, and most students are not used to discussing racism in an in-depth manner. Teachers interested in cross-racial dialogue must engage students in conversations about race, responding constructively to what they bring to the learning process. Particularly for white professors, awareness of the implications of our positionality, as well as honesty regarding our level of understanding of and attentiveness to race issues are imperative. Teaching about race requires pedagogical clarity, and an ability to ask hard questions of knowledge that may be widely accepted in our respective disciplines. Teachers must be clear about what they want their knowledge to do, and mindful of 'ethical and political referent[s].'[3] As teachers committed to cross-racial dialogue, whom do we seek to serve?

At a minimum, for teachers and learners to address race in concrete and meaningful ways, and to allow all students to engage themselves in the learning process, teachers must mark whiteness and open up the classroom to multiple levels of knowledge. They must draw attention to and explore routine expressions of white expectations, priorities, and knowledge in higher educational settings. Marking whiteness requires that teachers make visible patterns of behavior that are based on the assumption of white superiority.[4] Pointing out the European American bias of most textbooks, or limiting the comments of white students when those comments leave no time for the views of people of color, are two ways of marking whiteness.

For the most part, people in higher education have marked, and continue to mark, that which is outside of the dominant framework. They increasingly recognize the need to address particular racial/ethnic-related topics not found in mainstream research. A class on women's history may cover white women's commitment to suffrage in detail, and might also briefly address African American women's roles in the suffrage movement. Another women's studies class may have a section on women and difference, in which students read about women of color, working-class women, and women with disabilities. In both of these cases, there is a kind of core curriculum, and curricular additions. In many cases, the core curriculum is, in fact, knowledge that is most representative of and useful to white people.

Marking whiteness does not include throwing out all previous knowledge, disregarding work that does not specify its particularity, or ignoring white students' experiences and expertise. It does require identification of the existing bias toward European American assumptions and values in much college and university curricula; a recognition of how power works in the classroom and how business as usual often privileges European American knowledge at the cost of the knowledge and experiences of people of color; an ability to decenter white norms; and consideration of the ethical implications of a professor's choices in the classroom.

White professors must also recognize that 'racism is not a theory.'[5] Too often in the classroom, teachers and students treat race as a topic that can be fully explored through exclusively rational examination. Race becomes a topic that is convenient to hold at a distance, to keep thoroughly separate from our selves. In reality, race involves daily, lived experiences. Race is not always best understood as if we are analyzing an object we can at any time put down and leave behind. To think about racism and anti-racist practice, teachers and students must consider how race affects our own lives. Further, the realities of race exist at many levels. Racism involves pain, anger, confusion, and doubt. Expressions and interactions of race and racism are most often a tangle of reason and emotion. If educators are to teach well about race and racism, we must be able to express both reason and emotion, and encourage students to do the same.

The Place of Race and Culture in Higher Education

Racial and cultural differences have always been present in higher education. To understand the ways in which race plays out in current settings in higher education, it is important to identify how institutional standards and directions have affected educational representations of race. In particular, it is possible to trace a pervasive tendency toward assimilation of cultural values and frameworks of people of color into white norms instead of living with difference. Likewise, throughout the last several decades of knowledge production in higher education, there have been attempts, often highly successful, to manage diversity. Put another way, 'the effect of the proliferation of ideologies of pluralism in the 1960s and 1970s, in the context of the (limited) implementation of affirmative action in institutions of higher education, has been to create what might be called the Race Industry, an industry that is responsible for the management, commodification, and domestication of race on American campuses.'[6]

This domestication of race has led to a troubling paradox. Most people in higher education have learned to interact in a polite and professional manner about race and racism: we discuss issues, share information, and work together toward specific learning, curricular, or departmental goals. At the same time, frank and honest conversations about race, among students or among teachers, most often hover just below the surface of interactions. For example, it is common for faculty within a department to agree that all courses should include some attention to culture. It is rare for faculty in a department to talk concretely and at length about exactly how and to what extent teachers should include culture and race in the classroom.

Further, when students in a particular class or the faculty in a department do begin to address race, many assume that white objectives and norms for conversation and behavior will set the tone.[7] In a classroom in which students talk about race, white students may be

very comfortable expressing defensiveness and anger about the existence of racism. These same students may complain that students of
color are being too loud or unreasonably emotional when they point
out the existence of the racism that the white students have just questioned. Discussions of racism, particularly when European Americans
are in control of these discussions, tend to only go as far as most white
people are comfortable. Once the conversation pushes through certain
unspoken limits in either content or format, it may well quickly come
to an end. When white people are in the majority in higher educational
settings, the general unspoken rule is that the priorities and interac-
tional norms of people of color may only be present in mild and
unthreatening ways.

The model, then, is one of tolerating differences that do not fundamentally threaten the assumptions and values that have undergirded
higher education for years, and disallowing differences that do. Further, despite resistance from specific groups, this model has existed
with relative ease and without significant shifts for years. That is, the
parameters for addressing race in higher education are still largely the
same as they were a few decades ago: although professors in a few
departments may question and disagree with basic approaches to race
and cultural difference, administrators and teachers permit change
only in certain instances and almost never at a fundamental or structural level.

The assumed wisdom of assimilation and of managing difference
results in 'a superficial reading of difference that makes power relations invisible and keeps dominant cultural norms in place.'[8] Because
dominant cultural norms are able to stay so firmly in place, it can be
profoundly difficult and rare for approaches to education and knowledge production that do not fit the European American norm to surface at any level. For the most part, ways of teaching and learning
about race that do not fit white peoples' expectations and norms are
simply not present in higher education. To consider how cross-racial
dialogue can occur at several levels in higher education, it is necessary
to come to terms with widespread and longheld assumptions about
the best ways to deal with difference. We must understand the significance of historical treatment of difference to the contexts in which we
now work. Before educators can move forward toward cross-racial dialogue, we must recognize the ways in which ourselves, our departments, and our institutions are firmly entrenched in approaches to
education that manage diversity.

Historical Approaches to Race and Culture in Higher Educational Settings

Particularly in the educational and social work disciplines, scholars and teachers pay considerable attention to diversity among their students and clients.[9] Both of these fields have expanded the meaning of difference in racial and ethnic terms. Teachers and social workers have long studied the language and communication patterns, the routes to success or failure, and the particular cultural strengths of various racial groups. In many ways, the attention educators have paid to language and cultural difference has served as a way to 'cultivat[e] dominant Anglo-Saxon values among new immigrants and their offspring.'[10] Historically and into the present, schools have been a particularly useful place to 'cultivate norms of citizenship, to fashion a conformist American identity, and to bind together a population of diverse nations and origins.'[11]

From the 1800s into the 1970s, assimilation was the goal and centerpiece of U.S. educational institutions. Administrators and teachers openly worked at forcing American Indians, Latin Americans, Asian Americans, and African Americans to discard cultural characteristics that educators and administrators, usually white, considered in opposition to the dominant culture, and to offer these same groups 'the skills that would bring them to the level of the white middle class.'[12] This direction in education paralleled social practices on a broader level. In the 1920s and 1930s, the Chicago School of Sociologists asserted that all people of color and white immigrants went through a four-stage process that ended in assimilation.[13]

From the 1960s, however, people of color began to challenge educational models that valued assimilation, and in response, educational policy makers began to acknowledge cultural diversity. Because these policy makers had positions of power, they were able to conveniently package the critique people of color offered. While people of color focused on who controlled local educational institutions, the representation and staffing of people of color in schools, the lack of representation of people of color in the curriculum, and the connected dominance of European Americans, policy makers chose to focus on minority failure, language proficiency, and cultural characteristics that differed from those of middle-class white people.[14] In this way, policy makers were able to appear to be concerned with race and culture, to deflect issues of power and representation, and to maintain European American dominance.

Over time, white people's emphasis on the failures and deficits of people of color became increasingly unacceptable. In recent years, a focus on cultural deprivation has shifted to the 'positive qualities of minority cultural heritage.'[15] White people turned to praising people of color for specific cultural characteristics, lauding them for their ability to maintain cultural traditions, for their resiliency in hostile conditions, and for their adaptability in moving between their language and culture and that of the dominant white culture.

Yet white educators have rarely, if ever, given up control, or thoroughly adopted non-assimilationist models of education. Over the last hundred years, when it comes to addressing racial and cultural differences, white people have by and large maintained control of both the terms of the discussion and the direction and extent of change. Even as we rejected assimilationist approaches in theory, we embraced difference only to the extent that we could name, control, and predict it.

Recent Approaches to Race and Culture in Higher Education

In part because people of color continued to critique educational models that made much of language proficiency and cultural deficits, instead of tending to staffing and curricular patterns, it has been useful for white people to continue to deflect attention away from issues of power and access. Educational models that support cultural understanding, cultural competence, and cultural emancipation represent three primary responses to the critique from people of color. These three models point to the predominant ways of understanding difference in higher education. The cultural understanding model focuses on improving communication and assumes that all social and ethnic groups have formal equality. The idea that 'Despite our differences, we are all fundamentally the same' is common among people who endorse this model. In the context of higher education, the cultural understanding model emphasizes courses that promote the idea of racial tolerance. Advocates of this model do not take an active stance toward racial inequality in education.[16]

In the cultural competence model, values of cultural pluralism are central. Teachers are responsible for aiding the development of students' ethnic identities. The cultural competency of white teachers displaces educational and social change. The goals of this model include 'the preservation of minority languages and cultures.' Its supporters believe that 'cross-cultural interaction will contribute to reduced antagonism between majority and minority ethnic groups.'[17] Finally, cultural emancipation models stress the importance of changing teacher attitudes and curriculum in fostering the educational achievement of people of color. This model clearly states that there 'is a fundamental mismatch between the school curriculum and the life experiences and cultural backgrounds' of U.S. students of color, and that educational systems privilege white students.

It is possible to find examples of all three of these models in higher education classrooms. Most students and teachers can easily embrace the cultural understanding model and its focus on improved communication. For white students, bettering communication between groups is, at least on the surface, not a threat. At a secondary level, improving communication can have little to do with culture and much to do with improving students' chances in a corporate environment, which most students understand to be increasingly diverse. In this sense, white people desire cultural understanding to further their career, rather than to implement any significant cultural shifts.

The cultural understanding model's emphasis on changing attitudes is also relatively comfortable for white students. These students may readily and in theory agree on the inappropriateness of stereotypes and on the importance of treating everyone equally. Unfortunately, for white students, ideas about treating everyone equally are often predicated on a lack of knowledge of the lives and values of people of color. In the absence of this knowledge, equal treatment can mean the same treatment. There may be no attention given to the question of what equal means in concrete situations within the context of a history of racism, injustice, and unequal power.

People across academic disciplines, including psychology, business, social work, education, and public health, have eagerly embraced the cultural competence model, with its focus on language and the importance of learning a spectrum of particular cultural behaviors. Cultural competence emphases are reflected in social work classrooms that stress the importance of offering social services in different languages; in the value of white teachers understanding communication patterns of various racial groups; and in white students learning about racial histories, literatures, and cultural expressions different from their own. Again, although all of these areas require more time of white people, they do not call for any shift in fundamental assumptions and practices. Cultural competency can be reduced to a badge to earn, rather than a fundamental change in one's basic approach to education.

In cultural emancipation frameworks, educators enlarge the curriculum, adding on the lives and realities of people of color. Moving beyond the scope of cultural understanding and cultural competence, educators who embrace cultural emancipation focus on the inequality present outside of the classroom. Students might study the working conditions of Latino day laborers, and teachers might lecture on institutional social stratification and inequality. Although supporters of cultural emancipation models acknowledge the existence of racial inequality, these educators often pay inadequate attention to the material process of change. This model also assumes that reorganizing the curriculum results in more equitable relationships among racial groups.

Although these three models have drawn important attention to culture and to race, they have also legitimized assimilationist approaches and diverted attention from the need for a process that supports structural transformation. Significantly, none of these models fundamentally challenges the core of educational institutions. As a result, 'Discriminatory policies and the manifestations of racism in educational institutions have changed very little over the years.'[18] Further, it is common for 'celebratory embracings of diversity' to displace attention to 'structures of inequality and disparate power.'[19] In higher education, white students and teachers alike often become uncomfortable when talk turns to the relatively recent entry of people of color into the academy; to the overwhelming acceptance of theories and knowledge that white people have almost completely developed, critiqued, and controlled; to the limitations of white teachers who are racially privileged yet simultaneously hope to transcend that privilege; and to the possibility that white supremacy and the supposed superiority of European American values and norms are so ingrained that white people have difficulty even recognizing, let alone resisting, their existence.

The results of assimilationist approaches have profound implications. Proponents of the cultural understanding, cultural competence, and cultural emancipation models rarely examine, in an in-depth and sustained way, the intricacies of the realities and knowledge of people of color. Nor are they eager to consider the dominance of European American theories and educational priorities and the assumptions underpinning them. Belief in assimilationist approaches can also make it difficult to teach and learn about race in a frank and realistic manner. As long as educators consider assimilation desirable, little mandates the discussion of the challenges of non-assimiliationist approaches.

Current Pedagogical Challenges Related to Race

In the classroom, a historical reluctance to grapple with issues of power and access has created a vacuum for sustained conversations about race and racism. The cultural understanding, cultural competence, and cultural emancipation models have thoroughly condoned and rewarded inattention to and ignorance of racial injustice and issues of racially differentiated access to resources. 'Covert racism is ignored by those who have never experienced it, and denied by those who contribute to it.'[20] All three of these models, and particularly the first two, focus attention on language and on cultural differences – such as food, art, and dress – only as they can be celebrated. There is often a related lack of capacity among students and teachers to address race and racism in socio-structural terms.

Over time, persistent inattention – in many cases, over the entire educational life of college undergraduates – to issues of racial representation and institutional control has resulted in a lack of familiarity with and strong opposition to discussions that examine racial inequality. As the authors of one report state, 'Participation in a community drawn from multiple cultures and experiences calls on an inclination to engage and learn across difference that many students have had no opportunity to achieve. It requires skills that have not been practiced – or valued.'[21] Further, because cultural assimilationist models often deny institutional inequality and racism, and dodge questions of responsibility and accountability, students prefer to do the same. They view those who have the power to sustain institutionalized racism as well-intentioned, doing the right thing, and/or deserving to be excused for their acts.

In particular, two obstacles to discussing race can be linked to cultural assimilationist approaches. These obstacles include an unwillingness, mostly among white students, to acknowledge and confront systemic and institutionalized racism. Attached to this is an attendant lack of attention to responsibility and the consequences of particular choices, and an inability to reflect on and analyze racism and the possibility of change as part of the learning process. A second obstacle is the acceptance of European American knowledge and norms as superior and 'normal' and as therefore justifiably dominant.

Denial of Local and Institutionalized Racism

With respect to an inability to acknowledge the existence of institutionalized racism, many white students and teachers often place a significant amount of trust in public institutions. They may find particular faults with a specific public institution in their community, but, in general, they assume that that institution will not do them or their racial group significant harm. Further, when individuals do complain of harm, it must be their fault. In other words, 'If some people have been served well by this democratic system and others poorly, it is not surprising that some would judge it the best system in the world and others would feel alienated from it. In a system that is fundamentally process-oriented and focused on the protection of individual rights rather than reciprocal obligations, it is relatively easy to conclude that if one is treated well by the system, the system is working well. Concomitantly, those who are not treated well must have somehow failed to take advantage of the system.'[22] White students readily draw on this kind of analysis when it comes to race and to their immediate contexts.

In higher education, white students may be unhappy with one class or one professor in their department. However, there are usually enough other classes and teachers that meet their satisfaction to prevent them from becoming frustrated with the entire department. In contrast, it is quite possible for a student of color to take several classes within a department and never see his or her experience affirmed. White students, despite complaints regarding a particular professor or class, are able to maintain their trust in the department as a whole because of their experience overall. When they hear a complaint from a student of color, they may equate their own dissatisfaction with one class or professor with the dissatisfaction of the student of color. In fact, the dissatisfaction is qualitatively quite different. In this example, white students may be reluctant to question their assumptions regarding the department. As a result, they ignore the reality of the student of color. In this framework, for white students, racism becomes an isolated occurrence rather than a result of institutional structures.

This general trust of public institutions usually extends beyond the classroom. When I bring up the Tuskegee experiments,[23] or point out that the U.S. attorney general 'spoke glowingly of' a white supremacist journal,[24] students are usually surprised. 'How long ago did that happen?', 'Why didn't anyone say anything?', and 'How can that be allowed?' are common questions. It has been useful for white students to believe that their experience has been widely shared; not to believe so makes life complicated and messy. If students are unable or unwilling to even consider the possibility of institutional racism, it is unlikely that discussion of racism as widely problematic in public life will be possible.

When white students express surprise at the examples discussed above, they often insist that these are isolated cases. Rather than seeing them as institutionally based and condoned, the incidents are in a sense put to the side. An immediate result of this in connection to cross-racial dialogue is that students of color, who may or may not have been aware of the Tuskegee experiments and Ashcroft's support of a racist newspaper, and who are usually not surprised, are immediately aware that experiences and histories with which they may identify are not of primary importance, and that white students will question these experiences and see them as exceptions to the larger picture. Students who question Ashcroft's support of the *Southern Partisan Quarterly Review* send a message about their level of knowledge and acceptance of routine racism. Similarly, the students of color will make decisions in response to the assumptions and questions of white students. In other words, 'women and students of color may see privilege reflected in the very questioning of social facts that are at odds with one's experiences.'[25] The reaction of the professor will also send a message to both groups about what knowledge is relevant in that classroom.

Finally, in part because European American students see racist realities as isolated, and because such claims actively deny the experiences of many students of color, sustained discussions in the classroom about race and racism are difficult and rare. The differences in experiences and viewpoints can in themselves seem to disrupt the learning process. When this does happen, the teacher may opt to abandon the discussion and ensuing conflict, rather than work through students' differences. Indeed, in the minds of some teachers, resolution of a topic may not be a priority, and may be perceived as impossible in a conversation about race. Even when a small number of students and professors are willing to look hard at racist practices, there is often a reluctance to do so in the contexts in which we work and live. It is difficult for white students to question their own complicity in racism, and their parallel embrace of privilege. At the same time, students of color may be quite aware of the European Americans students' race ignorance. As one author states, 'although privilege is often obscured from these students who enjoy the most advantages, these same privileges can be quite glaring to nonprivileged students.'[26]

Consider the following example. A discussion of the lack of media images of people of color in a persuasion class may lead white students to grudgingly admit that this is a problem. However, when we move to why students rely on the news sources they do – often NBC, CBS, and ABC – it is quite a different issue to understand this reliance as an indication of white privilege. In fact, white students can and do rely on the major news networks because, particularly when the students come from middle- or upper-class backgrounds, these networks have served them well – they have mirrored assumptions and values that make sense. White students, and many times, white professors, rarely have frameworks to understand and critique the beliefs and resulting choices that constitute systems of white supremacy in their own lives.

Students must be able to disagree constructively, and must develop an aptitude for ethical analysis and for connecting choices to their consequences. Many students, particularly those privileged by race and/ or class, may not have a thorough understanding of their own value system, or of the assumptions with which they work in regard to race and racism. Teachers can generate open and strong resistance from students when we ask them to think hard about what they take for granted. When the subject at hand is race, white students especially are skilled at dodging the questions.

'Aren't things getting better?' 'People don't sit around in a room and try to be racist,' and 'Its not my fault' are common responses in discussions that address European American complicity in racist interactions and in racist representations of people of color. When the discussion continues to provoke discomfort, students may make jokes or ridicule the people involved: once someone is the object of ridicule, students do not need to take the person or topic seriously. Finally, making connections between choices and their implications is particularly challenging for teachers and students. In classes that clearly address race and racism and the possibility of anti-racist change, students and teachers must learn to link the goals of a particular organization or institution with actual change.

Dominance of European American Norms

A second barrier to discussing race is the power of European American approaches in defining what is normal, expected, and legitimate in university classrooms. Three primary areas in which this occurs are curriculum and the representation of knowledge; patterns of interaction; and the presence and absence of cultural referents. As stated previously, higher education in the United States has been fairly monocultural for most of its existence.[27] In concrete terms, one result of this is that white people have authored the vast majority of classroom texts. Because they are usually a large part of the knowledge base that most have in common, texts ensure that European American knowledge is the measuring stick for all other knowledge, despite vast differences in context and priorities. The centrality of texts written primarily by white people and for such audiences immediately establishes all other knowledge as peripheral and as legitimate only to the extent that it does not contradict the knowledge represented in the text.[28] As one writer states, 'Western knowledge is encaged in historical and institutional structures that both privilege and exclude particular readings, voices, aesthetics, authors, representation, and forms of socialization.'[29] These cages generally contain white norms and exclude those of people of color.

Another way in which the centrality of European American knowledge makes it difficult to talk about race is the legitimacy of generalizable theories that often discount people who are not in the white and middle-class norm. Even when white students have strong analytical skills, generalizations can be a refuge from hard-edged and uncomfortable truths. In communication and media classes, an important topic is often the relevancy of media and images to social relations in the United States. Middle-class white students in particular are often reluctant to criticize the narrow control of media images, and the widespread European American acceptance of this control. Even when white people are aware of this control, they continue to consume these images with a false hope of neutrality.

In considering the issues of responsibility and change white men or women often argue at length about the presence of a democracy and the potential for all people to participate, and if they wish, to complain and alter the structures of media control. At this point, students' comments often become fairly unspecific. They make vague references to gains in the representation of people of color, to the possibility of using public access television, and to the existence of media owned by people of color. The vast gap in access to and control of images suddenly becomes irrelevant. Further, at this point, students often consider it fair to make general statements that have little if anything to do with practice.

Such generalizations and departures from actual practice on any range of topics are common. When students or a professor offer knowledge in this way, it can be difficult for other students to disagree. Indeed, higher education most often honors knowledge that is generalizable, regardless of what that knowledge might leave out. It follows, then, that in the classroom students may accept such generalizations unproblematically. In this way, systems and processes that have worked for years to the advantage of white people are justified and even praised for their potential ability to serve everyone well. Displacing the basic goodness and normality of these systems and processes in the minds of many students and some professors then becomes a serious challenge.

At another level, norms of interaction privilege white students. The example used above demonstrates the comfort with which white men and women offer sweeping generalizations rather than address concrete social interactions. 'Aren't things getting better?' is a comment students repeatedly offer in discussions about racism in the United States. Generalizations most often favor the group in power. Unless teachers insist on concrete supporting evidence for such generalizations and accord value to the choice to start with the specific and then move to the general, rather than the other way around, many students will assume that generalizations are both appropriate and desirable.

One result of working in an institution in which white people constitute at least two-thirds of the classroom and students of color constitute one-third or less is, quite simply, that European Americans get more air time. In part because representation of knowledge often affirms their reality, white students will usually feel particularly comfortable responding to that knowledge. This can lead to patterns of interaction in which white students speak often and at length. Students of color may not respond as quickly.[30] They may choose not to put themselves in the position of educating white people, or not to risk sharing their ideas in a space where those ideas may not be welcome. Further 'members of less privileged groups are often accustomed to silence and avoidance as resistance strategies ... these students may carry scars of years in classrooms when teachers' perspectives differed from their own.'[31]

Finally, higher education privileges European American norms in the area of cultural referents, the symbols and norms that give meaning and context to one's cultural reality. Teachers most frequently rely on what they know when making examples, telling jokes, and relating stories. At one level, this offering of personal experiences can enhance learning. But if a teacher's cultural referents derive overwhelmingly from a monocultural perspective, this can limit what students perceive as appropriate in the classroom.[32] Because 'teaching is a form of mediation between different persons and different groups of persons ... we can't be good mediators unless we are aware of what the referents of the mediation we engage in are.'[33] As a first step, teachers must be cognizant of the referents they lack.

An African American student I knew was taking a course on media in which the professor made several references in every class to popular television shows he found humorous. While the rest of the class laughed, the African American student did not. When the professor asked, in front of the class, why that student was not laughing, the student replied that he did not find the teacher's jokes and references funny. In this particular class, the teacher set a student apart because he did not share the teacher's sense of humor. That teacher never had to explain why he consistently relied on a certain set of shows to make jokes. Since most sitcoms are about white people and draw on people of color primarily as objects of derision, as the butt of the dominant society's jokes, and as supporters of the development of white characters in the show, such references and jokes are often particularly harmful to people of color.

Cultural referents are one way for teachers to demonstrate their own knowledge base, and in a sense, they can establish parameters for what is acceptable in the classroom. White professors who boast about their knowledge of Latin American music or Asian American film are probably more likely to be demonstrating their need to be accepted by students than they are to be expanding the space for cultural referents. At a minimum, teachers must have a sense of the variety of cultural referents present in the classroom. Cultural referents, when repeatedly and overwhelmingly European American, further contribute to dynamics that center white knowledge and realities, and leave little room for the contributions and expertise of teachers and students of color.

Consider a discussion in a persuasion class. One of my primary objectives for this class is that students become more aware of how images work. Students often assume that they understand how they take in, process, and act on images. I am explicitly concerned with how the students and I process images of people in relation to racial representation. How does mental awareness of the inappropriateness of existing images of people of color in the media intersect with our emotional, gut-level reaction when we interact with people of color?

How does our internalization of images persuade us to act in certain ways?

I usually introduce this topic a couple of weeks into the term. In the specific class from which this example comes, I began by offering some ideas about how images work in relation to the media and public policy.[34] I drew these ideas primarily from a book by K. Sue Jewell, *From Mammy to Miss America and Beyond*. I presented them as concepts with which the students could agree or disagree. The required reading for that day provided the students with information about signs and symbols; after discussing the reading during the first half of the class, we moved to my presentation on images.

This was a Wednesday; toward the end of that class, I asked students to think about the five points raised over the next few days, and to see if their own experience with images supported the concepts discussed in Jewell's book or not. I asked them to spend ten to twenty minutes a day on this and to make a chart that listed the person in the image, groups to which the person likely belonged, and the values associated with the image. Their knowledge and observations would then form the basis for our discussion during the next class on Monday. I also asked the students to pay particular attention to gender, race, and class, and to what kinds of messages the images they saw offered about people in groups based on these identity categories.

On Monday, we began by reviewing the five points I had extracted on Wednesday from Jewell's book. We then started to discuss what the students had seen in the images they observed. It quickly became apparent that perhaps one-third of the class had seen part or all of the Superbowl, which had aired the Sunday before our Monday class, and which I had not watched. This became a point of reference about which many students shared knowledge. Students remembered the ads in detail. They could respond to each other, agree and disagree, and supply details another student may have forgotten. For at least twenty minutes, the conversation was easy and fluid. I started to fill in the columns on the board: person, group or groups to which he or she belongs, and values associated with image. Students readily provided information. They also offered different interpretations of the values column, and discussed why and how certain actions conveyed specific values.

After about twenty minutes, we had not said a word about race or class. In contrast, there was a general ease, if not always agreement, in talking about gender. In almost every ad the students mentioned, men and women in the class discussed the significance of gender. For example, students laughed about a woman vacuuming up her couch-potato husband in one advertisement. After twenty minutes, I asked, 'What about race and class? No images related to either? In the ads you just mentioned, were there any people of color?' The students were not as forthcoming with their responses.

'I guess everyone in those commercials was white.'

'There wasn't one ad with people who did not appear to be middle or upper class, or who were clearly people of color?' I asked.

'Everyone in the ads was pretty wealthy,' one student admitted. 'You know, nice cars ...'

I waited, left some silence. No one had a comment about race. Again, I asked, 'What about people of color? Not in one ad?' After another minute or so of silence, one student responded, 'There was one ad that I remember with African Americans.' After another silence – perhaps some students were hoping this would be enough discussion on race – several students comfirmed this with nods or 'yesses.' I waited.

Another student offered, 'Yeah, one African American man and one African American woman.' The ease and fluidity formerly present had vanished. In a second, I could have shut this conversation down and moved on. Many students seemed to be hoping for an easy and gentle resolution. The mood of minutes before, when the students were laughing and full of contributions, turned into one of being on hold. While they did not seem to be quite finished with the discussion, the students were no longer eager participants. Many seemed slightly embarrassed: they were now caught by that which had formerly been humorous.

After a period of silence, I asked, 'So, what was the ad about, what were they doing?' One student reluctantly described the ad. 'The man had two beers, one in each hand. The tops were off, and he was spraying them at the woman. He was kind of goofy-looking, out of control, clumsy.' Another student immediately asked, 'What was the woman doing?' 'Not much.' I asked, 'What do we know about these two people? About the African American man and the African American woman, from their actions?' No one responded. The discussion had become plainly uncomfortable. I had been careful not to accuse, not to set up the students. It is important that part of our discussion relied on their knowledge, that they could be agents in this kind of analysis.

The students did not want to voice that which had become obvious. One student offered, 'He looks a little silly.' I summed up what had not been said: 'The African American man is uncoordinated, a social idiot, completely immature, disrespects women in general and the woman in this ad in particular, and can't even hold a beer bottle, or fix a problem that would have been easy to correct. The African American woman tolerates stupidity, and apparently accepts and/or deserves disrespect.'

A brief pause ensued, and then there was no more silence. 'It's just a beer commercial.' 'It's supposed to be funny.' 'Beer commercials always make fun of people.' 'Think of all the white men who look stupid in beer commercials.' At this, the students began to share their recollections of all the beer commercials they have seen in which white people look foolish. 'It's only one commercial.' 'Who's ever seen a serious beer commercial?!' 'The people who made that commercial know people will laugh. That's what they want.' 'Those few people working on that ad can't be responsible for every image. They're just selling beer.' 'It's not their fault.' 'What, you think those people who made the commercial sat in a room and decided to be racist?'

After this thorough attempt by several white students to normalize the discussion and ad, and to eliminate any hint of wrongdoing, a white student in the back, who had said little, spoke: 'The makers of that commercial know they're selling to a primarily white and middle-class audience, an audience that likely has some familiarity with black-face and minstrelsy shows. It fits right into their expectations of black people.' I asked this student to tell us what he knew of blackface and minstrelsy shows. He did, and this provided some context and a clearly different read than that offered by the students who had spoken so far.

This example demonstrates many of the challenges teachers face when they aim for in-depth discussions of race. It also reveals the limitations of past attention to race in contexts of higher education. More than placing blame or regretting what the students do not know, it is important to identify barriers to discussing race and racism. In this situation, most of the students had at least hoped that advertisers had done the right thing. When it became clear they had not, the students quickly moved to justify and excuse their behavior. If students can see racism as an oversight or an exception, they can almost make it disappear. Their reluctance to bring this ad into the discussion at all demonstrates that, at least on the surface, it is entirely appropriate and desirable to ignore race. If I had not insisted, European American norms and images would have constituted the entire discussion. Finally, the students were openly opposed to addressing responsibility.

They were eager to remove blame, to relativize the images of African Americans, and to avoid all discussion of accountability.[35]

The example provided above is fairly mundane on a number of levels: it did not directly involve any of the students in the classroom as active in relation to the ad, and the students were not agents in the creation of the ad. Further, the disservice of the corporate media to communities of color is not a particularly new concept, and because corporations are known for prioritizing profit, it would not have been a large jump to attribute the demeaning images of African Americans to profit. Indeed, the students did not have a problem doing this in their discussion of images related to gender. Also, for the most part, emotions were not right on the surface. At the same time, this discussion demonstrates the challenges students and teachers face in addressing racism and working toward anti-racist practice. We will need to find ways to address those challenges, and to acquire a greater level of agility when it comes to discussing race, racism, and responsibility.

Facing Race in the Classroom: Pedagogical Possibilities

Addressing race in the classroom is never easy. Students and teachers enter the learning context with a range of experiences of race and racism. In any given classroom, some students may perceive race as completely irrelevant to course subject matter. Other students may see race as undeniably linked to that same subject matter. Addressing race at in-depth levels may be new for many students; further, many students and teachers perceive the emotions that accompany discussions of race as foreign to and inappropriate in a classroom setting.[36]

In this context, two strategies for addressing race and racism in the classroom are particularly relevant. In order for teachers and students to devote consistent and in-depth attention to racism, and to make the learning process more democratic, teachers especially must learn to make whiteness visible. The assumption of whiteness as normal and as the standard by which all else should be judged poses an enormous barrier to addressing race. As long as students and teachers fail to see the problems inherent in current processes in higher education that are related to a near-monopoly of European American knowledge, values, and theories, it will be difficult, if not impossible, to support dialogue regarding race and racism. A second step is for teachers and students to construct classroom spaces in which experience and affective knowledge become necessary parts of the learning process, much in the same way that theories and book knowledge are now. Racism is far more than a theory. It acts on bodies and relationships in ways that traditional theories may not be able to account for. Teachers need to open up the routes to knowledge so that messy and painful realities are welcomed as a necessary part of learning. Working at these two strategies can facilitate classroom dialogues about race and racism.

Making Whiteness Visible

Marking whiteness can be part of the process of addressing and undoing racist practices in higher education.[37] In a broad sense, whiteness is a 'sociohistorical form of consciousness [that] constitutes and demarcates ideas, feelings, knowledge, social practices, cultural formations, and systems of intelligibility that are identified with or attributed to white people.'[38] In other words, whiteness includes habits of being that white people have learned, and that we practice with ease. In the classroom, whiteness reigns when white students have no time for the views of students of color in the classroom. White peoples' eagerness to evaluate realities particular to a specific group of people of color, with little or no contextual information about that group, is an expression of whiteness. Using theories constructed out of and for European American individuals and groups to analyze American Indians is likewise an expression of whiteness. When white people have near total lack of knowledge regarding what people of color are saying about any given issue, this is an example of whiteness as well. Finally, when white students express a sense of entitlement – to be called on first, to take up most of the class discussion time, to defensively interrupt students of color who may disagree with them on issues of race – they are expressing whiteness.

The discourse of color blindness is another form of whiteness. Color-blindness, the view that color does not matter at all, and that all people are the same, is attractive to students who want to deny the relevance of racial difference. In this framework, where everyone is the same, attention to race is always problematic and divisive. A related, common form of whiteness is white students' comfort with learning about the experiences of people of color as long as these experiences are related to art, literature, food, holidays, celebrations, music, or fashion. Once those experiences turn to injustice, racism, or colonialism, white people may respond defensively and feel offended. Because white people may have been able to maintain a comfortable distance from or total ignorance of most of the racist interactions that people of color experience, it is easier to continue this denial.[39] Whiteness is always a location of structural advantage, a standpoint from which white people look at themselves and others, and a set of unmarked and unnamed cultural practices.[40]

At its core, whiteness is a belief in European American superiority. This belief is often profoundly invisible to European American eyes. Whiteness often includes behaviors so normalized in the minds of white people, and sometimes in the minds of people of color as well, that it can be extremely difficult to identify and undo these behaviors. Whiteness makes sense for white people: it offers privileges and rewards, it is historically justified, and it is in large part a prism through which whites make sense of the world.

The previously discussed example of analyzing advertisements and images in relationship to gender, race, and class makes this process of exclusion visible. Most of the students involved were reluctant to admit that the absence of images of people of color overall in advertising during the Superbowl, and the presence of people of color looking ridiculous, could be an example of racism. Rather, they openly stated their preference to view a connection between the one advertisement with people of color and the ridicule of those people as racially irrelevent. It was 'just like all the other beer commercials,' since all beer commercials make fun of people. They quickly denied the possibility that the creators of this advertisement realized the significance of their choices. The students did not have a framework with which to examine issues of responsibility in the production of racial images and stereotypes.

These arguments rely on several assumptions, all of which build on notions of white superiority. First, the students were not willing to acknowledge the possibility of white people intentionally acting in a racist manner. Further, the comments made decontextualize individual advertisements: it is permissible if the one advertisement about people of color makes fun of people of color because all beer ads make fun of people; the overall representation of people of color in which this one ad is situated is irrelevant. Such comments also devalue systems of accountability. The students were eager to defend the ad creators' actions. The overall direction of the students' comments set the tone. If students with different views are not confident expressing their views, or do not believe that other students will respect those views, it is the teacher's responsibility to intervene. If the teacher is not prepared to clearly and thoroughly address the assumptions surveyed above, the views of the most vocal students are what remains.

EXPRESSIONS OF WHITENESS IN THE CLASSROOM

In the classroom, the ideology and practice of European American superiority leads directly to particular expressions of whiteness. Identification of these expressions can help teachers understand the context of student comments and facilitate discussions about race that lead to change. Whiteness triumphs when white students have no need to hear from students of color in the classroom. When students and teachers are convinced of the superiority of one way of being and thinking, there is really no need for a democratic process. If one way is superior, other ways are at best an interesting distraction and at worst a useless nuisance. In this framework, students and teachers value competition as a way to get to the best knowledge.

Those students who speak longest and most often, and with elaborate theoretical language, are good students. Those who do not participate are unprepared, slow, or not interested. Further, air time becomes irrelevant. As one author states, 'a key feature of a pedagogy of whiteness involves inducing white people as a key aspect of their analysis of their subjectivity to listen to [people of color] as they explain issues [related to race]. Such a process will be difficult in Western societies where the dominant culture has encouraged speaking over listening and has rewarded domination over sensitivity to the position of others.'[41] It is common for a few of the white students to speak often and at length, with seemingly no regard for or interest in the participation of other students. One aspect of whiteness is an utter lack of need or respect for the voices of people of color.

A second expression of whiteness is forthright denial of systemic racism. Most white people, and particularly those who are middle class, have benefitted from the existing operation of social institutions, which, for the most part, serve their needs well. White people often exhibit a deep-seated unwillingness to admit that there may be fundamental problems with these institutions, and that they may have hurt others while helping us. The resulting denial has profound results. Ignorance of and silence about racism becomes entirely legitimate, as does a total lack of consideration of how systems that help us may hurt others. As argued above, the assumption is made that if systems hurt others, those who are hurt are doing something wrong.

A third expression of whiteness that stems from the idea that European American knowledge is superior is the removal of knowledge from context, the parallel divide between practice and theory, and the willingness to accept theories as authoritative regardless of whom they hurt and exclude. If European American knowledge is superior to all other knowledge, generalizations are appropriate and justified, and consideration of how these generalizations misrepresent or exclude is unimportant. When people believe that European American knowledge is superior, they assume that other knowledges and realities should fit into European American frameworks, rather than existing on their own. Knowledge that is apparently good for everyone, although it derives from specific experiences and supports specific norms, ceases to be questioned and students fail to see its shortcomings. Further, because this knowledge usually serves most white teachers and students well, at least on a surface level, students can view questions about who it is not serving well as inappropriate. It is critical for teachers to develop ways of naming these expressions of whiteness, and of decreasing their presence in the classroom, if productive discussions of race and racism are to occur.

An example of the normality of and trouble with whiteness in the classroom is the treatment of gender and corresponding lack of attention to race in many communication textbooks. In many areas of communication, such as interpersonal, organizational, and group communication, it is generally accepted that men and women communicate differently. Often, texts will devote a few pages, or even a chapter, to these differences. Quantitative and qualitative studies have documented gender differences in communication and texts cover a variety of theories that account for the different ways in which women as a group and men as a group communicate.

Comparable attention to communication differences among various racial groups is notably absent. Texts rarely go beyond a few paragraphs or pages in addressing the difference in communication patterns among different racial groups. Often, this attention is superficial, with little recognition of difference beyond particular behaviors, such as the idea that members of some cultural groups may not look directly at someone they perceive as having more authority. A corresponding lack of quantitative and qualitative studies minimizes the importance or even awareness of the existence of these cultural differences. In these texts, for example, theoretical presentations of how American Indian communication patterns, differ from Latin American communication patterns, or from Asian American communication patterns, are rare, if they exist at all.

Consequently, many white students will not recognize or be open to the possibility and existence of varied communication patterns among different cultural groups. Furthermore, white students in particular will assume that, where communication patterns are concerned, it is useful and accurate to view women and men as separate, cohesive groups. Moreover, because virtually no attention is paid to specific cultural groups other than white people, it becomes difficult if not impossible for white students to even imagine the possibility of people of color working with different norms and expectations. In reality, in particular communication interactions, there may be an affinity between white women and men regarding communication patterns, and enormous differences between white men and American Indian men, for example, or between African American women and Latin American women. As long as communication texts continue to address only gender-based communication differentials, it is easy to ignore the reality of cross-racial differences, particularly when students do not experience this reality themselves.

Whiteness in the classroom is profoundly ordinary, and unfortunately invisible to many white people. The practice of generalizations and of not accounting for groups and individuals that dominant theories exclude renders students unable to see such knowledge as problematic. The assumption present in most classrooms is that discussions should move forward with ease and without interruption. If someone cannot find a space in European American frameworks or notices their shortcomings, that person, and not the frameworks themselves, is the problem. Another result is the readiness of white students to mimic such generalizations, without using examples or referring to context.

These three expressions of whiteness in the classroom – the absence of the need for democratic processes and participation, the denial of systemic racism, and the acceptability of removing knowledge from context – all contribute to the difficulty of shifting this frame with students who hold onto it. Exposing these assumptions can cause anger, resistance, and complaints, as well as a sense of loss. Students must ask themselves to let go of what they did not even know they were holding: a trust in the order of things that served them well while hurting others. This often happens whenever teachers confront students with new knowledge. At the same time, because paying attention to the intricacies of race is new to most white students, identifying the racial contours and content of such assumptions and experiences of loss becomes even more important.

White supremacy and privilege afford white students many benefits. These benefits can literally block learning about structural realities when that learning threatens to expose these benefits as unfair advantages. Consider the following example. In one of the classes I frequently teach, I ask students to identify how their beliefs, attitudes, and values prompt them to rely on certain news sources. I ask the question early in the term, in a review of the reading. They must summarize the reading material on beliefs, attitudes, and values, and then discuss how these three facets of persuasion affect their reliance on certain news sources.

During one semester of this class, several white students wrote that they relied on a specific news source, usually the local paper or network news, because the newscaster demonstrated a sense of humor, because he or she dressed nicely, or because the organization had been in business for a long time. White students wrote that the sense of humor made the person seem human, and that the person's sincere attitudes gave the impression that he or she really cared about the news reported. When I raised this issue toward the end of one class meeting, I pointed out that these reasons for reliance make sense as long as the news serves you well. I made my concerns with their responses plain: 'These reasons make sense at one level, but are they enough to demonstrate that you are attentive to how the media persuades you? What if these news sources had not served your community well – would it be enough that someone dressed well or had a sense of humor? Also, you must be assuming that these sources serve everyone well. How do you know that?'

I was glad the students had been clear about the reasons with which they were working, and said so. I also expressed my desire that they think harder, that they consider how their values are active when they choose to allow the media to persuade them. After class, several students came to the front. One young white woman asked, 'What was I supposed to write? Those were really my reasons.' I reassured her that it was a place to start, and said again that I wanted to encourage her to think harder. Another student was more forthcoming with her frustration: 'Why do you ask us those questions? It's a lot to think about. I can't answer that question in twenty minutes.'

It was clear that this student was angry. She did not feel I had asked a fair question. I stated that in a class on persuasion, I considered this an important question to consider over the course of the term. It was important to begin to think about how we ourselves are engaging in persuasive processes, as the one trying to persuade or as the receiver of persuasion. I stated that the question was central to understanding how persuasion works, and that if we can understand how it works in our own lives, we might better understand how it works in other situations. She was persistent, and not satisfied with my response. For ten minutes, in front of several other students, she challenged my right to ask, and reiterated the difficulty of answering such a question. The student who had approached me first after class responded to the second student, and said the question was fair. I felt supported by her comment, and worn out.

On the surface, this discussion was never about race. Yet the need for such a discussion, and the student's anger, were built on white privilege, and are examples of the practice of whiteness. The assumption that white institutions are for the most part benevolent was firmly in place. Further, I was plainly wrong, in the student's mind, to question that benevolence. It was implicitly appropriate for her to generalize and make assumptions from her experience: if the media is serving her well, it must be serving everyone well. Also, her reliance on primarily European American sources for her information was not problematic; she did not miss the absence of a range of peoples', including peoples' of color, input.

Such resistance still catches me unaware, making sense only after it occurs. In spite of my own hard thinking about race, I am not always ready. My emotional expectations have not caught up to my mental capacity to understand. Perhaps they never will catch up; I grew up with white supremacy and privilege, and I benefit from them now. I am always and everywhere white. I am learning to accept and work with the resulting emotional and spiritual stretching that come when I challenge whiteness, even as I am unable to completely walk away from the practice myself – my own surprise is sign of this. I am not always entirely confident with my questions. When a student challenges me, I wonder: Was the question appropriate? Was it too much? Have I been unfair? Facing race and whiteness in the classroom require clarity of purpose and agenda, a willingness to live with the rough patches inherent in the process of learning about racism and white supremacy, and a humility that can accept tiredness and struggle.

IDENTIFYING WHITENESS IN THE CLASSROOM

Marking whiteness is possible. It can also begin to open up, for students and teachers, the doors that hide racism, particularly from European American eyes. Four concrete pedagogical practices will help teachers and students pay attention to whiteness and begin to understand how it supports undemocratic and racist knowledge. One step is defining and describing whiteness. Identification is critical. Demonstrating how and when whiteness works, what it does, and how it can be interrupted and changed is of primary importance. Offering readings on whiteness, making examples of whiteness, and asking students to consider the possibility of whiteness in their own lives is a beginning. Often, especially when white students are unfamiliar with the idea of whiteness, it is necessary to proceed slowly and step by step. Denial, at least by some students, is inevitable. For many students, talking about race means talking about specific behaviors of people of color, and not about the ways in which white people practice white supremacy. For example, white students may be comfortable talking about what is appropriate in sharing a meal with someone from a country in Africa, or how to do business with an Asian American. Shifting the frame to consider whiteness, to analyze the behavior and choices of white people, is less likely to be comfortable for white students, and may not be comfortable for all of the students of color.

In many cases, students and teachers have a language for discrimination. We can talk about the effects of racism for people of color, about the problems racism causes for African American families, about the loss of culture and language connected to white genocide of American Indians, about Proposition 227 in California and the issue of language for Spanish-speaking students, or about the low-paid Asian garment workers in U.S. factories. Tending to whiteness requires attention to how whites benefit from all of the above practices.

A language of whiteness will make clear to white students how they benefit from white supremacy, and will place the results of race discrimination next to the practices of white supremacy. For example, a language that can identify whiteness might have resulted in white students accepting and questioning their privilege when it comes to media institutions that serve them well. When students understand whiteness, they will be able to address how communities of color are hurt by particular news coverage, and how white communities benefit from this same coverage.

A second pedagogical practice that will help address whiteness is consistent attention to power and access, historically and in the present. Addressing who controls various institutions will help students see race discrimination and privilege in relational terms, rather than leaving out the doers.[42] When teachers represent knowledge, constant attention to questions of control and self-determination of the people involved will support recognition of whiteness. Identification of who is writing about whom, of who controls whose images, of who is speaking for whom and why, of whom particular theories speak, of whom theories serve well and whom they leave out, of the results of exclusion, and of who benefits from exclusion and in what ways, will help bring issues of control and power to the forefront. Asking, for example, who can write about whom may upset those who thought they had control over a certain subject area. At the same time, even the appearance of democracy requires that subjects have the means to represent themselves in a variety of forms.

A teacher's lack of knowledge about theories and ideas from people of color can have hurtful consequences in the context of marking whiteness and democratic education. If a white teacher is not aware of theories from people of color that inform the issues in her discipline, she will probably teach European American knowledge as if it were everything in that field. If she is not familiar with and versed in, for example, what people of color have said and are saying about topics covered in her class, she will be unable to even begin to address control and access. Another concrete benefit of consistently addressing issues of power is that teachers can move away from representing people of color as victims, without agency and the ability to resist. Systems of institutional racism have damaging effects, but people of color are never the sum of those effects. Understanding power relationships may help teachers present white people and people of color as agents and as doers who make choices in specific contexts, choices that are in part related to and affected by institutional racism and white supremacy.

A third pedagogical practice is the act of pivoting the center, an act in which students and teachers 'analytically and affectively reflect on another experience and evaluate it by its own criteria, without comparison or adoption of those criteria.'[43] This requires students and teachers to acknowledge complex and years-old ways of thinking that have little if anything to do with European American norms and expectations, and equally to acknowledge that measuring everything with a European American ruler is inappropriate and will not support democratic analysis or research. American Indians or Asian American people have reasoned systems of communication that exist independently of white communication patterns and ideas, systems that differ again among tribes and among Asian countries of origin, and it is wrong to try to fit those systems into a European American mold. Rather, they should stand on their own, with thorough attention paid to their historical contexts.

Pivoting the center also moves students and teachers away from comparing and ranking. Efforts to compare are most often related to the need for generalization, or to establish superiority of one way over another, and usually flatten or ignore some part of a group's existence. In the European American mind, comparison is often necessarily tied to ranking. Systems cannot simply be different; one must be better, more useful, more relevant, or more widespread than another. Pivoting the center asks that students and teachers analyze theories and ideas on their own terms, in the absence of comparison or ranking.

A fourth way of marking whiteness for students and teachers involves clarifying and addressing ethical choices and their implications. Dialogue and learning in the interests of changed social practice rarely simply happen. Students' choices matter. When teachers encourage consideration of how choices matter, students may be more willing to consider the reach and significance of their own actions in particular contexts. In our discussion of the Superbowl advertisements, most European American students were eager to distance advertising executives from the consequences of their choices. Comments such as 'It's not their fault' and 'It wasn't their intention to be racist, was it?' demonstrate the dis-ease when issues of responsibility and accountability come full circle. After this particular class, a white woman approached me. 'I work for an advertising agency, and am always bugging my colleagues about including women. Now I realize I haven't been thinking at all about people of color.' Such comments mark a beginning. Sustaining this level of concern is a different matter.

Interrupting and undoing racism is not easy, and it is not an activity that all white people will pursue. In a system in which business as usual regularly privileges whites and misrepresents or excludes people of color, it is critical for those interested in cross-racial dialogue to link choices and their consequences, to bring together values and practices. Often, whiteness moves just under the surface of our thinking. An offhand comment made by a white student after watching a video on corporate control of the judicial system – 'The situation might be more conservative now, but it will swing back. It always does, and for the most part, everyone comes out all right' – demonstrates the ease with which we justify business as usual. Attention to ethics stresses that the choices of those inside 'for the most part' in that student's comment are necessarily linked to those who continue to live outside of his 'for the most part.' His comment reveals a subtle acceptance and resulting affirmation of unjust conditions that may not be part of his own experience. Ethics, critical attention to and reflection of how we choose to be together in intersecting and material communities, offers a passageway into cross-racial dialogue for white people.

'Who benefits, who gets hurt, and to whom and what are we loyal?' I risk wearing out these questions with students, and stress that we make decisions about such issues all the time, even though we do not realize or acknowledge those choices. Marking whiteness requires loyalty to a process of change and to the possibility of cross-racial dialogue, neither of which often bring immediate rewards or benefits.

'Who benefits, who gets hurt, and to whom and what are we loyal?' Students are angry and resist. They reluctantly offer up their loyalties for scrutiny. These questions turn upside down allegiances to long-held assumptions, to ideas that have made sense for years, to an unexamined trust in their beliefs that may suddenly appear naive and empty. Usually by the time of offering up the term is nearly over. I hope that they will remember the shape and weight of these questions in their own lives.

Teachers, particularly those of us who are white, must also work through our own issues of loyalty in moving toward cross-racial dialogue. How has our own pursuit and representation of knowledge relied on assumptions and on our acceptance of basic ideas in our disciplines? If we believe that systems of education have discriminated against people of color, have we considered how this discrimination continues in the classes we teach, and how we will respond? Publicly asking such questions can legitimize their importance, for other teachers and for students.

'I keep thinking about that question, about who speaks for whom,' a white student told me in a meeting she requested. This student had taken one of my classes, and was now taking a class on American Indian history. The instructor had assigned a primary text written by a white person, the teacher was white, and most of the students were white as well. According to the student, the most vocal of her classmates were European American men. She did not know if there were any American Indians in the class.

She continued, 'Two years ago, I wouldn't have cared, but now I am uncomfortable. Every class, I get a little more uneasy. It seems so simple – hearing from American Indians themselves – a reading, a guest speaker who is American Indian, maybe ideas from an American Indian student. We talk and talk and talk, all these big ideas about American Indians. I should be able to ask, "What about what American Indians are saying?" but I can't. I feel small in the class, the ideas are so big, and it feels like my question has nothing to do with the rest of the class. I am afraid they will just turn around and stare, and go on with their big ideas.'

We talked, discussed some possible strategies for her to be an agent and participant in that class. I told her I was glad she was thinking about the issue, that I was proud of her questions and discomfort. Her comments also reminded me that the seeming order of things threatens to overwhelm potential acts of resistance. Her concerns presented me with the knowledge that as teachers, we must establish different frameworks so that cross-racial dialogue and the gift of hearing from American Indians in a class on American Indian history is not dependent on one student's potential question. Teachers committed to cross-racial dialogue and the democratic representation and production of knowledge will not leave it up to a student risking her grade and sense of self to insert the possibility of disagreement.

'Who benefits, who gets hurt, and to whom and what are we loyal?' In the example just discussed, the teacher was loyal to business as usual, to processes that leave out the agency and participation of the subjects of the discussion. For the most part, white people benefitted – they got to speak often and at length, act as authorities, and validate their own ideas and those of other whites. The professor's choice to teach a class on American Indians from the perspective of European American men thoroughly excludes American Indian perspectives, theories, and ideas about American Indian history. Loyalty to white frameworks and knowledge as the cornerstone of all learning is damaging at many levels. American Indian students in the course who speak up risk a low grade, and also open up the possibility that students and the professor will expect them to speak for all American Indians and to be authorities on American Indian history, in as much as their knowledge confirms what is in the text. Attention to ethics, to who benefits and who gets hurt, offers those committed to cross-racial dialogue a way to hold onto the necessary questions, to remember the profound importance of considering choices and their consequences in all social interactions.

'Racism Is Not a Theory': The Importance of Affect in Learning about Race

In addition to marking whiteness, facing race in the classroom also requires the acknowledgment, at all levels of teaching and learning, that 'racism is not a theory.'[44] These five words stopped me short in a conversation I was having with my doctoral adviser. I was struggling to understand my ability to discuss race at length in theory-bound graduate seminars, and my corresponding inability to confront racism when I see it in my friends and in myself on Saturday nights. I was frustrated with this inability, and felt slightly ashamed to be talking about this with my adviser, an African American woman.

Her patience was a gift and her words made sense. 'Racism is not a theory,' she said, and I realized that the ability to sustain anti-racist practice must be more than a series of calculations in my head. I must begin to pay attention to how racism acts at emotional, physical, and spiritual levels. To act against white supremacy in myself and in institutions, and to talk about change with students, I must know white supremacy as a system that moves through all levels of our existence.

'Racism is not a theory.' These words opened a performance I wrote and did in a class. The performance lasted about thirty minutes. I used my words and what lay behind them, along with a few props, to communicate what I was learning about racism and acting against it. I centered the performance on a Saturday night of hanging out with other students, a Saturday night that happened several weeks before the performance. On that Saturday night, I was with a few friends and we were talking about a teacher we all knew, a teacher who was at the time my adviser. All of us had taken at least one class from her. I had known her for five years.

Quickly, our praise for this teacher began to sexualize her. She was someone who 'had an iron hand and a velvet glove,' and who 'seduced us into taking her classes.' I knew, immediately after these words were spoken, that sexualizing an African American woman when addressing her ability to teach is racist. Our comment had roots in cultural imagery which assigns the stereotype of hypersexuality to all African Americans. White people are comfortable sexualizing black bodies, and have been for years. Our inability to see that professor as a knowledgeable and effective teacher displaced her ability to teach with manipulation. Our comments essentialized her, made it impossible for her to be an individual, and placed her in a classification that was easy for us to look down on and disregard. We could not let her be an effective professor. Rather, we had to place her in the racially essentialized category of seducer.[45]

On that Saturday night, the comment was filling me up, and I chose not to say anything. I had known my adviser for five years. She believed in my ability to offer something of value to the conversation about race in higher education. I let the image of her stand. The conversation moved on. But the comment and my inaction remained in front of me like a billboard for weeks. I wanted to write a paper about this. I had to tell my adviser because it would be clear about whom I was talking and I thought she should know and have her say before I decided whether to make this story public.

'I knew it was racist and I said nothing,' I said to her. 'Racism is not a theory,' she responded. She neither blamed nor excused me. The conversation was brief. I knew this mess was of my making and likewise mine of which to make sense. When the conversation was over, I was left with my mess, with the hole of my inaction, and with the despair that comes with dishonoring someone you respect.

'Racism is not a theory.' I say these words out loud and I am performing my inaction and the context that surrounded that choice. I rehearsed this performance for weeks – my growing up learning to be at worst superior to and at best ambivalent toward the Mexican Americans at my high school, learning to swallow resistance to the status quo, learning to deny the confusion that came when those around me said Mexicans were lazy and African Americans did not like to work. I rehearsed the Saturday night, rehearsed my inaction, rehearsed the words of Toni Morrison[46] that address images, the paradox of closeness and distance white people maintain when it comes to people of color, including those we know well. In this case, our closeness was embodied by our eagerness to sexualize her body, and our distance was marked by our inability to leave her as the person she was. I rehearsed, also, different endings to the story of my inaction, different ways to respond to racist images among friends on Saturday night.

'Racism is not a theory.' Over and over, I practiced, moving the words and the script from my head into my body. I was nervous. I was a doctoral student, comfortable with theories and ideas, polite and well-spoken about racism, unsure of the wisdom of revealing my racism, again, this time in front of a crowd.

'Racism is not a theory,' I began, and I knocked over the stack of books on the floor beside me. These books had taught me much about race and images and what I do about them, but not enough to fill the hole of my inaction as it swallowed me on a Saturday night. 'Racism is not a theory,' I said to those in front of me, and I was angry, disappointed, hesitant, and hopeful at turns. Racism and the possibility of moving beyond it were no longer just in my head. There is now a small and new space for my emotions, for witnessing the damage I have done to my own soul by choosing inaction, for giving the proper weight and ridicule to the lessons of racism and white supremacy that I have learned well.

By the end of that thirty minutes, I was exhausted, but I had gained new knowledge. I had learned that words on paper are a small piece of the realities of racism, that boldly spoken anger and righteous indignation have a place in moving toward anti-racism, and that my caring for my adviser and my own part in her representation moved me to act, even if after the situation. I had learned that I have feelings about race and racism and not only thoughts, that all my thinking about race was a beginning and would in itself never be enough, and that my frameworks for thinking and learning about race in public places were painfully narrow and inadequate.

It is this knowledge that insists on the necessity of expanded pedagogical frameworks for teaching and learning well about race. Change often requires an investment that is more than a mental commitment to or understanding of an issue. When professors teach with the agenda of changing social interactions or of giving their students the tools to do so, learning requires more than the ability to think well. Students and teachers must practice the ability of affective reflection alongside critical analysis: what matters, why, and to what lengths are we willing to go to change the contexts in which we live? In regard to race, an already complicated and weighty topic, teachers must develop pedagogical strategies that allow all students to bring in what they know about race and anti-racist practice. As I learned through my performance, that knowledge will often entwine emotions and rationality in a manner that is both realistic and that offers hope for change.

Once race is on the table, knowledge may be present in stark and unfamiliar ways. In one class, we read a novel about African

American-European American relationships in the 1920s, and students take sides with various characters, deeply engaged in those characters' choices and actions. In another class, during a discussion of racial profiling, a student volunteers that as a security guard at a local mall, he has been directed by his superviser to follow African American men in that mall. He explains that he understands the rationale for this and does not feel uncomfortable doing this. Students' responses are quick and to the point. 'Isn't that stereotyping?' 'What if I came in dressed in a certain way – are you going to follow me too?'[47] Often, the unwritten rules of class discussion prevent race from coming to the table at all. When it comes to talking about race, silence may be the loudest refrain.

In higher education classrooms, the best of situations include professors who value interaction and students' experiences, and students who are familiar with learning on several levels. Even in these cases, university classrooms do not present themselves as locations that easily accept emotions, pain, and the combination of affective reflection and critical analysis that is required for social change. In most classes, students are expected to be in control of their thoughts, and feelings are best when absent. To express weakness or confusion, or to make a mistake, will likely invite ridicule from other students, or inspire fear of that ridicule. Learning is clean and scheduled; forty-five minutes for a lecture, thirty minutes for discussion. When difficult issues arise, students often make fun of part of the issue to create distance and to find a comfort zone for themselves.

Further, because students' experiences and emotions are rarely an open part of the learning process, invitation of the two can be complicated. In a class I taught on the Ethical Dimensions of Race, Gender, and Class, several European American women students wanted me to untangle their confusion and ambivalence about race. Once I had articulated the importance of being able to analyze our own lives and interactions, students who had little practice in this skill had difficulty combining their experience with the broader sociological historical context in which they lived. This inability surfaced over and over in the classroom. I am still learning to balance what students bring so that learning is possible.

The challenge, then, is to represent the range and specificity of experiences and knowledge about race in ways that contribute to the learning process for as many students as possible, if not for all of them. Students, including white students, who often use guilt and defensiveness to block new knowledge and practice, must see themselves as agents who can contribute to change. Teachers must replace the constant refrain from white students and some students of color that race dynamics are improving in the United States with attention to concrete, material conditions in particular contexts.

Three particular pedagogical practices can lead to classrooms in which learning at a variety of levels is possible. When teachers give value to emotions, to affective learning, and to knowledge that is complicated and messy, students may be more likely themselves to approach learning with an eye toward their own stake in and their feelings about the topic. Second, a willingness on the part of the teacher to address his or her own vulnerability and caring in connection with race matters and class content can open up the learning process. Finally, choosing to base at least part of the classroom learning on students' own experiences can result in students bringing a wider range of knowledge to the table.

All of these suggestions carry risks. They take practice, and a commitment to the process of facing race in higher education. They may not bring quick rewards. Often, working at these three practices may feel like it brings more trouble than gain. Further, I know best how these practices work from my own positionality as a teacher, which is as a white person. Although hard-and-fast rules regarding the significance of a teacher's race to how students learn do not exist, I believe my raciality in the classroom matters.[48] How it matters largely depends on how I represent myself and the material, on the students themselves, and on the topics we address. At a minimum, I have learned the importance of pedagogical clarity when it comes to addressing race in the classroom, with specific attention to how my positionality, role, and contributions match the learning objectives over the course of a term and within one class meeting.

VALUING AFFECTIVE AND COMPLICATED KNOWLEDGE

Combining social analysis with affective reflection can encourage movement toward anti-racist practice and cross-racial dialogue. Social analysis includes examination of course material that considers power and access to resources, to societal norms and expectations and who they exclude, and to issues of representation, including who controls images of whom, and who speaks for whom. Many teachers would say that this kind of analysis is a goal of their teaching. Affective reflection includes attention to ethics, to who benefits and who gets hurt, to our own stake in and caring for the issue at hand, and to how a topic matters to students and teachers.

When my then-adviser told me that racism is not a theory, I understood this at the level of social analysis. I could address how images and stereotypes worked, the history of white representation of African Americans, and the relatively recent presence of people of color in institutions of higher education. It was far more difficult for me to articulate the affective level of the issue. I struggled to find an appropriate way to talk about the confusing intensity of my anger, at myself and at the group as a whole; my frustration with my own inability to link such situations with my research; and my sense of profoundly betraying a teacher and ideals that I knew to be important. Further, I was at a loss as to how to make sense of this whole process in the context of the classroom. I was aware of the value of my struggle with that Saturday night event to talking about race, but had no means to make sense of that conflict with others in a way that would help us move toward cross-racial understanding and dialogue.

In the interests of cross-racial change, both social analysis and affective reflection are critical. On their own, each may contribute pieces of what is required for cross-racial change. However, analysis and affective reflection together can make it possible to discuss, at micro- and macro-levels, material conditions, and how individuals who are part of institutions can contribute to change. Further, careful attention to how students feel about concrete social interactions makes it far more likely that students and teachers will address the intricacies and complications of race.

For me, the key issue with that Saturday night conflict was my lack of response. A classroom discussion about images and stereotypes would have been possible with no reference at all to this lack of response. However, talk about change requires talk about the details. Highlighting the variety of possible perceptions about what occurred, and the possible responses, allows those in a classroom to discuss actual change, and how it happens in practice rather than only in theory. Further, revealing how that Saturday night behavior is played out in similar ways throughout the contexts in which students live helps to demonstrate the way in which our choices are part of larger social structures.

Teachers must be willing to value affective knowledge as much as we value social analysis. We must not retreat from the complications of real life that satisfy no theory but that do speak to how people live. We must value different interpretations of messy situations, always with an eye toward material conditions, power relationships, and what we and our students want to change.

THE ROLE OF VULNERABILITY AND CARING

As a white teacher working at anti-racist practice, I routinely make mistakes and trip on my good intentions. I am in no way immune from benefitting from and enjoying white supremacy and white privilege. Despite my work at understanding race and anti-racist change, I have not arrived. At the same time, I believe strongly in the value of cross-racial dialogue. I want students to understand how race works in their own lives, and how it affects broader social structures. I hope that my teaching moves myself and my students toward these ends.

My demonstration of my vulnerability and commitment when it comes to cross-racial change can be a doorway through which white students might enter the conversation. Identification of myself as white and as a person who routinely makes choices about race might encourage these students to see themselves as white and as racial agents. Further, I have seen that it is often in retelling my mistakes, and my resolve to unlearn that behavior, that white students are willing to pick up the topic of race. The stories of when I have tripped and thought about how to keep on walking forward can provide places for white students to begin considering race. In the midst of my mistakes and my resolve to act differently next time, there is little room for guilt and defensiveness. Rather, the issue is how to adopt different practice so that I am not supporting white supremacy.

'Racism is not a theory,' I said in my performance, and then told of how I saw racist images standing in front of me and let them be. In the performance, I asked in a variety of ways: What images do we respond to? How do we respond? What is familiar to us? What is not? Do we know how to resist racist representation? Do we know how to be silent? Do we have the nerve to interrupt on Saturday night with friends, on Monday mornings at work, on Wednesday afternoons in class? Do we risk disturbing the comfort to name that which is ordinary and racist? In between mistakes and the possibility of different practice, students may find a way into conversations about race and anti-racist change.

THE ROLE OF STUDENT EXPERIENCE IN TALKING ABOUT RACE

When the purpose of education is social change, it is not enough to study change and how it happens from a distance. In as much as learning involves an internalization of ideas and practice so that people may act on new knowledge, the classroom can be one place where students consider how they will apply that new knowledge in concrete situations. Incorporating students' experiences into the learning process can encourage talk about racism and anti-racist change in several ways. Marking students' experiences as relevant to and a part of the learning process identifies students as agents in relationship to the topic itself; lends a materiality to the subject of race; allows those in the classroom to represent race matters in complex and conflicting ways; and encourages a holistic analysis that can include theory and practice, and analytical and affective learning.

When students understand their own experience as a starting point for analysis and change, they often look at the subject matter differently than when that experience is absent from the learning process. Further, when the goal of learning is changed practice, students can see themselves as actors in relationship to that goal. They are no longer passive and neutral, but are significant to the topic and to how they live it. In the exercise in which students had to observe and classify certain aspects of advertisements, they became authorities in relation to their observations, and responsible for their interpretation of course material. But it is also critical for the teacher to provide relevant information so that the students' knowledge can be tailored to specific learning objectives.

A second benefit to drawing on students' experiences in the learning process is that class discussion will stay close to material reality. Again, this obviously carries specific risks. Depending on students' positionality in terms of race, their experiences, and their perceptions of these experiences, the material and knowledge they bring may represent a particularly narrow piece of reality. Further, white students may have readings of their experience that are themselves racist. It is extremely important for the teacher to have an in-depth understanding of the context of the knowledge to be addressed, and a clear grasp of his or her learning objectives relevant to that knowledge. When both of these are in place, beginning with students' experiences lends a layer of reality to the material that may have not been present before.

A related benefit of this concreteness is that students are usually more able to think about different and conflicting experiences in a constructive way than when their experiences are absent. When it is clear that agreement and a single correct understanding are not necessary or even desired, students might learn to let difference stand, to accept another's interpretation of an event, and to consider how different interpretations lead to different ends. Treating students' experience as a part of classroom knowledge can in itself send the message that there are several ways into class material, and that no one topic is neatly bounded or simply understood. Further, learning is not so much about right or wrong as it is about working with what one knows, including experience, book knowledge, and what comes out of class discussion, and making sense of that knowledge as it supports specific practice.

In connection with race matters, this approach can allow students to take the risk of entering unfamiliar territory. It also opens up the possibility of, for example, a white student listening to a person of color talk about race in ways that directly contradict that white student's views. That student may be better able to hear the student of color if she knows she is not required to give up her own experience.

Again, risks with this approach are inevitable. Any student can represent her experiences in ways that interrupt classroom learning. In the case of race, white students may not be interested in learning, and may be far more committed to using classroom time to cover over assumptions or lack of knowledge, to excuse themselves of responsibility, or to work through feelings of guilt. It is critical to be clear about movement toward changed practice, and how classroom learning can support changed social interactions. For this to be possible, the teacher must be certain about what she wants from the course meeting. Teachers may be compelled to ask students of color to share their experiences. Such asking is unfair; it may simultaneously serve the teacher's goals and ignore the right of the students of color to speak when they choose without the pressure of a teacher's question.

All teachers, in the act of teaching, establish a certain direction or course that the learning takes, even if the establishment of that direction is not intentional or clearly thought out. Teaching about race requires that professors know the direction in which they want to go, and that they take an active part in ensuring that the class moves in that direction. Further, these practices are most relevant in the context of anti-racist practice. Talking about race solely for the purpose of talking about race – because it is interesting or exotic, because you want to check it off a list, or because you know that students will respond to the topic – will not move a class toward anti-racist knowledge and practice. Further, because race and racism are topics that involve the potential to cause pain and to shut down learning, to talk about race without a clear direction in mind is irresponsible and dangerous.

Finally, working with students' experiences as an integral part of the learning process can bring learning full circle for everyone involved. Students learn to integrate their experience into the theories relevant to course material. After practice, they may become more adept at linking local social interactions of which they are a part to broader social structures. Further, they can bring together the analytical and the affective. It makes particular sense, when viewing one's own experience as relevant to the learning process, to think about change and one's stake in the issue. In connection with race, students can perhaps learn to bring together a new or enlarged understanding of institutional racism and white supremacy with their own agency and commitment to change.

'Racism is not a theory.' It is not an easy lesson for white people to learn. It is also a difficult lesson for groups of people in higher education to learn, as we cling to safe and predictable routes to knowledge. Changes in the classroom and in higher education are not easy either. They will come only with costs, heavy at times. People in higher education have absorbed assimilationist approaches to education, and we are comfortable with them. Adoption of these approaches offers meaningful rewards. Institutions and colleagues may not support plain talk about structural inequality, including inequality in our own institutions and departments. It is unlikely that moving away from an exclusive focus on language and specific cultural characteristics of particular racial-ethnic groups will be a popular endeavor. Resistance may seem to come from all corners.

Yet it is with such plain talk about racism and structural inequality that anti-racist practice and democratic education can begin. Engaging in this process with students requires attention to whiteness, and an ability to bring together analytical and affective learning. 'Racism is not a theory,' my then-adviser said, and I know that lasting change will require far more than ideas. 'Racism is not a theory,' she said, and I struggle to find the place for caring and a commitment to change in the process of teaching and learning.

Appendix:
Discussion Questions, Exercises,
and Assignments

Guidelines for Discussion Questions, Exercises, and Assignments

1 These questions will best facilitate learning about race when the teachers who use them have an agenda for the course meeting and clearly articulate course meeting learning objectives. Introducing these questions separate from course learning objectives, and without contextual knowledge on the part of the teacher, may support general conversation but will not likely promote learning for the class as a whole.

2 In my experience, it works best if the teacher opens and closes the discussion with substantive and prepared commentary. It is crucial for all teachers to articulate to students the reasons for the discussion in the context of the course, as well as the three or four main points the teacher wants to make that relate to her learning objectives for that course meeting.

3 Preparation on the part of the teacher should provide the backdrop for the questions and exercises outlined below. For example, if you choose to use the discussion questions on the topic of Race Words, you should come prepared with definitions for all of these words, as well as with clear ideas about your own thoughts on them. If you do Exercise 2, it will be useful to spend time before class making your own lists, and to spend time thinking through the mechanisms of race privilege and discrimination in each item on your list.

4 A list of ground rules and guidelines can be very useful. If I have to

articulate these ground rules to students, I always remind the students that certain guidelines can help to ensure that everyone has a chance to learn. A preliminary list of guidelines might include:
- Don't interrupt. Let people finish what they want to say.
- Consider air time: if there are thirty people in the class, am I taking up about one-thirtieth of the overall class time?
- Jokes about others' experiences or comments are inappropriate.
- Silence, reflection, and listening are all essential components in the learning process.

5. Use examples to ground conversations. When discussions about race become conflicted and uncomfortable, white students often retreat to analysis of purely hypothetical situations. For example, in a discussion that focuses on racial profiling, students may want to talk about how people would respond if African American law enforcement officials repeatedly pulled over white people because of their race. They may even argue that this has happened to them. Students may also begin to talk in very abstract terms. Concrete examples can help hold the discussion to lived, material conditions. In teaching to promote cross-racial dialogue, discussions that exclusively focus on abstract ideas and hypothetical examples have limited utility.

6. Achieving cross-racial dialogue and anti-racist practice requires long-term investment at many levels. These questions and exercises are a beginning, and are one piece of the process. Structures in higher education will change when large numbers of people in this setting, and particularly when large numbers of people who hold institutional power, are invested in anti-racist practice.

Chapter One. Introduction: Race and Higher Education

Questions for Discussion

1 *Racial Identity*
- What is your racial identity?
- When do you think about race?
- When do you pay attention to race?
- How old were you when you first thought about race?
- Ruth Frankenberg writes that 'Race shapes white women's lives.' If you are a person of color, how has your racial identity shaped

how you live? If you are white, how has being white shaped how you live?

2 *Talk about Race*
- When is the last time you had a conversation about race?
- Who was involved?
- How long did it last?
- What was it about?
- How did you feel during this conversation? Why did you feel this way?
- Did the conversation change anything? For whom, and how?

3 *Race Words*
- How do you feel when you hear the following words: race, racist, racism, white supremacy, white privilege? Why do you feel this way?
- What do these words mean?
- Do they have anything to do with you? Why or why not, and in what ways?
- How does this chapter define white supremacy?
- Do you agree with the idea that white supremacy 'most determines how white people in this society (irrespective of their political leanings to the right or left) perceive and relate to black people and other people of color?'[1] Why or why not?

4 *Race Issues*
- Make a list of social issues that involve race. You might start with social issues that are relevant in your particular community.
- Are these issues important to you? Why or why not?
- Do these issues limit or otherwise directly affect how you live? How?
- What is the connection of these issues to your education and taking classes?
- Do these issues have anything to do with your college or university? Why or why not?

5 *Race Relations*
- If you are a person of color, are you often the 'honorary [insert race] friend' of many of your white friends? How do you feel and/or respond when a white person says this to you?

- If you are a person of color, what are some of the assumptions that white people make about you?
- If you are a white person, do you make any assumptions about people of color, both people you don't know and people you know well, based on their race? Why or why not?
- If you are a white person, do you think about the race of your friends or acquaintances? Why or why not?
- If you are a person of color, do you think about the race of your friends or acquaintances? Why or why not?
- Do you see any connection between individual race relations and larger social issues? Why or why not? Make examples.
- How does your acquaintance and/or friendship with people from racial groups different from your own change what you think and how you act?
- How do race and racism affect your friendships and acquaintances with people from racial groups other than your own?
- Is it important for you to have friends and acquaintances from different racial groups? Why or why not?

6 *Race Knowledge*
- What do you know about race and race issues?
- Where did you learn this? What are the sources of your knowledge about race issues and racism?
- Do you seek out knowledge about racial groups different from your own? Why or why not?
- Is your own racial group well represented in the media you rely on and the classes you take? Why or why not?
- Is information about racial groups different from your own easily available in the local media?
- Particularly if you are white, how often do people of color control and/or have a major role in the sources you rely on for knowledge and information? Provide examples.
- Particularly if you are a person of color, how often do white people control and/or have a major role in the sources you rely on for knowledge and information? Provide examples.

7 *Race and Responsibility*
- In the Preface and in chapter 1, the author of this book clearly connects her interest in the topic to a sense of responsibility toward racism and race issues. If you go back to the list of race issues you

made, who do you think is responsible in connection with each of these for changing race relations? Why?

- If you think about race issues at your college or university, who is responsible for addressing these issues?
- Is thinking about race and racism, and working at change, a priority for you? Why or why not?
- If you are invested in learning about race and racism, and in working at change and at anti-racist practice, why are you invested? What do you have to gain? What do you have to lose?

Class Exercises and Assignments

The first of these three exercises requires that students spend time outside of class working on the exercise; the last two may be done entirely in class.

1 *Survey of Local Race Issues*
  In groups of three or four, students should survey the last six months of local newspapers for attention to race issues in your local community. These newspapers might include the city newspaper(s), the campus paper, and papers that come out of particular racial/ethnic groups in your community. For example, you might assign three groups to cover the city paper, with each group covering two months.
      Students should return with a list of the issues they discovered, a brief description of each issue (one-half to one page), a list of the groups connected to that issue, and a list of issues at stake for each group.
      Each small group should present its findings in class. This project might take a few weeks, or could be spread out over the whole term, with groups doing assessments and analyses of their findings. During this time, the teacher might also talk with professors or community advocates who have a stake in race issues in the community. This might begin to give the teacher a sense of what the local media is leaving out. Students might also be able to contribute to the discussion of what the media is leaving out, and the teacher should offer structured time for individual students to add to what groups have found.

2 *Identifying Race Privilege and Race Discrimination*
  This exercise corresponds to the questions on racial identity listed

above. Students should have a few days to answer the racial identity questions individually, and they should write their answers outside of class. After students have done this, as a group, the class should list examples of race privilege and race discrimination. The teacher might lay out some categories: employment, politics, educational, media, and day-to-day (shopping, banking, public transportation, neighborhood) settings.

The list should include a column for discrimination and a column for privilege. Throughout the exercise, the class should fill in both columns, even if individuals speak to only one side of the table. For example, if a student mentions that an employee always follows him or her at the local music store, the recorder should write in the same row, privilege column, the privilege of not being followed and suspected as a thief.

Students might also consider examples of race privilege and race discrimination at that university.

As a final part of this exercise, students can discuss how to create change in one or two of the situations listed. First, what is it that those in the class want to change? What should be different? Does change need to happen at the situational level only? For example, is it enough that the one employee know it is not fair to follow people who are African American? Or are there institutional issues that affect the situation? In the store example, do supervisors and management expect employees to follow African Americans? How might someone in the classroom who is in the situations listed respond?

3 *Race in Disciplinary Contexts* (particularly relevant to upper division undergraduate and graduate classes)
Students should make a list of all the theories they have learned in different classes in the department in which the class is offered. They might include names of theorists and of theories, and brief descriptions of different theories and concepts that are common to that department.

In groups, students should discuss how each of these theories addresses race or not. Drawing on a concrete situation that raises issues relevant to the field and that involves race, they should discuss how these theories and concepts speak to this situation. Students might draw on one of the examples from Exercise 2.

As students identify which theories and ideas do or do not account for race in the situation they discuss, they should begin considering how theories and concepts common to the discipline might better account for race. Each group might take one theory or concept, together with one concrete situation, and articulate how that theory would look if it were thoroughly responsive to the situation and to race issues.

Chapter Two. Resisting 'Sympathy and Yet Distance':[2] The Connection of Race, Memory, and History

Questions for Discussion

1 *Individual Race History*
- What is your first memory of race? Is this memory a pleasant or unpleasant one, or both? Why?
- What messages did you hear about race while growing up, from parents, siblings, extended family members, and people who held authority in your life (teachers, community leaders, faith-based leaders)? How did you feel about these messages? Did you ever 'talk back,' either directly or indirectly, and if so, how?
- When did you begin to identify as a person with a race? What shaped this identification?
- What messages did you receive about race generally? Was race routinely present in your life and familial and social interactions? How?

2 *Race, History, and Community*
- What issues involving race do you remember from the community/ies in which you grew up? From your high school?
- Were there racial issues in the community about which you were not supposed to ask, or about which your parents or others expected you to remain quiet? How does this affect your views on those issues now?
- Where was race present in your community? How did race issues occupy public and private spaces?

3 *Lessons about Race*
Consider your current ideas about race in terms of:
- Dialogue about race. Is talk about race acceptable dinner conversation? Why or why not? Is race frequently a topic with family and friends? A topic you generally avoid?

- Current social issues. For example, racial profiling; affirmative action; or the level of racism in the media, your professional life, and your community.
- Your own social practice. This should include interactions with people of different racial groups than your own, and the topics and degree of closeness in those interactions; how often you talk about race for an extended period of time and in an in-depth manner.
- Where did you learn your ideas and practices relevant to all of the above? What lessons persisted, and why? About which issues identified above do you have strong feelings, and why?

4 *Historical Race Knowledge*
- Consider your history and civics classes throughout your education. What racial issues were prevalent in these classes? What did you learn about particular historical issues, such as Asian immigration laws, the Japanese internment camps, the United States-Mexican war, boarding schools, the activities of the Klu Klux Klan, and/or school integration? If you had to write a page based on your knowledge about any of these issues, what would you include?
- From what sources did you acquire your knowledge? In which cases did the groups involved control and present the information and history upon which you rely? Does the source of the knowledge matter? Why or why not?
- How did these histories present particular racial groups? How did the authors handle issues of ethics, accountability, and responsibility? How does this history present European Americans: as saviors, oppressors, givers of charity, innocent and/or neutral bystanders, and/or ignorant but well-intentioned observers? How does this history present American Indians and people of Asian, African, and Latin American descent: as victims, resisters, trouble makers, exceptions to the norm, social change agents, people dependent on white peoples' assistance, and/or autonomous actors? What are other categories/roles present in the history you know?

Class Exercises and Assignments

1 *Individual Race History*
Students should write individual racial autobiographies. These

should track the development of their racial identification and address their memories of race or its absence in their growing up. They should also address the messages about race they received from parents, siblings, extended family, and community members; the development and background of their own ideas about race; their sources for information and lessons about race; and any conflicts about or challenges to their ideas about race.

2 *Community Race History*
This is a semester-long project in which students investigate and report on race issues in their local area. As a whole, the class might investigate a time period of fifty years; small groups might examine ten-year periods. Sources of information might include local newspapers (including mainstream and racial/ethnic publications), social activists, long-standing community members, faith-based and/or business leaders who have lived in the community for at least fifteen to twenty years, university or community archives, neighborhood association archives, and so forth. Student groups might present their findings in class as well as preparing a written report. If there is interest in follow-up work, students might prepare educational presentations for local high school, junior high school, or elementary school classrooms. If the student work does extend beyond the university, it may be worthwhile for the professor to establish a feedback panel of university and community representatives knowledgeable about local history to review student work.

3 *Disciplinary Race History*
Students should trace the history of their discipline with particular attention to race issues. In the late 1800s and early 1900s (or earlier, if relevant), were people of color in any way a part of disciplinary formation? How did major contributors to the discipline respond to prominent racial issues such as eugenics, immigration policy, and the European American push toward assimilation of all people of color in the late 1800s and early 1900s? Considering prominent social issues throughout the 1900s, how did the discipline respond (or not) to these issues, particularly those most relevant to the discipline? How did the discipline respond to the social and cultural movements of American Indians, African Americans, Latin Americans, and Asian Americans in the 1960s? As colleges and universities hired more people of color, how did this affect disciplinary content and method?

Chapter Three. We Are Not Enough: Epistemology and the Production of Knowledge

Discussion Questions

1 *Race Knowledge*
   • When did you begin learning about race? From whom?
   • What do you know from book learning about race? What do you know from experience about race? Are these two kinds of knowledges intertwined? Why or why not, and if so, how?
   • In terms of what you have read about race, is the knowledge most often produced by those most affected by the topic at hand?
   • How important is location to knowledge about race? In regard to your answers to the above questions, what is the relationship between the knowledge produced and the location of the people producing the knowledge?
   • What are some of the ways in which white people discriminate against people of color in your community? In each of these examples, where is it most likely that you might find yourself?
   • How does your experience of racial discrimination and race privilege affect your feelings about race? How do these feelings affect your beliefs about racism and your willingness and ability to learn more about race and racism?

2 *Knowledge Practices*
   • Make a list of the routine ways in which you use race knowledge.
   • Do you have a theory or philosophy of knowledge? What is it? How do you move from idea to knowledge, from having an idea about something to knowing something?
   • When you think about your own race knowledge, do you generalize this knowledge or speak for others? When is generalizing this knowledge appropriate or useful? When is it not appropriate or not useful? When is it hurtful? Why?
   • What is the best way to correct the absence of knowledge about race in your field or discipline? Is it sufficient to 'add on' new ideas and information, or are more fundamental changes necessary? Why or why not? Provide examples.

3 *Knowledge and Social Institutions*
   • Consider social institutions that regularly produce and/or repre-

sent knowledge about racial groups. These institutions might include media organizations, schools, and faith-based organizations. What messages do each of these institutions send about particular racial groups?

- Do the institutions considered in the previous question generally send a favorable message about the racial group with which you identify? If they send no message at all, why might this be the case? Do these institutions offer a realistic picture of the racial group with which you identify? Why or why not, and if so, how? Provide examples.
- Consider the classes you have taken in your major or graduate program. Does the knowledge that people and course materials present in these classes appear specific to a racial group? If the knowledge appears to be equally relevant to all racial groups, is this actually the case? What racial groups are present in the knowledge in your major or field, and in what ways are they present? What racial groups are absent?

4 *Knowledge Interests*
- In your mind, what is the purpose of knowledge? What should knowledge do? Provide examples.
- When you encounter knowledge that is new, unfamiliar, or threatening, how do you evaluate that knowledge? When someone presents you with knowledge about a topic on which you have strong feelings (for example, affirmative action, racial profiling, or immigration) how do you judge that knowledge? How do your socialization, loyalties, and values affect that judgment?
- If you are a white person, when you hear knowledge that reflects unfavorably on white people, does this seem strange or upsetting? Why or why not? What is your first response when you hear this knowledge? What are some of the reasons for this response? Provide examples. If you are a person of color, when you hear knowledge that reflects unfavorably on the racial group with which you identify, does this seem strange or upsetting? What is your first response when you hear this knowledge? What are some of the reasons for this response? Provide examples.
- Chapter 3 discusses the concept of standpoint and 'better' or 'less distorted' knowledge. Does standpoint matter? Why or why not, and if so, how? Provide examples.

5 *Knowledge, Race, and Higher Education*
  - Chapter 3 articulates three assumptions made by whites when it comes to race and knowledge: (1) book learning can offer the entirety of knowledge on any given subject; (2) since book learning can provide the entirety of knowledge on any given subject, an organization can be cross-cultural if the white people in that organization learn enough; and (3) knowledge operates in a neutral space. Do you agree that these assumptions are operative? Provide examples.
  - In your own mind, what does it take for an individual to have cross-cultural knowledge? For an organization to have cross-cultural knowledge?
  - In your own experience, are cultural inappropriateness and/or racism routine in your department/school/community, or an exception? Provide examples.
  - Chapter 3 concludes by stating (1) that knowledge is particular, and (2) that the production of cross-racial knowledge will require a cross-racial group of people. Do you agree or disagree with these conclusions? Why or why not?

Class Exercises and Assignments

1 *Students Producing Knowledge*
  The teacher should choose any recent controversial political or social issue or event in your community that involves race. Students should, individually, do enough outside research about this issue or event to allow them to write a page on this topic. Students must list their sources of information, including personal conversations. Once students have completed this page, the teacher should place them in race-based groups of three or four students (white students should be in the same groups; groups made up of students of color might be constituted by one racial-ethnic group, or might include a cross-section of students of color). Each student should bring the page they have written. The students should then together write one page on which they can all agree, representing what they know about this particular topic. When completed, students should hand this in. Finally, the teacher should place students in cross-racial groups of three or four. Students should bring the page they wrote individually, as well as the collective page they wrote in the first group. Again, groups must write one page on the topic or event. When completed,

the class can look at the variety of pages written by the groups. In addition to looking at the different knowledge produced, the teacher and students should also consider the processes of producing knowledge. How was it different writing as an individual, in a monoracial group (for the white students and for students of color), in a group of only people of color, and in a cross-racial group? How did the sources of information change depending on who was involved? What was easy, hard, frustrating, challenging, interesting, exciting? What did this process teach the participants about knowledge?

2 *Students and Curriculum Design*
This exercise is particularly for upper division undergraduate and graduate students. In groups, students must design a diversity class required for all students during their first year. The teacher should first provide a rational for such a class, relying on existing university curricular policy or borrowing such policy from another university. This rationale should provide students with a basic understanding of the reasons for and parameters of the policy. Students should articulate the topical organization of the course and assignments; who should be involved in teaching the course (an individual, team, or series of lecturers); and course objectives.

Chapter Four. 'The Challenges and Possibilities of Cross-racial Dialogue'

Discussion Questions

1 *Talk about Race*
  - In your day-to-day experience, when is it appropriate to talk about race? When is it inappropriate?
  - When do you talk about race? With whom? About what? When do you initiate conversations about race, and why do you initiate these conversations?
  - When is the talk you hear/speak about race defensive? Excited? Angry? Hopeful? How often and when do you hear talk about race that addresses, in an in-depth manner, social injustice and racism?
  - Is some of your talk about race only for those in your own racial group? How does your talk about race change depending on if you are: with friends or family, in class, or at work?

- In your mind, do people need specific skills to talk about race? Is talking about race different from talking about other subjects (such as sports, movies, or what is going on at work)?
- In class, what would make it easier for you to talk about race? What makes it difficult?

2 *Talk about Change*
   - How does this chapter define dialogue? Do you agree with this definition? Why or why not?
   - This chapter assumes that people participating in cross-racial dialogues need to challenge the status quo. Do you agree with this idea? Why or why not? In what ways are you a part of the status quo? In what ways do you challenge the status quo?
   - According to this chapter, cross-racial dialogue requires that white people know themselves as subjects within the context of race, that they know people of color as subjects, that they learn to share space rather than control it, and that they enter the conversation knowing that change is necessary. If you are white, can you make examples of each of these requirements from your own life (when you have acted on these requirements, and when you have not)? If you are a person of color, can you provide examples of when white people you know have taken each of these steps (or not)?
   - In thinking about race issues in concrete situations, what do you want to change? Are you interested in dialogue? Why or why not?

Classroom Exercises and Assignments

1 *Classroom Dialogues about Race*
   In groups, students are responsible for setting up and facilitating classroom dialogues about race and a specific topic, perhaps relevant to the local community. Topics might include affirmative action, racial profiling, media images of people of color and white people, or income disparities related to race. The topics might be discipline-related; students should choose a topic that has immediate relevance to the university and/or the community. Each dialogue should fill one class session. Students should use the guidelines provided at the end chapter 4. Clear attention should be paid to changed practice. Students should also be responsible for providing historical and contextual information, and for providing a structure and ground rules for the dialogue. Each group should articulate an area for changed

practice at the start of the class session. Students should submit an outline of the planned dialogue at least a week in advance of the dialogue itself. Teachers should ensure that the outline meets learning goals.

2 *Public Dialogues about Race*
In groups, students should research and report on public models of dialogue about race at a local, state, or national level. The purpose of this exercise is to enable students to become aware of, offer a critique of, and present on race dialogues. Such dialogues might include the Clinton administration-initiated Dialogue on Race, or a local group specifically devoted to race issues (for example, a diversity committee on campus or at a student's workplace). Students should research and report on: participants in the dialogue, objectives of the dialogue (according to a range of people), structure of the dialogue (including frequency of meetings, ground rules, etc.), and internal and external critique of the dialogue. If the dialogue group disbanded earlier than planned, or before the participants realized the dialogue objectives, students should explain why this happened. Groups should also offer their own analysis of what these dialogues accomplished, and how they made, or failed to make, a contribution to those in the group and to the broader community.

Chapter Five. 'Racism Is Not a Theory:'[3] Race Matters in the Classroom

Discussion Questions

1 *Race in the Classroom*
- Make a list of the times you remember talking about race in the classroom. How did these conversations begin? How did they end? For how long did conversations specifically addressing race issues last? Who was involved? What did you learn from these discussions?
- How have the readings in your classes addressed race? Has race seemed like a subject tacked on to the core material, or like a central part of the material? Provide reasons for your answer.
- Chapter 5 argues that most efforts in higher education that address race have been aimed at 'managing diversity.' What has

been your experience with your department or school's approach
to race?

- When discussions in the classroom significantly challenge ideas
  that you or other students hold, what happens? What are your
  thoughts regarding discussions in which there is a wide range of
  conflicting opinions, and which may become heated or difficult?

2 *Race in Disciplinary Contexts: Assimilation and Structural Change*
- In your major or field, how have the textbooks you have read
  treated race? Has there been a tendency toward the relevance of
  language differences, racial tolerance, and/or cultural understanding; an emphasis on structural injustice, unequal power, and
  institutional change; neither; or both? In what ways? Provide
  examples.
- What is the relevance of the concept of cultural competence to
  your discipline? How has your discipline defined this term? If no
  attention is given in your field to cultural competence, are there
  concepts with parallel significance? If ideas about race are for the
  most part absent from your field, why is this?
- Discuss the significance of the cultural understanding, cultural
  competence, and cultural emancipation models to your discipline.
  Provide examples of how each of these is present in concrete ways
  in your field or discipline. If these models are absent from your
  field, explain.

3 *Existence of Local Racisms*
- Make a list of local institutions whose intentions or practices you
  question (for example, the police department, media organizations, educational institutions, city hall (including city agencies),
  health care facilities, and local businesses). What are your reasons
  for questioning these institutions? Make a second list of institutions that did not make the first list. What distinguishes the institutions on the first list from those on the second? Do these
  distinctions have anything to do with race? Why or why not, and
  if so, how?
- Provide examples of specific practices you question and do not
  question relative to each institution on your two lists. For example, the police department may or may not take a complaint about
  safety issues in your neighborhood seriously. Then consider issues
  of ethics and responsibility. Connect the institutions, practice, and

person/group/agency responsible. In the case of institutions and practices that you and/or your classmates question, is it possible to agree on issues of responsibility?

4 *Racial Norms*
  • Consider your knowledge about race, patterns of interaction, and cultural referents. What have been your sources for each?
  • Has there ever been a need for you to put aside your knowledge, interaction patterns, and/or cultural referents to make room for someone else's? When did/does this occur? When does this seem appropriate and when does it seem inappropriate?

5 *Marking Whiteness*
  • Make a list of some examples of whiteness in the classroom discussed in chapter 5, in the section 'Making Whiteness Visible.' Add your own examples to this list. Do you agree that these are examples of the ways in which white people assert their norms and social assumptions?
  • In your mind, do the practices outlined above serve to exclude people or ideas? Why or why not?
  • Identify how these practices privilege some students and discriminate against others.
  • With respect to the practices of whiteness that you decided serve to exclude people or ideas, what are your suggestions for change? How would you create an environment in which these practices are less prevalent?
  • Make a list of the effects of racial discrimination. This list might include a wide variety of examples, such as (1) a lack of positive images of people of color leads young people of color in particular to question their value and worth; (2) unfair lending practices result in people of color receiving fewer loans; or (3) the stereotype of Asian Americans as strong in the sciences leads to decreased support for Asian Americans in the humanities and social sciences. For each item on this list, identify the related privilege(s). For example, (1) young white people are able to rely on the images around them to instill a positive sense of self-worth, (2) white people can count on receiving loans when they meet basic expectations and on the fact that their race will give them an advantage in applying for loans; and (3) white people will receive encouragement for a range of professions and jobs and their race will be an

asset in this process. For each of these sets of privileges and acts of discrimination in the examples you made, discuss possible short-term and long-range effects.

6 *The Role of Affective Learning*
   • In thinking about race, racism, and changed practice, what is your investment in doing things differently? Is this work a class assignment, a reading or two, some credits to complete, a minor annoyance, or a long-term commitment? Why?
   • What do caring and emotions have to do with your education? When you change how you approach a topic or certain situation, why do you change?
   • In thinking about race, racism, and changed practice, what do you have to gain? What do you have to lose? If you ignore these issues, will it matter? Why or why not, and if so, how?

Class Exercises and Assignments

1 *Media Images and Race*
   Students should individually make a log of the images they consume in the media (including television, radio, print, as well as movies, billboards, etc.). They should fill in a chart that includes several columns: person or group in the particular media representation (which might be an advertisement, thirty-minute television show, news program, etc.); gender, race, age, and class of the persons and/or group; what people in the representation are doing; words students would use to characterize their actions; and value/meaning associated with those actions. The students should keep this log for at least a week, and possibly for two or three weeks. After a few days, the teacher might check in to see how this exercise is going, and if the students have questions. Once the time assigned for the exercise has passed, discuss the students' findings in class. Make a chart on the board, and begin to fill it in. Encourage students to think about patterns, who is present in what ways, and who is absent in media images. This exercise could be extended so that groups of students focus on particular media. Groups might focus on, for example, local television, radio, and print news organizations.

2 *Race, Education, and Change*
   Now that students have completed reading this chapter (or perhaps

the entire book), what would they like to offer as a response? This exercise might resemble a capstone project, in which students in groups choose a particular issue to research or address. The issue chosen might derive from previous exercises. Do they want to start a reading group? Would they like to prepare a report for the campus radio station on a particular topic related to race and the local community? Would they like to do an oral history related to particular issue? Do they believe it is important to make their opinions known more broadly and in a formal manner? Is there a project at work they would like to take on? Teachers should encourage all students, and particularly white students, to consider why they may or may not make a commitment to continuing to think about race in their education or in other arenas. If they do want to make this choice, how will they act on it? How will they ensure that they carry it out? What kinds of accountability systems will they put in place to make sure that they are receiving a variety of views?

Notes

1 Introduction: Race and Higher Education

1 Aída Hurtado, *The Color of Privilege: Three Blasphemies on Race and Feminism* (Ann Arbor: University of Michigan Press, 1996), 24–37.
2 As discussed later in this chapter and in chapter 2, women of color have long been linking oppressions including, at a minimum, sexism, racism, and classism.
3 Ruth Frankenberg, *White Women, Race Matters: The Social Construction of Whiteness* (Minneapolis: University of Minnesota Press, 1993), 1; Nancie Caraway, *Segregated Sisterhood: Racism and the Politics of American Feminism* (Knoxville: University of Tennessee Press, 1991); Vron Ware, *Beyond the Pale: White Women, Racism and History* (London: Verso, 1992); Barbara Hilkert Andolsen, *'Daughters of Jefferson, Daughters of Bootblacks': Racism and American Feminism* (Macon, GA: Mercer University Press, 1986); Becky Thompson, *A Promise and a Way of Life: White Antiracist Activism* (Minneapolis: University of Minnesota Press, 2001).
4 Hurtado, *The Color of Privilege*, 42.
5 bell hooks, *Killing Rage: Ending Racism* (New York: Henry Holt, 1995), 100.
6 European American feminist theory often ignores the work of women of color that is directly relevant to the topic at hand, and also veers into areas that have little relevance to the lives of women of color.
7 M. Annette Jaimes, 'American Racism: The Impact on American-Indian Identity and Survival,' in *Race*, ed. Steven Gregory and Roger Sanjek (New Brunswick: Rutgers University Press, 1994), 41–61 at 41–5. While I believe white men held much of the socio-economic power in these histories, I also believe white women possessed agency. My attention to white racism against people of African, Asian, and Latin American descent and against

American Indians is not intended as a history of white supremacy in this country. I do want to stress that racist beginnings have effected and scarred all cross-racial relationships between European Americans and U.S. people of color, including those among women.

8 Patricia Hill Collins, *Black Feminist Thought: Knowledge, Consciousness and the Politics of Empowerment* (Boston: Unwin Hyman, 1990), 48–52.

9 Helen Zia, *Asian American Dreams: The Emergence of an American People* (New York: Farrar, Straus, and Giroux, 2000), 35–52.

10 Patricia Zavella, 'Reflections on Diversity Among Chicanas,' in *Race*, ed. Steven Gregory and Roger Sanjek (New Brunswick, NJ: Rutgers University Press, 1994), 199–212 at 203.

11 Frankenberg, *White Women, Race Matters*, 1–2.

12 Imelda Whelehan, *Modern Feminist Thought* (New York: New York University Press, 1995), 108–9.

13 Elizabeth V. Spelman, *Inessential Woman: Problems of Exclusion in Feminist Thought* (Boston: Beacon Press, 1988), 11.

14 See Michelle M. Tokarczyk and Elizabeth A. Fay, *Working-Class Women in the Academy: Laborers in the Knowledge Factory* (Amherst: University of Massachusetts Press, 1993) and Sherry Lee, ed., *Teaching Working Class* (Amherst: University of Massachusetts Press, 1999). One aim of this book is to contribute to a growing body of scholarship that fully recognizes and incorporates the relevance of social difference to all theory and practice. I do not seek to place race in competition with social class or with gender as a 'more significant' issue. I also believe the change I call for in regard to anti-racism requires thorough and specific attention to racism in the academy, and to its historical origins and contemporary expressions.

15 Andolsen, *Daughters of Jefferson*, Caraway, *Segregated Sisterhood*, and Ware, *Beyond the Pale*.

16 Frankenberg, *White Women, Race Matters*, 1.

17 Becky Thompson and White Women Challenging Racism, 'Home/Work: Antiracism Activism and the Meaning of Whiteness,' in *Off White: Readings on Race, Power, and Society*, ed. Michelle Fine, et al. (New York: Routledge, 1997), 354–66; and Mab Segrest, *Memoir of a Race Traitor* (Boston: South End Press, 1994).

18 Trudier Harris, comp., *Selected Works of Ida B. Wells-Barnett* (New York: Oxford University Press, 1991); and Anna Julia Cooper, *A Voice from the South: By a Black Woman of the South* (Xenia, OH: Aldine Printing House, 1892).

19 Cherríe Moraga and Gloria Anzaldúa, ed., *This Bridge Called My Back: Writings by Radical Women of Color* (New York: Kitchen Table Women of Color

Press, 1981); Gloria Anzaldúa, ed., *Making Face Making Soul: Creative and Critical Perspectives by Women of Color* (San Francisco: An Aunt Lute Foundation Book, 1990).

20 Evelyn Brooks Higgenbotham, 'African American Women's History and the Metalanguage of Race,' *Signs: Journal of Women in Culture and Society* 17, no. 2 (1992): 251–74 at 251.

21 White women frequently turn to European American feminist theory for an essay on literary criticism, and rely on well-known fiction writers, such as Alice Walker or Toni Morrison, for experimental work by women of color. While they often find metaphors or fictional images of women of color useful, they are reluctant to draw on theoretical work by women of color.

22 There are exceptions to Higgenbotham's claim, many of which have been previously cited. Further, race is only one marker of difference. For work on exclusions of class and nationality in European American feminist theory, see Michelle M. Tokarczyk and Elizabeth A. Fay, *Working-Class Women in the Academy: Laborers in the Knowledge Factory* (Amherst: University of Massachusetts Press, 1993), and Chandra Talpade Mohanty, Ann Russo, and Lourdes Torres, eds., *Third World Women and the Politics of Feminism* (Indianapolis: Indiana University Press, 1991).

23 For an excellent discussion of white feminist appropriation of the work of women of color, see Paula M.L. Moya, *Learning from Experience: Minority Identities, Multicultural Struggles* (Berkeley: University of California Press, 2002), 28–37.

24 See especially Andolsen, *Daughters of Jefferson*, and Paula Giddings, *When and Where I Enter: The Impact of Black Women on Race and Sex in America* (New York: Bantam Books, 1984), 57–74 and 119–31; Lugones, 'On the Logic of Pluralist Feminism,' 43.

25 I model my use of this technique on Kamala Visweswaran's chapter, 'Betrayal: An Analysis in Three Acts,' in her book *Fictions of Feminist Ethnography* (Minneapolis: University of Minnesota Press, 1994), 41. Visweswaran writes, 'This analysis is framed as theater, not only to emphasize agency as performance, but also to underscore the contructedness and staging of identity.'

26 Liz Stanley and Sue Wise, *Breaking Out Again: Feminist Ontology and Epistemology* (London: Routledge, 1993), 190–2.

27 Velina Hasu Houston, *The Politics of Life: Four Plays by Asian American Women* (Philadelphia: Temple University Press, 1993), 5.

28 Michael Omi and Howard Winant, *Racial Formation in the United States: From the 1960s to the 1990s* (New York: Routledge, 1994), 55. For a discussion of the social constructionist nature of race, and specifically the political, glo-

bal, and historical dynamics, see Michael Omi and Howard Winant, 'On the Theoretical Concept of Race,' in *Race, Identity, and Representation in Education*, ed. Cameron McCarthy and Warren Crichlow (New York: Routledge, 1993), 3–10 at 6–9.

29 Omi and Winant, 'Theoretical Concept,' 5.

30 Omi and Winant, *Racial Formation*.

31 David L. Wheeler, 'A Growing Number of Scientists Reject the Concept of Race,' *Chronicle of Higher Education* 41, no. 23 (17 February 1995), A8–9, 15.

32 Omi and Winant, *Racial Formation*, 162.

33 Virginia R. Harris and Trinity A. Ordoña, 'Developing Unity among Women of Color: Crossing the Barriers of Internalized Racism and Cross-Racial Hostility,' in *Making Face Making Soul: Creative and Critical Perspectives by Women of Color*, ed. Gloria Anzaldúa (San Francisco: An Aunt Lute Foundation Book, 1990), 304–16 at 304.

34 Eduardo Bonilla-Silva, *White Supremacy and Racism in the Post Civil Rights Era* (Boulder, CO: Lynne Rienner Publishers, 2001), 22.

35 David Roediger, *Towards the Abolition of Whiteness* (London: Verso, 1994), 184.

36 Ibid., 184.

37 Ibid., 187.

38 Ibid., 192.

39 Bonilla-Silva, *White Supremacy*, 38.

40 Peggy McIntosh, *White Privilege and Male Privilege: A Personal Account of Coming to See Correspondences through Work on Women's Studies* (Wellesley, MA: Center for Research on Women, 1988).

41 hooks, *Killing Rage*, 185.

42 Eileen O'Brien, *Whites Confront Racism: Antiracists and Their Paths to Action* (Lanham, MD: Rowman and Littlefield, 2001), 5.

43 hooks, *Killing Rage*, 35. For a discussion regarding how white supremacy functions, see Bonilla-Silva, *White Supremacy*, esp. 199–200.

44 For a helpful description of this body of work by European American women, see the first four chapters of Whelehan, *Modern Feminist Thought*.

45 Throughout this book, I use the term 'American Indian' to refer to tribal people living in the United States. As the authors of an essay on the writing of American Indian women state, '*Native American* is a term invented in academe and is the term of the moment. It was invented to replace the term *American Indian*. This is a serious misnomer. In our communities we first name ourselves by tribe, but the general term commonly used is *Indian* in the United States and *native* in Canada.' Joy Harjo and Gloria Bird, 'Introduction,' in *Reinventing the Enemy's Language: Contemporary Native Women's Writing of North America*, ed. Joy Harjo and Gloria Bird (New York: W.W. Norton, 1997), 19–31 at 20.

46 Houston, *Politics of Life*, 5.

47 Values involve a choice one makes freely; require that one makes a choice from alternatives; occur only after careful and deliberate thought; contain a positive aspect (something in which we take pride, care about, and know as important); require public affirmation; incite action and doing; and occur consistently and regularly rather than haphazardly, occasionally, or haltingly. This definition draws on a lecture by Toinette M. Eugene, Chicago Theological Seminary, Spring 1991.

48 Digest of Education Statistics, 2001, chap. 3, 'Postsecondary Education.' National Center for Education Statistics website (http://nces.ed.gov// pubs2002/digest2001/ch3.asp), accessed 30 September 2002.

49 U.S. Department of Education, Office of Educational Research and Improvement, 'Tenure Status of Postsecondary Instructional Faculty and Staff, 1992–98' (July 2002), 36.

50 Mary Romero and Debbie Storrs, '"Is That Sociology?": The Accounts of Women of Color Graduate Students in Ph.D. Programs,' in *Women Leading in Education*, ed. Diane M. Dunlap and Patricia A. Schmuck (New York: State University of New York Press, 1995), 71–85 at 75.

51 bell hooks, 'Representing Whiteness in the Black Imagination,' in *Cultural Studies*, ed. Lawrence Grossberg, Cary Nelson, and Paula Treichler (New York: Routledge, 1992), 338–46 at 339.

52 Later in this book, I will further explore anti-racist praxis. At this point, I want to stress the value of any form of anti-racism in the academy in a context in which whites routinely deny the existence of racism, and in turn, the need for anti-racism.

53 For discussion regarding this displacement, see Elsa Barkley Brown, '"What Has Happened Here": The Politics of Difference in Women's History and Feminist Politics,' in *'We Specialize in the Wholly Impossible': A Reader in Black Women's History*, ed. Darlene Clark Hine, Wilma King, and Linda Reed (Brooklyn: Carlson Publishing Company, 1995), 39–54.

54 David Theo Goldberg, 'Introduction: Multicultural Conditions,' in *Multiculturalism: A Critical Reader*, ed. David Theo Goldberg (Oxford: Blackwell, 1994), 1–41 at 20–4.

55 The *Minnesota Review*, an academic journal, put out a 1996 call for papers on 'post-whiteness.' It is extremely problematic that academics have spent hundreds of years on 'blackness,' pause at the possibility of whiteness, and then are eager to jump to 'post-whiteness.'

56 María Lugones, 'On the Logic of Pluralist Feminism,' in *Feminist Ethics*, ed. Claudia Card (Lawrence: University Press of Kansas, 1991), 35–44 at 40.

57 Ibid., 38–40.

2   Resisting 'Sympathy and Yet Distance'

1 Tessie Liu, 'Teaching the Differences Among Women from a Historical Perspective: Rethinking Race and Gender as Social Categories,' in *Unequal Sisters: A Multicultural Reader in U.S. Women's History,* ed. Vicki L. Ruiz and
Ellen Carol DuBois (New York: Routledge, 1994), 571–83 at 581. Further discussion of this citation occurs later in the chapter.

2 Antonia I. Castañeda, 'Women of Color and the Rewriting of Western History: The Discourse, Politics, and Decolonization of History,' *Pacific Historical Review* 61, no. 4 (1992): 501–33 at 501–2; and Evelyn Brooks
Higgenbotham, 'African American Women's History and the Metalanguage of Race,' *Signs: Journal of Women in Culture and Society* 17, no. 2 (1992):
251–74.

3 Paula Giddings, *When and Where I Enter: The Impact of Black Women on Race
and Sex in America* (New York: Bantam Books, 1984), 121–31.

4 Barbara Hilkert Andolsen, *'Daughters of Jefferson, Daughters of Bootblacks':
Racism and American Feminism* (Macon, GA: Mercer University Press, 1986),
1–20.

5 Mary Church Terrell, 'Lynching from a Negro's Point of View,' in *Black
Women in White America: A Documentary History,* ed. Gerda Lerner (New
York: Vintage Books, 1992), 205–11 at 210.

6 M. Annette Jaimes, *The State of Native America: Genocide, Colonization, and
Resistance* (Boston: South End Press, 1992), 331–4.

7 Devon A. Mihesuah, 'Commonality of Difference: American Indian Women
and History,' *American Indian Quarterly* 20, no. 1 (1996): 15–27 at 17–18.

8 Patricia A. Carter, '"Completely Discouraged": Women Teacher's Resistance in the Bureau of Indian Affairs Schools, 1900–1910,' *Frontiers* 15, no. 3
(1995): 53–86 at 55.

9 Ibid., 30.

10 Ibid., 55.

11 Higgenbotham, 'African American Women's History,' 251–8.

12 See Helen Zia, *Asian American Dreams: The Emergence of an American People*
(New York: Farrar, Straus, and Giroux, 2000); Asian Women United of Cali-
fornia, *Making Waves: An Anthology of Writings by and about Asian American
Women* (Boston: Beacon Press, 1989); Melvina Johnson Young, 'Exploring
the WPA Narratives: Finding the Voices of Black Women and Men,' in *Theo-
rizing Black Feminisms: The Visionary Pragmatism of Black Women,* ed. Stanlie
M. James and Abena P.A. Busia (London: Routledge, 1993), 55–74; Gerda
Lerner, ed., *Black Women in White America: A Documentary History* (New
York: Vintage Books, 1992); Devon A. Mihesuah, *Cultivating the Rosebuds:
The Education of Women at the Cherokee Female Seminary, 1851–1909* (Urbana:

University of Illinois Press, 1993); and Gloria Anzaldúa, *Borderlands/La Frontera: The New Mestiza* (San Francisco: Aunt Lute Books, 1999). These are a few examples of historical work by women of color.

13 Elsa Barkley Brown, '"What Has Happened Here": The Politics of Difference in Women's History and Feminist Politics,' in *'We Specialize in the Wholly Impossible': A Reader in Black Women's History*, ed. Darlene Clark Hine, Wilma King, and Linda Reed (Brooklyn: Carlson Publishing Company, 1995), 39–54 at 42.

14 Nancy A. Hewitt, 'Beyond the Search for Sisterhood: American Women's History in the 1980s,' in *Unequal Sisters: A Multicultural Reader in U.S. Women's History*, ed. Ellen Carol DuBois and Vicki L. Ruiz (New York: Routledge, 1990), 1–14 at 11.

15 Vicki L. Ruiz and Ellen Carol DuBois, 'Introduction to the Second Edition,' in *Unequal Sisters: A Multicultural Reader in U.S. Women's History*, ed. Vicki L. Ruiz and Ellen Carol DuBois (New York: Routledge, 1994), xi–xvi at xi.

16 Kathleen Blee, *Women of the Klan: Racism and Gender in the 1920s* (Berkeley: University of California Press, 1991); Peggy Pascoe,'Home Mission Women, Race, and Culture: The Case of "Native Helpers",' chap. 4 in *Relations of Rescue: The Search for Female Moral Authority in the American West, 1874–1939* (New York: Oxford University Press, 1990); Louise Michele Newman, *White Women's Rights: The Origins of Racial Feminism in the U.S.* (New York: Oxford University Press, 1999); and Beth Roy, *Bitters in the Honey: Tales of Hope and Disappointment across Divides of Race and Time* (Fayetteville: University of Arkansas Press, 1999).

17 Liu, 'Teaching the Differences,' 571, 572, and 575.

18 Ibid., 572.

19 Scholars important to work in memory studies include Maurice Halbwachs, *The Collective Memory*, trans. Francis J. Ditter, Jr and Vida Yadzi Ditter (New York: Harper and Row, 1980); Barbie Zelizer, 'Reading the Past Against the Grain: The Shape of Memory Studies,' *Review and Criticism* (June 1995): 214–39; and Pierre Nora, 'Between Memory and History: *Les Lieux de Mémoire*,' *Representations* 26 (Spring 1989): 7–25. By racial memory, I am referring to frameworks people rely on to interpret racial pasts.

20 Nora, 'Between Memory and History,' 24.

21 Zelizer, 'Reading the Past Against the Grain,' 235; Nora, 'Between Memory and History,' 13; Omer Bartov, 'Intellectuals on Auschwitz: Memory, History, and Truth,' *History and Memory* 5, no. 1 (1993): 87–129 at 113–15; and Robert O'Meally and Geneviève Fabre, 'Introduction,' in *History and Memory in African American Culture*, ed. Geneviève Fabre and Robert O'Meally (New York: Oxford University Press, 1994), 2–17 at 5–9.

22 Susan A. Crane, '(Not) Writing History: Rethinking the Intersections of Per-

sonal History and Collective Memory with Hans von Aufsess,' *History and Memory* 8, no. 1 (1996): 16–29 at 20.

23 Zelizer, 'Reading the Past Against the Grain,' 216.

24 Ibid., 226.

25 Seth Mydans, 'One Last Deadly Crossing for Illegal Aliens,' *New York Times*, 7 January 1991, A1.

26 Ruth Frankenberg, *White Women, Race Matters: The Social Construction of Whiteness* (Minneapolis: University of Minnesota Press, 1993), 166–7.

27 Michael Omi and Howard Winant, *Racial Formation in the United States: From the 1960s to the 1980s* (New York: Routledge, 1994), 83, 186 n.51; bell hooks, *Killing Rage: Ending Racism* (New York: Henry Holt, 1995), 185–8.

28 Dorothy Sterling, *Black Foremothers: Three Lives* (New York: Feminist Press, 1988), 81.

29 Andolsen, *Daughters of Jefferson*, 16.

30 Giddings, *When and Where I Enter*, 126.

31 L. Mun Wong, 'Dis(s)-secting and Dis(s)-closing "Whiteness,"' in *Shifting Identities Shifting Racisms: A Feminism and Psychology Reader*, ed. Kum-Kum Bhavnani and Ann Phoenix (London: Sage Publications, 1994), 133–53 at 136.

32 bell hooks, *Feminist Theory: From Margin to Center* (Boston: South End Press, 1984), 9; Barbara Smith, 'Toward a Black Feminist Criticism,' in *All the Women Are White, All the Blacks Are Men, But Some of Us Are Brave: Black Women's Studies*, ed. Gloria T. Hull, Patricia Bell Scott, and Barbara Smith (New York: Feminist Press, 1982), 157–75 at 157–9.

33 K. Sue Jewell, *From Mammy to Miss America and Beyond: Cultural Images and the Shaping of U.S. Social Policy* (London: Routledge, 1993), 21.

34 Paulette Childress White, 'Getting the Facts of Life,' in *Memory of Kin: Stories about Family by Black Writers*, ed. Mary Helen Washington (New York: Anchor Books, 1991), 132.

35 Ibid., 133.

36 Ibid., 135–6.

37 Ibid., 140.

38 Ibid., 133.

39 Wong, 'Dis(s)-secting and Dis(s)-closing "Whiteness,"' 136; Frankenberg, *White Women, Race Matters*, 41–2; Cherríe Moraga, 'La Güerra,' in *This Bridge Called My Back: Writings by Radical Women of Color*, ed. Cherríe Moraga and Gloria Anzaldúa (New York: Kitchen Table Women of Color Press, 1981), 27–34 at 30, 33; Ann Russo, 'We Cannot Live without Our Lives: White Women, Antiracism, and Feminism,' in *Third World Women and the Politics of Feminism*, ed. Chandra Talpade Mohanty, Ann Russo, and Lourdes Torres (Indianapolis: Indiana University Press, 1991), 297–313 at 299–300.

40 O'Meally and Fabre, 'Introduction,' 3.
41 bell hooks, 'Representing Whiteness in the Black Imagination,' in *Cultural Studies*, ed. Lawrence Grossberg, Cary Nelson, and Paula Treichler (New York: Routledge, 1992), 338–46 at 339.
42 Cheng Imm Tan, 'Thinking about Asian Oppression and Liberation,' in *Skin Deep: Women Writing on Color, Culture and Identity*, ed. Elena Featherston (Freedom, CA: Crossing Press, 1994), 46.
43 Frankenberg, *White Women, Race Matters*, 6.
44 Ibid., 1.
45 In addressing issues of history, I am speaking specifically to *race* matters left out of history. There are marginalized groups within the broader category of 'white' who must also reconstruct their history (for example, Jewish people and queer people). It is relevant to note here that Jewish people have not always been considered 'white.' In the early 1900s, ethnic groups, including Jewish and Italian people, were considered more 'black' than 'white.' Whiteness is not a monolithic way of representation; it is always contested and contingent on socio-historical factors. See chapter 1 for additional discussion of this issue.
46 Jennifer S. Simpson, 'Easy Talk, White Talk, Back Talk: Some Reflections on the Meanings of Our Words,' *Journal of Contemporary Ethnography* 25, no. 3 (1996): 372–89.
47 Sucheta Mazumdar, 'General Introduction: An Woman-Centered Perspective on Asian American History,' in *Making Waves: An Anthology of Writings by and about Asian American Women*, ed. Asian Women United of California (Boston: Beacon Press, 1989), 1–22 at 3–4.
48 Tan, 'Thinking About Asian Oppression and Liberation,' 46.
49 Crane, '(Not) Writing History,' 20–1; Virginia Scharff, 'Else Surely We Will All Hang Separately: The Politics of Western Women's History,' *Pacific Historical Review* 61, no. 4 (1992): 535–55 at 537; and Antonia I. Castañeda, 'Women of Color and the Rewriting of Western History: The Discourse, Politics, and Decolonization of History,' *Pacific Historical Review* 61, no. 4 (1992): 501–33 at 533.
50 Castañeda, 'Women of Colour,' 503–4, 514–22.
51 Robert Famighette, ed., *The World Almanac and Book of Facts 1995* (Mahwah, NJ: World Almanac An Imprint of Funk and Wagnalls Corporation, 1994), 20–31; United State. Immigration and Naturalization Service, *1993 Statistical Yearbook of the Immigration and Naturalization Service* (Washington, DC: U.S. Government Printing Office, 1994), 12–20.
52 bell hooks, *Yearning: Race, Gender, and Cultural Politics* (Boston: South End Press, 1990), 40.
53 Young, 'Exploring the WPA Narratives,' 55–7.

54 Marisa Nordstrom, interview with author, April 1995, Evanston, Illinois. Author's notes.

55 Carol Boyce Davies, *Black Women, Writing and Identity: Migrations of the Subject* (London: Routledge, 1994), 56; Norma Alcarón, 'The Theoretical Subject(s) of *This Bridge Called My Back* and Anglo-American Feminism,' in *Making Face, Making Soul Haciendo Caras: Creative and Critical Perspectives by Women of Color*, ed. Gloria Anzaldúa (San Francisco: An Aunt Lute Foundation Book, 1990).

56 Manju S. Kurian, 'Negotiating Power from the Margins: Lessons from Years of Racial Memory,' *Women and Language* 19, no. 1 (1996): 27–31 at 28.

57 Ibid.

58 Elizabeth Alexander, 'Memory, Community, Voice,' *Callaloo* 17, no. 2 (1994): 408–21 at 410.

59 Crane, '(Not) Writing History,' 23.

60 Liu, 'Teaching the Differences,' 573.

61 Patricia Hill Collins, *Black Feminist Thought: Knowledge, Consciousness, and the Politics of Empowerment* (Boston: Unwin Hyman, 1990), 14–15.

62 Joanna Kadi, 'A Question of Belonging,' in *Working Class Women in the Academy: Laborers in the Knowledge Factory*, ed. Michelle M. Tokarczyk and Elizabeth A. Fay (Amherst: University of Massachusetts Press, 1993), 87–96 at 89–95; Pam Annas, 'Pass the Cake: The Politics of Gender, Class, and Text in the Academic Workplace,' in *Working Class Women in the Academy*, 165–78 at 175–7.

63 Russo, 'We Cannot Live Without Our Lives,' 299.

64 See Willi Coleman and Patricia Harris, 'The Trouble with Change: A Conversation between Colleagues,' in *Women Leading in Education*, ed. Diane M. Dunlap and Patricia A. Schmuck (New York: State University of New York Press, 1995), 225–34.

65 Scholars have noted the problems when scholars in the United States construct 'a glorious African past while accepting European notions of what that past should look like.' See E. Frances White, 'Africa on My Mind: Gender, Counter Discourse, and African-American Nationalism,' *Journal of Women's History* 2, no. 1 (1990): 73–97.

3 We Are Not Enough

1 Liz Stanley and Sue Wise, *Breaking Out Again: Feminist Ontology and Epistemology* (London: Routledge, 1993), 188.

2 Patricia Hill Collins, *Fighting Words: Black Women and the Search for Justice* (Minneapolis: University of Minnesota Press, 1998), 277.

3 Sara Ruddick, 'Maternal Thinking,' *Feminist Studies* 6, no. 2 (1980): 342–67 at 347.
4 Ibid., 342–3.
5 Ibid., 346.
6 Sue Jackson, 'Crossing Borders and Changing Pedagogies: From Giroux and Freire to Feminist Theories of Education,' *Gender and Education* 9, no. 4 (1997): 457–67 at 457–67; Susan Hekman, 'Truth and Method: Feminist Standpoint Theory Revisited,' *Signs* 22, no. 2 (1997): 341–65.
7 Jackson, 'Crossing Borders,' 465.
8 Hekman, 'Truth and Method,' 353.
9 Ibid., 353.
10 Paula Giddings, *When and Where I Enter: The Impact of Black Women on Race and Sex in America* (New York: Bantam Books, 1984), 119–31; Nancie Caraway, *Segregated Sisterhood: Racism and the Politics of American Feminism* (Knoxville: University of Tennessee Press, 1991), 154.
11 Caraway, 'Segregated Sisterhood,' 245 n. 117.
12 Ruth Frankenberg, *White Women, Race Matters: The Social Construction of Whiteness* (Minneapolis: University of Minnesota Press, 1993).
13 Patricia Hill Collins, 'Learning from the Outsider Within: The Sociological Significance of Black Feminist Thought,' *Sociology* 33, no. 6 (1986): 40–65 at 56–7.
14 Collins, *Fighting Words*, 95.
15 Patricia Hill Collins, *Black Feminist Thought: Knowledge, Consciousness, and the Politics of Empowerment* (Boston: Unwin Hyman, 1990), 203–4; Stanley and Wise, *Breaking Out Again*, 27–44; Sandra Harding, 'Introduction: Is There a Feminist Method?', in *Feminism and Methodology*, ed. Sandra Harding (Bloomington: Indiana University Press, 1987), 1–14 at 3–10; Jane Flax, *Thinking Fragments: Psychoanalysis, Feminism, and Postmodernism in the Contemporary West* (Berkeley: University of California Press, 1990), 40–1; Paula M.L. Moya, 'Learning from Experience: Politics, Epistemology, and Chicana/o Identity,' Dissertation, Cornell University, 1998; Uma Narayan, 'The Project of Feminist Epistemology: Perspectives from a Nonwestern Feminist,' in *Gender/Body/Knowledge: Feminist Reconstructions of Being and Knowing*, ed. Alison M. Jaggar and Susan R. Bordo (New Brunswick, NJ: Rutgers University Press, 1989), 256–69 at 256; and Mary Crawford and Jeanne Marecek, 'Feminist Theory, Feminist Psychology: A Bibliography of Epistemology, Critical Analysis, and Applications,' *Psychology of Women Quarterly* 13 (1989): 477–91 at 477–9.
16 Stanley and Wise, *Breaking Out Again*, 27; Sandra Harding, 'Conclusion:

Epistemological Questions,' in *Feminism and Methodology*, ed. Sandra Harding (Bloomington: Indiana University Press, 1987), 181–90 at 181–2.

17 Crawford and Marecek, 'Feminist Theory,' 478.

18 Narayan, 'Project of Feminist Epistemology,' 256.

19 Ibid., 257; Collins, *Black Feminist Thought*, 203–5.

20 Lucy Sprague Mitchell, *Two Lives: The Story of Wesley Claire Mitchell and Myself* (New York: Simon and Schuster, 1953), 186. See also Dorothy Ross, 'New Models of American Liberal Change,' chap. 9 in *The Origins of American Social Science* (Cambridge: Cambridge University Press, 1991), for an excellent discussion of this issue.

21 Collins, *Fighting Words*, 103–4.

22 Narayan, 'Project of Feminist Epistemology,' 257.

23 See James B. McKee, *Sociology and the Race Problem: The Failure of a Perspective* (Urbana: University of Illinois Press, 1993); Kum-Kum Bhavnani and Ann Phoenix, 'Shifting Identities Shifting Racisms: An Introduction,' in *Shifting Identities Shifting Racisms: A Feminism and Psychology Reader*, ed. Kum-Kum Bhavnani and Ann Phoenix (London: Sage Publications, 1994), 5–18; and George W. Stocking, Jr, *Race, Culture, and Evolution: Essays in the History of Anthropology* (Chicago: University of Chicago Press, 1982).

24 Kathryn Pyne Addelson, 'Knowers/Doers and Their Moral Problems,' in *Feminist Epistemologies*, ed. Linda Alcoff and Elizabeth Potter (New York: Routledge, 1993), 265–94 at 266.

25 Flax, *Thinking Fragments*, 148.

26 Ibid., 148.

27 Ibid., 149.

28 Ibid., 150.

29 Sheryl Gay Stolberg, 'Link Found Between Behavioral Problems and Time in Child Care,' *New York Times*, 19 April 2001 (accessed from the web: http://www.nytimes.com/2001/04/19/health/19CHIL.html).

30 Addelson, 'Knowers/Doers,' 267.

31 David Theo Goldberg, 'Introduction: Multicultural Conditions,' in *Multiculturalism: A Critical Reader*, ed. David Theo Goldberg (Oxford: Blackwell, 1994), 1–41 at 3–6.

32 Daniel P. Moynihan, *The Negro Family – A Case for National Action* (Washington, DC: Office of Policy Planning and Research, United States Department of Labor, 1965).

33 Wade W. Nobles, 'African American Family Life: An Instrument of Culture,' in *Black Families*, ed. Harriette Pipes McAdoo (Newbury Park, CA: Sage, 1988), 45.

34 Henry A. Giroux, *Border Crossings: Cultural Workers and the Politics of Education* (Routledge: New York, 1992), 90.

35 Dorothy E. Smith, 'Women's Perspective as a Radical Critique of Sociology,' in *Feminism and Methodology,* ed. Sandra Harding (Bloomington: Indiana University Press, 1987), 84–96 at 89–90.

36 Sandra Harding and Merrill B. Hintikka, 'Introduction,' in *Discovering Reality: Feminist Perspectives on Epistemology, Metaphysics, Methodology, and Philosophy of Science,* ed. Sandra Harding and Marrill B. Hintikka, ix–xix (Boston: D. Reidel, 1983), x.

37 Joan Kelly Gadol, 'The Social Relation of the Sexes: Methodological Implications of Women's History'; Carolyn Wood Sherif, 'Bias in Psychology'; Smith, 'Women's Perspective'; Heidi L. Hartmann, 'The Family as the Locus of Gender, Class and Political Struggle: The Example of Housework,' in *Feminism and Methodology,* ed. Sandra Harding (Bloomington: Indiana University Press, 1987).

38 Sandra Harding, 'Women, Science, and Society,' *Science* 281, no. 5383 (09.11.98): 1599–1600 at 1599.

39 Ibid., 1599–1600.

40 Douglas A. Lorimer, 'Nature, Racism, and the Late Victorian Science,' *Canadian Journal of History* 25, no. 3 (1990): 369–85 at 369.

41 Ibid., 369–70.

42 Richard J. Herrnstein and Charles A. Murray, *The Bell Curve: Intelligence and Class Structure in American Life* (New York: Free Press, 1994); and Rose M. Brewer, 'Knowledge Construction and Racist 'Science,' *American Behavioral Scientist* 39, no. 1 (1995): 62–73.

43 Brewer, 'Knowledge Construction.'

44 Boston Women's Health Collective, *The New Our Bodies, Ourselves* (New York: Touchstone, 1992), esp. chap. 25.

45 See Susan Reverby, ed., *Tuskegee's Truths: Rethinking the Tuskegee Syphilis Study* (Chapel Hill: University of North Carolina Press, 2000).

46 See chap. 25, 'The Politics of Women and Medical Care,' in *The New Our Bodies, Ourselves;* and National Academy of Science, Institute of Medicine, Division of Health Care Services, *Health Care in a Context of Civil Rights: A Report of a Study,* no. 1804 (Washington, DC: U.S. Government Printing Office, 1981).

47 Renato Rosaldo, *Culture and Truth: The Remaking of Social Analysis* (Boston: Beacon Press, 1993), 31.

48 Michelle Zimbalist Rosaldo and Louise Lamphere, 'Introduction,' in *Women, Culture, and Society,* ed. Michelle Zimbalist Rosaldo and Louise Lamphere (Stanford: Stanford University Press, 1974), 1–15 at 2.

49 Rebecca Mead, '"We Are Your Sisters,"' *Oral History Review* 23, no. 1 (1996): 47–56 at 47.

50 Susan Sheridan, 'Feminist Knowledge, Women's Liberation, and Women's Studies,' in *Feminist Knowledge: Critique and Construct*, ed. Sneja Gunew (London: Routledge, 1990); Sandra Harding, 'Rethinking Standpoint Epistemology: What Is "Strong Objectivity"?,' in *Feminist Epistemologies*, ed. Linda Alcoff and Elizabeth Potter (New York: Routledge, 1993), 49–82.

51 Adrienne Rich, 'Women's Studies – Renaissance or Revolution?: A Paper Read at University of Pennsylvania Women's Studies Conference, November 15, 1974,' *Women's Studies* 3 (1976): 121–6 at 123. See also Sharon L. Sievers, 'What Have We Won, What Have We Lost?' *Frontiers* 8, no. 3 (1986): 43–6 at 43; Sherna Berger Gluck, 'Reflections on Linking the Academy and the Community,' *Frontiers* 8, no. 3 (1986): 46–9 at 46; Johnnella E. Butler, 'Complicating the Question: Black Studies and Women's Studies,' in *Women's Place in the Academy: Transforming the Liberal Arts Curriculum*, ed. Marilyn R. Schuster and Susan R. Van Dyne (Totowa, NJ: Rowman and Allenheld Publishers, 1985), 73–86 at 75; Karen M. Merritt, 'A Braid of Associations: Ten Years of Women's Studies in Wisconsin,' *Frontiers* 8, no. 3 (1986): 20–5; and Victoria Robinson, 'Introducing Women's Studies,' in *Thinking Feminist: Key Concepts in Women's Studies*, ed. Diane Richardson and Victoria Robinson (New York: Guilford Press, 1993), 3.

52 Sondra Hale, 'Our Attempt to Practice Feminism in the Women's Studies Program,' *Frontiers* 8, no. 3 (1986): 39–43 at 39–40.

53 Marilyn J. Boxer, 'For and About Women: The Theory and Practice of Women's Studies in the United States,' *Signs* 7, no. 3 (1982): 661–95 at 668–9.

54 Combahee River Collective, 'The Combahee River Collective Statement,' in *Home Girls: A Black Feminist Anthology*, ed. Barbara Smith (New York: Kitchen Table Women of Color Press, 1983), 272–82; Cherríe Moraga and Gloria Anzaldúa, ed., *This Bridge Called my Back: Writings by Radical Women of Color* (New York: Kitchen Table Women of Color Press, 1981); Kate Shanley, 'Thoughts on Indian Feminism,' in *A Gathering of Spirit*, ed. Beth Brant (Ithaca, NY: Firebrand Books, 1988), 213–15.

55 Imelda Whelehan, *Modern Feminist Thought* (New York: New York University Press, 1995), 5.

56 Ibid., 9–20.

57 Ibid.

58 Harding, 'Conclusion,' 182.

59 L.S. Fidell, 'Empirical Verification of Sex Discrimination on Hiring Practices in Psychology,' *American Psychologist* 25, no. 12 (1970): 1094–8 at 1096.

60 Helen Longino, 'Subjects, Power and Knowledge: Description and Pre-

scription in Feminist Philosophies of Science,' in *Feminist Epistemologies*, ed. Linda Alcoff and Elizabeth Potter (New York: Routledge, 1993), 101–20 at 114.
61 Lynn Hankinson Nelson, *Who Knows? From Quine to a Feminist Empiricism* (Philadelphia: Temple University Press, 1990), 39.
62 Ibid., 22.
63 Ibid., 35.
64 Nancy Tuana, 'The Radical Future of Feminist Empiricism,' *Hypatia* 7, no. 1 (Winter 1992): 100–13. It is useful to clarify that Lynn Hankinson Nelson refers often (although not exclusively) to contemporary empiricism in the context of scientific communities and discourse. Indeed, much of the debate about empiricism has been carried out by scholars in the scientific community. At the same time, feminist empiricists demonstrate that the discussion about empiricism is clearly relevant beyond the scientific community.
65 Nelson, *Who Knows?*, 39.
66 Ibid.
67 Harding, 'Introduction,' x.
68 Harding, 'Rethinking,' 54.
69 Bonnie Zimmerman, 'Seeing, Reading, Knowing: The Lesbian Appropriation of Literature,' in *(En)gendering Knowledge: Feminists in Academe*, ed. Joan Hartman and Ellen Messer-Davidow (Nashville: University of Tennessee Press, 1991), 85–99.
70 Kathryn Gutzwiller and Ann Michelini, 'Women and Other Strangers: Feminist Perspectives in Classical Literature,' in *(En)gendering Knowledge: Feminists in Academe*, ed. Joan Hartman and Ellen Messer-Davidow (Nashville: University of Tennessee Press, 1991).
71 Harding 'Rethinking,' 54–5.
72 Ibid., 56.
73 Ibid., 54.
74 Ibid., 55–6.
75 Harding, 'Conclusion,' 185.
76 Nancy C.M. Hartsock, 'Feminist Standpoint: Developing the Ground for a Specifically Feminist Historical Materialism,' in *Feminism and Methodology*, ed. Sandra Harding (Bloomington: Indiana University Press, 1987), 159.
77 In her 1987 essay, Nancy C.M. Harstock usefully applies feminist standpoint theory to the sexual division of labor. But her essay is also significant to any discussion of feminist epistemology in that it plainly turns away from differences among women within this context. She writes, 'In addressing the institutional sexual division of labor, I propose to lay aside the

important differences among women across race and class boundaries and instead search for central commonalities.' She then proceeds to draw on psychoanalytic theory to explore the 'complex relational world inhabited by women,' and does not address the existence of significantly different frameworks among women for understanding such concepts as family, mothering, human development, and individuation. Harstock, 'Feminist Standpoint,' 164, 167–8.

78 Ibid., 173.

79 María Lugones, 'On the Logic of Pluralist Feminism,' in *Feminist Ethics*, ed. Claudia Card (Lawrence: University Press of Kansas, 1991), 35–44 at 43.

80 Although Addelson does not specifically address race, her comments regarding the connection of epistemology to accountability and responsibility are instructive to this chapter. See 'Knowers/Doers,' esp. 267–70.

81 Flax, *Thinking Fragments*, 30–1.

82 Jane Flax, 'The End of Innocence,' in *Feminists Theorize the Political*, ed. Judith Butler and Joan W. Scott (New York: Routledge, 1992), 445–63 at 450. Flax's argument contains an important contradiction. Stating that postmodernists have displaced the 'Western sense of self-certainty' disguises the fact that many postmodernists are Westerners. Thus, it would be more accurate to state that postmodernists have displaced the universalist tendencies and claims of positivist thinkers. Further, postmodernism is in part a discourse that Westerners (usually white Europeans and European Americans) articulate, arguably to maintain control of the conversation while appearing to recognize difference and subjective knowledge. As one sociologist aptly states, '... one might asks who benefits from a methodology that appears unable to construct alternative explanations for social phenomena suitable for guiding political action; legitimates its own authority via exclusionary language; and dismantles notions of subjectivity, tradition, and authority just when Black women are gaining recognition for these attributes.' Collins, *Fighting Words*, 145.

83 Flax, 'End of Innocence,' 450.

84 Ibid., 450–5.

85 Whelehan, *Modern Feminist Thought*, 211.

86 Judith Butler, 'Contingent Foundations: Feminism and the Question of Postmodernism,' in *Feminists Theorize the Political*, ed. Judith Butler and Joan W. Scott 19–38 at (New York: Routledge, 1992), 3–21 at 16.

87 Nancy Fraser and Linda Nicholson, 'Social Criticism without Philosophy,' in *Feminism/Postmodemism*, ed. Linda Nicholson (London: Routledge, 1990), 19–38 at 35.

88 Flax, 'Thinking Fragments,' 220.
89 Ibid., 230–1.
90 Ibid., 232.
91 Trudier Harris, comp., *Selected Works of Ida B. Wells-Barnett* (New York: Oxford University Press, 1991); Combahee River Collective, 'Statement.'
92 Richard H. Dana and Joan Dayger Behn, 'A Checklist for the Examination of Cultural Competence in Social Service Agencies,' *Research on Social Work Practice* 2, no. 2 (1992): 220–33 at 221.
93 Ibid., 221.
94 Sherene H. Razack, *Looking White People in the Eye: Gender, Race, and Culture in Courtrooms and Classrooms* (Toronto: University of Toronto Press, 1998), 61.
95 According to Kimberle Crenshaw, Neil Gotànda, Gary Peller, and Kendall Thomas, 'Critical Race Theory embraces a movement of left scholars, most of them scholars of color, situated in law schools, whose work challenges the ways in which race and racial power are constructed and represented in American legal culture, and, more generally, in American society as a whole.' See Kimberle Crenshaw, Neil Gotanda, Gary Peller, and Kendall Thomas, eds., *Critical Race Theory: The Key Writings That Formed the Movement* (New York: New Press, 1995), xiii.
96 In this section, I am primarily relying on Angela P. Harris, 'Race and Essentialism in Feminist Legal Theory,' *Stanford Law Review* 42, no. 3 (1990), 581–616; and Catharine A. MacKinnon, 'From Practice to Theory, or What Is a White Woman Anyway?' in *Critical White Studies: Looking behind the Mirror*, eds. Richard Delgado and Jean Stefancic (Philadelphia: Temple University Press, 1997), 300–4.
97 MacKinnon, 'From Practice to Theory,' 302.
98 Ibid., 302.
99 Ibid., 303.
100 Collins, *Fighting Words* and *Black Feminist Thought*; Elsa Barkley Brown, 'African American Women's Quilting: A Framework for Conceptualizing and Teaching African-American Women's History,' *Signs* 14, no. 4 (1989): 92–9; Aída Hurtado, *The Color of Privilege: Three Blasphemies on Race and Feminism* (Ann Arbor: University of Michigan Press, 1996); Sherene Razack, 'Revolution from Within: Dilemmas of Feminist Jurisprudence,' *Queen's Quarterly* 97, no. 3 (1990): 398–413; Mari J. Matsuda, *Where Is Your Body? And Other Essays on Race, Gender, and the Law* (Boston: Beacon Press, 1996); and Devon A. Mihesuah, 'Commonality of Difference: American Indian Women and History,' *American Indian Quarterly* 20, no. 1 (1996): 15–27.

101 Peggy McIntosh, *White Privilege and Male Privilege: A Personal Account of Coming to See Correspondences through Work on Women's Studies* (Wellesley, MA: Center for Research on Women, 1988); and Deborah King, 'Multiple Jeopardy, Multiple Consciousness: The Context of a Black Feminist Ideology,' *Signs* 14, no. 1 (1988): 42–72.

102 Harris, 'Race and Essentialism,' 585.

103 Ibid., 605.

104 Ibid., 605.

105 Ibid., 606.

106 Ibid., 609.

107 Ibid., 612.

108 Ibid., 612.

109 bell hooks, *Killing Rage: Ending Racism* (New York: Henry Holt, 1995), 51–61.

110 See Shirley Goek-Li, 'Feminist and Ethnic Literary Theories in Asian American Literature,' *Feminist Studies* 19, no. 3 (1993): 571–95; *Making Waves: An Anthology of Writings by and about Asian American Women*, ed. Asian Women United of California (Boston: Beacon Press, 1989); and *Making More Waves: New Writing by Asian Women*, ed. Elaine H. Kim and Lilia V. Villanueva (Boston: Beacon Press, 1997).

111 Joy Harjo and Gloria Bird, 'Introduction,' in *Reinventing the Enemy's Language: Contemporary Native Women's Writing of North America*, ed. Joy Harjo and Gloria Bird (New York: W.W. Norton, 1997), 19–31; Devon A. Mihesuah, 'A Few Cautions at the Millennium on the Merging of Feminist Studies with American Indian Women's Studies,' *Signs* 25, no. 4 (2000): 1247–51; and Devon A. Mihesuah, ed., *Natives and Academics: Researching and Writing about American Indians* (Lincoln: University of Nebraska Press, 1998).

112 Edna Acosta-Belén and Christine E. Bose, 'U.S. Latina and Latin American Feminisms: Hemispheric Encounters,' *Signs* 25, no. 4 (2000): 1113–19; Monica Russell y Rodriguez, 'Confronting Anthropology's Silencing Praxis: Speaking of/from a Chicana Consciousness,' *Qualitative Inquiry* 4, no. 1 (1998): 15–40.

113 Collins, *Fighting Words*, 11–43.

114 Brown, 'African American Women's Quilting,' 10.

115 Whelehan, *Modern Feminist Thought*, 2.

116 Robyn Wiegman, *American Anatomies: Theorizing Race and Gender* (Durham, NC: Duke University Press, 1995), 2.

117 Frances Richardson Keller, review of Wiegman, *American Anatomies*, *American Historical Review* 102, no. 1 (1997): 220–1 at 220.

118 Jennifer DeVere Brody, review of Wiegman, *American Anatomies, American Literature* 68, no. 3 (1996): 656–7 at 656.

119 Wiegman, *American Anatomies*, 1.

120 Ibid., 6–7.

121 Ibid., 76.

122 Michael Berube, review of Wiegman, *American Anatomies, African American Review* 31, no. 2 (1997): 317–20 at 317–18.

123 Amy Kaplan, review of Wiegman *American Anatomies, Signs* 23, no. 1 (1997): 220–5 at 224.

124 Ibid., 77.

125 Ibid., 202.

126 Trinh T. Minh-ha, *Woman, Native, Other: Writing Postcoloniality and Feminism* (Bloomington: Indiana University Press, 1989), 2.

4 The Challenges and Possibilities of Cross-Racial Dialogue

1 Bob Herbert, 'In America, Lessons in Reality.' *New York Times*, 21 February 2000, A19.

2 This definition draws on work by bell hooks. See hooks, *Talking Back: Thinking Feminist Thinking Black* (Boston: South End Press, 1989), 131.

3 Lorraine Bethel, 'What Chou Mean *We*, White Girl?' *Conditions Five* 11, no. 2 (1979): 86–92; and Audre Lorde, *Sister Outsider: Essays and Speeches* (Freedom, CA: Crossing Press, 1984).

4 Aída Hurtado, *The Color of Privilege: Three Blasphemies on Race and Feminism* (Ann Arbor: University of Michigan Press, 1996), 42.

5 Liz Stanley and Sue Wise, *Breaking Out Again: Feminist Ontology and Epistemology* (London: Routledge, 1993), 120.

6 Lorde, *Sister Outsider*, 115.

7 Cherríe Moraga, Title of presentation unknown, paper presented at workshop on cross-cultural feminism, DePaul University, Chicago, Illinois, 1997.

8 Renato Rosaldo, *Culture and Truth: The Remaking of Social Analysis* (Boston: Beacon Press, 1993), xii.

9 Deborah J. Wilds and Reginald Wilson, *Minorities in Higher Education 1997–1998* (Washington, DC: American Council on Education, 1998), 42.

10 In the general U.S. population, according to the 2000 census, 12.5 per cent of people indicated they were of Hispanic origin, 12 per cent were African American, nearly 4 per cent were Asian American, and 1 per cent were American Indian. United States Census Bureau, Census 2000 Briefs, 'Overview of Race and Hispanic Origin,' 12 March 2001; and 'The Hispanic Population,' 10 May 2001 (accessed from the web).

11 K. Sue Jewell, *From Mammy to Miss America and Beyond: Cultural Images and the Shaping of U.S. Social Policy* (London: Routledge, 1993).

12 Ibid., 6.

13 From this situation, I learned that when using this text, I need to provide one or two articles that address African American gender roles in an African American framework. As much as possible, as professors, we need to think through what contextual information is necessary to reach pedagogical goals.

14 Elsa Barkley Brown, 'African American Women's Quilting: A Framework for Conceptualizing and Teaching African-American Women's History,' *Signs* 14, no. 4 (1989): 921–9 at 922.

5   'Racism Is Not a Theory'

1 Elizabeth Higgenbotham, 'Getting All Students to Listen: Analyzing and Coping with Student Resistance,' *American Behavioral Scientist* 40, no. 2 (1996): 303–11 at 203–4.

2 Students of color can best educate white students about race when these white students are ready to learn. A readiness to learn about race is not always present in white people.

3 Henry A. Giroux, *Border Crossings: Cultural Workers and the Politics of Education* (New York: Routledge, 1992), 154.

4 In his article, 'Decentering Whiteness,' Peter McLaren offers a useful discussion of whiteness and how it relates to individuals and institutions. In *Multicultural Education* 5 (Fall 1997): 4–11 at 8–9.

5 Toinette M. Eugene, interview with author, April 1995, Evanston, Illinois, Author's notes.

6 Chandra Talpade Mohanty, 'On Race and Voice: Challenges for Liberal Education in the 1990s,' in *Between Borders: Pedagogy and the Politics of Cultural Studies*, ed. Henry A. Giroux and Peter McLaren (New York: Routledge, 1994), 145–66 at 148.

7 Margaret L. Hunter and Kimberly D. Nettles, 'What about the White Women: Racial Politics in a Women's Studies Classroom,' *Teaching Sociology* 27 (October 1999): 385–97 at 388.

8 Sherene H. Razack, *Looking White People in the Eye: Gender, Race, and Culture in Courtrooms and Classrooms* (Toronto: University of Toronto Press, 1998), 9.

9 Carl A. Grant and Judyth M. Sachs, 'Multicultural Education and Postmodernism: Movement Toward a Dialogue,' in *Critical Multiculturalism: Uncommon Voices in a Common Struggle*, ed. Barry Kampol and Peter McLaren (Westport, CT: Bergin and Garvey, 1995), 89–105. Anna R. McPhatter, 'Cul-

tural Competence in Child Welfare: What Is It? How Do We Achieve It? What Happens Without It?' *Child Welfare* 76, no. 1 (1997): 255–77.

10 Cameron McCarthy, 'Multicultural Policy Discourse on Racial Inequality in American Education,' in *Anti-Racism, Feminism, and Critical Approaches to Education*, ed. Roxana Ng, Pat Staton, and Joyce Scane (Westport, CT: Bergin and Garvey, 1995), 21–44 at 23.

11 Ibid., 22.

12 Herbert M. Kliebard, *The Struggle for the American Curriculum 1893–1958* (Boston: Routledge and Kegan Paul, 1986), 126.

13 Much of the discussion in this section draws on Cameron McCarthy's 'Multicultural Policy Discourses on Racial Inequality in American Education.'

14 Ibid., 24.

15 Ibid., 25.

16 Ibid., 25–8.

17 Ibid., 28–31.

18 María de la Ruz Reyes and John J. Halcón, 'Racism in Academia: The Old Wolf Revisited,' in *Facing Racism in Higher Education*, ed. Nitza M. Hildago, Caesar L. McDowell, and Emilie V. Siddle (Cambridge: Harvard Educational Review, 1990), 80.

19 American Commitments National Panel, *The Drama of Diversity and Democracy: Higher Education and American Commitments* (Washington, DC: American Association of Colleges and Universities, 1995), 7.

20 Reyes and Halcón, 'Racism in Academia,' 72. These authors usefully identify several forms of covert racism, which include 'tokenism, the type-casting syndrome, the one-minority-per-pot syndrome, the brown-on-brown research taboo, and the hairsplitting concept,' 72.

21 American Commitments National Panel, *Drama of Diversity*, xv.

22 Ibid., 16.

23 See Susan Reverby, ed., *Tuskegee's Truths: Rethinking the Tuskegee Syphilis Study* (Chapel Hill: University of North Carolina Press, 2000). From 1932 to 1972, 'as part of its study of the long-term effects of syphilis, the United States Public Health Service (PHS) denied treatment to 399 poor African American men suffering from the tertiary effects of the disease. Researchers and physicians involved in Tuskegee chose not to inform the study's participants that they were infected with syphilis or educate them regarding its treatment or prevention.' Amy L. Fairchild and Ronald Bayer, 'Uses and Abuses of Tuskegee,' *Science* 284, no. 5416 (7 May 1999): 919–21 at 919.

24 Bob Herbert, 'In America, Unseemly Alliances,' *New York Times*, 18 January 2001, A23.

25 Higgenbotham, 'Getting All Students to Listen,' 207.

26 Ibid., 207.
27 David Theo Goldberg, 'Introduction: Multicultural Conditions,' in *Multi-culturalism: A Critical Reader*, ed. David Theo Goldberg (Oxford: Blackwell, 1994), 1–41 at 3–6.
28 Authors of many standard textbooks might argue that, in fact, they are addressing a very different audience than that which existed twenty or thirty years ago. However, addition of a few pages, chapters, or examples that speak to the realities of students of color does not constitute any fundamental shift. In most cases, it merely represents a brief nod to critiques of monoculturalism and to texts that have little to do with the realities of many students.
29 Giroux, *Border Crossings*, 24.
30 A quick response to a question or comment from the professor can come out of the assumption that class discussion is of a competitive, rather than collaborative, nature. As a professor, I am often reluctant to leave spaces of silence during discussion; I do not want to lose the engagement of students. However, I am acutely aware that moving at a fast pace can give the impression of a competitive environment, and one in which listening, reflection, and waiting are unnecessary for and irrelevant to learning.
31 Higgenbotham, 'Getting All Students to Listen,' 207.
32 It is also crucial to note that the answer to a monocultural perspective is not to appropriate or pretend familiarity with another culture. Trying to pass off shallow or recently gained knowledge about another culture as a badge of being part of the culture is often insincere, or a perhaps well-intentioned attempt to make up for a lack of knowledge. As a white person, I can know about other racial and ethnic groups, but never from the inside of that experience. I have found it is most effective to use examples that explicitly attend to power and that always affirm my location as a white person, rather than to hide or move beyond that location.
33 Giroux, *Border Crossings*, 17.
34 I expanded on the following ideas: (1) images help us make sense of world we live in; (2) the mass media has the power to define and legitimize entitlements, including goods, money, and resources, and who does and who does not deserve these entitlements; (3) the mass media often produce and sustain images that attribute a lack of goods, money, and resources to individual and group deficiencies; (4) images nearly always simplify, mask, and/or distort some piece or pieces of the reality which they represent, while presenting the image as Truth; and (5) groups who control images will most often create images that represent their group favorably and others unfavorably, particularly when these groups have different social standing. See K. Sue Jewell,

From Mammy to Miss America and Beyond: Cultural Images and the Shaping of U.S. Social Policy (London: Routledge, 1993), chapters one and two.

35 It is also important to note here that white students often ignore the reality that there are a range of images of white people, and a paucity of images of people of color. The students' comment that all people look stupid in beer commercials, including white people, may be true. However, the range of images of white people ensures that even after viewing a beer commercial, I can draw on a nearly unlimited bank of images to show me that white men and women are intelligent, kind, thoughtful, socially adept, smart, and competent. This range does not exist for specific groups of people of color, or for people of color as a whole, and thus the advertisements that ridicule people in these groups are of more import than comparable advertisements featuring white people.

36 Jane Fried, 'Bridging Emotion and Intellect: Classroom Diversity in Process,' *College Teaching* 41, no. 4 (1993): 123–8 at 123.

37 Those in activist and scholarly circles have given increasing attention to whiteness and whiteness studies in the past few years. In my view, studies and critiques of whiteness should always remain in the context of understanding racism and achieving anti-racist practice. That is, I do not advocate whiteness studies whose primary aim is to understand white raciality or ethnicity for its own sake. See also Richard Delgado and Jean Stefancic, ed., *Critical White Studies: Looking behind the Mirror* (Philadelphia: Temple University Press, 1997): Henry A. Giroux, 'Rewriting the Discourse of Racial Identify: Toward a Pedagogy and Politics of Whiteness,' *Harvard Educational Review* 67 (Summer 1997): 285–320; and Nelson M. Rodriguez, 'Projects of Whiteness in a Critical Pedagogy,' in *Dismantling White Privilege: Pedagogy, Politics and Whiteness*, ed. Nelson Rodriguez and Leila Villaverde (New York: P. Lang, 2000), 1–24.

38 Peter McLaren, 'Decentering Whiteness,' *Multicultural Education* 5 (Fall 1997), 4–11 at 8–9.

39 Hunter and Nettles, 'What About the White Women?' 392–4.

40 Ruth Frankenberg, *White Women Race Matters: The Social Construction of Whiteness* (Minneapolis: University of Minnesota Press, 1993), 1.

41 Joe L. Kincheloe and Shirley R. Steinberg, 'Constructing a Pedagogy of Whiteness for Angry White Students,' in *Dismantling White Privilege: Pedagogy, Politics and Whiteness*, ed. Nelson Rodriguez and Leila Villaverde (New York: P. Lang, 2000), 178–97 at 193.

42 I am still surprised by my own ability, and the ability of other writers, teachers, and students, to use the passive voice when discussing racism, and to then drop the subject from the end of the sentence. 'Genocide was

carried out against American Indians' conveys a different message than 'European Americans committed genocide against American Indians.' It is convenient and attractive to simply leave out the doer when we talk about racism. Over time, this practice becomes an obstacle to anti-racist efforts.

43 'Pivoting the center' is a term Bettina Aptheker uses in *Tapestries of Life: Women's Work, Women's Consciousness and the Meaning of Daily Life* (Amherst: University of Massachusetts Press, 1989) in chapter 1. Elsa Barkley Brown also provides a useful discussion of the concept in 'African American Women's Quilting: A Framework for Conceptualizing and Teaching African American Women's History,' *Signs* 14, no. 4 (1989): 921–9.

44 Conversation with Toinette Eugene, Winter 1996.

45 Jewell, *From Mammy to Miss America*, 46.

46 Toni Morrison, 'Introduction: Friday on the Potomac,' in *Race-ing Justice, En-gendering Power: Essays on Anita Hill, Clarence Thomas, and the Construction of Social Reality*, ed. Toni Morrison (New York: Pantheon Books, 1992), vii–xxx at xiv–xv.

47 This response indicates a departure from race. Often, when white students are confronted with race matters, they are quick to divert the discussion from race itself.

48 Higgenbotham, 'Getting All Students to Listen,' 204.

Appendix: Discussion Questions, Exercises, and Assignments

1 bell hooks, *Killing Rage: Ending Racism* (New York: Henry Holt, 1995), 185.

2 Tessie Liu, 'Teaching the Differences Among Women from a Historical Perspective: Rethinking Race and Gender as Social Categories.' In *Unequal Sisters: A Multicultural Reader in U.S. Women's History*, ed. Vicki L. Ruiz and Ellen Carol DuBois (New York: Routledge, 1994), 581.

3 Toinette M. Eugene, interview with author, April 1995, Evanston, Illinois. Author's notes.

Bibliography

Acosta-Belén, Edna, and Christine E. Bose. 'U.S. Latina and Latin American Feminisms: Hemispheric Encounters.' *Signs* 25, no. 4 (2000): 1113–19.

Addelson, Kathryn Pyne. 'Knowers/Doers and Their Moral Problems.' In *Feminist Epistemologies*, ed. Linda Alcoff and Elizabeth Potter, 265–94. New York: Routledge, 1993.

Alcarón, Norma. 'The Theoretical Subject(s) of *This Bridge Called My Back* and Anglo-American Feminism.' In *Making Face, Making Soul Haciendo Caras: Creative and Critical Perspectives by Women of Color*, ed. Gloria Anzaldúa, 356–69. San Francisco: An Aunt Lute Foundation Book, 1990.

Alexander, Elizabeth. 'Memory, Community, Voice.' *Callaloo* 17, no. 2 (1994): 408–21.

American Commitments National Panel. *The Drama of Diversity and Democracy: Higher Education and American Commitments*. Washington, DC: American Association of Colleges and Universities, 1995.

Andolsen, Barbara Hilkert. *'Daughters of Jefferson, Daughters of Bootblacks': Racism and American Feminism*. Macon, GA: Mercer University Press, 1986.

Annas, Pam. 'Pass the Cake: The Politics of Gender, Class, and Text in the Academic Workplace.' In *Working Class Women in the Academy: Laborers in the Knowledge Factory*, ed. Michelle M. Tokarczyk and Elizabeth A. Fay, 165–78. Amherst: University of Massachusetts Press, 1993.

Anzaldúa, Gloria. *Borderlands/La Frontera: The New Mestiza*. San Francisco: Aunt Lute Books, 1999.

Anzaldúa, Gloria, ed. *Making Face Making Soul: Creative and Critical Perspectives by Women of Color*. San Francisco: An Aunt Lute Foundation Book, 1990.

Aptheker, Bettina. *Tapestries of Life: Women's Work, Women's Consciousness and the Meaning of Daily Life*. Amherst: University of Massachusetts Press, 1989.

Asian Women United of California. *Making Waves: An Anthology of Writings by and about Asian American Women*. Boston: Beacon Press, 1989.

Bartov, Omer. 'Intellectuals on Auschwitz: Memory, History, and Truth.' *History and Memory* 5, no. 1 (1993): 87–129.

Berube, Michael. Review of *American Anatomies: Theorizing Race and Gender*, by Robyn Wiegman. In *African American Review* 31, no. 2 (1997): 317–20.

Bethel, Lorraine. 'What Chou Mean *We*, White Girl?' *Conditions Five* 11, no. 2 (1979): 86–92.

Bhavnani, Kum-Kum and Ann Phoenix. 'Shifting Identities Shifting Racisms: An Introduction.' In *Shifting Identities Shifting Racisms: A Feminism and Psychology Reader*, ed. Kum-Kum Bhavnani and Ann Phoenix, 5–18. London: Sage Publications, 1994.

Blee, Kathleen. *Women of the Klan: Racism and Gender in the 1920s*. Berkeley: University of California Press, 1991.

Bonilla-Silva, Eduardo. *White Supremacy and Racism in the Post Civil Rights Era*. Boulder: Lynne Rienner Publishers, 2001.

Boston Women's Health Collective. *The New Our Bodies, Ourselves*. New York: Touchstone, 1992.

Boxer, Marilyn J. 'For and About Women: The Theory and Practice of Women's Studies in the United States.' *Signs* 7, no. 3 (1982): 661–95.

Brewer, Rose M. 'Knowledge Construction and Racist "Science."' *American Behavioral Scientist* 39, no. 1 (1995): 62–73.

Brody, Jennifer DeVere. Review of *American Anatomies: Theorizing Race and Gender*, by Robyn Wiegman. In *American Literature* 68, no. 3 (1996): 656–7.

Brown, Elsa Barkley. 'African American Women's Quilting: A Framework for Conceptualizing and Teaching African-American Women's History.' *Signs* 14, no. 4 (1989): 921–9.

– '"What Has Happened Here": The Politics of Difference in Women's History and Feminist Politics.' In *'We Specialize in the Wholly Impossible': A Reader in Black Women's History*, ed. Darlene Clark Hine, Wilma King, and Linda Reed, 39–54. Brooklyn: Carlson Publishing Company, 1995.

Butler, Johnnella E. 'Complicating the Question: Black Studies and Women's Studies.' In *Women's Place in the Academy: Transforming the Liberal Arts Curriculum*, ed. Marilyn R. Schuster and Susan R. Van Dyne, 73–86. Totowa, NJ: Rowman and Allenheld Publishers, 1985.

Butler, Judith. 'Contingent Foundations: Feminism and the Question of Postmodernism.' In *Feminists Theorize the Political*, ed. Judith Butler and Joan W. Scott, 3–21. New York: Routledge, 1992.

Caraway, Nancie. *Segregated Sisterhood: Racism and the Politics of American Feminism.* Knoxville: University of Tennessee Press, 1991.

Carter, Patricia A. '"Completely Discouraged": Women Teacher's Resistance in the Bureau of Indian Affairs Schools, 1900–1910.' *Frontiers* 15, no. 3 (1995): 53–86.

Castañeda, Antonia I. 'Women of Color and the Rewriting of Western History: The Discourse, Politics, and Decolonization of History.' *Pacific Historical Review* 61, no. 4 (1992): 501–33.

Coleman, Willi, and Patricia Harris. 'The Trouble with Change: A Conversation between Colleagues.' In *Women Leading in Education,* ed. Diane M. Dunlap and Patricia A. Schmuck, 225–34. New York: State University of New York Press, 1995.

Collins, Patricia Hill. *Black Feminist Thought: Knowledge, Consciousness, and the Politics of Empowerment.* Boston: Unwin Hyman, 1990.

– *Fighting Words: Black Women and the Search for Justice.* Minneapolis: University of Minnesota Press, 1998.

– 'Learning from the Outsider Within: The Sociological Significance of Black Feminist Thought.' *Sociology* 33, no. 6 (1986), 40–65.

Combahee River Collective. 'The Combahee River Collective Statement.' In *Home Girls: A Black Feminist Anthology,* ed. Barbara Smith, 272–82. New York: Kitchen Table Women of Color Press, 1983.

Cooper, Anna Julia. *A Voice from the South: By a Black Woman of the South.* Xenia, OH: Aldine Printing House, 1892.

Crane, Susan A. '(Not) Writing History: Rethinking the Intersections of Personal History and Collective Memory with Hans von Aufsess.' *History and Memory* 8, no. 1 (1996): 16–29.

Crawford, Mary, and Jeanne Marecek. 'Feminist Theory, Feminist Psychology: A Bibliography of Epistemology, Critical Analysis, and Applications.' *Psychology of Women Quarterly* 13 (1989): 477–91.

Crenshaw, Kimberle, Neil Gotanda, Gary Peller, and Kendall Thomas, ed. *Critical Race Theory: The Key Writings That Formed the Movement.* New York: New York University Press, 1995.

Dana, Richard H., and Joan Dayger Behn. 'A Checklist for the Examination of Cultural Competence in Social Service Agencies.' *Research on Social Work Practice* 2, no. 2 (1992): 220–33.

Davies, Carol Boyce. *Black Women, Writing and Identity: Migrations of the Subject.* London: Routledge, 1994.

Delgado, Richard, and Jean Stefancic, ed. *Critical White Studies: Looking behind the Mirror.* Philadelphia: Temple University Press, 1997.

Eugene, Toinette M. Interview with author, April 1995, Evanston, Illinois. Author's notes.
– 'Values.' Lecture presented at Chicago Theological Seminary, Chicago, Illinois, Spring 1991.
Fairchild, Amy L. and Ronald Bayer. 'Uses and Abuses of Tuskegee.' *Science* 284, no. 5416 (7 May 1999): 919–21.
Famighette, Robert, ed. *The World Almanac and Book of Facts 1995*. Mahwah, NJ: World Almanac An Imprint of Funk and Wagnalls Corporation, 1994.
Fidell, L.S. 'Empirical Verification of Sex Discrimination on Hiring Practices in Psychology.' *American Psychologist* 25, no. 12 (1970): 1094–8.
Flax, Jane. 'The End of Innocence.' In *Feminists Theorize the Political*, ed. Judith Butler and Joan W. Scott, 445–63. New York: Routledge, 1992.
– *Thinking Fragments: Psychoanalysis, Feminism, and Postmodernism in the Contemporary West*. Berkeley: University of California Press, 1990.
Frankenberg, Ruth. *White Women, Race Matters: The Social Construction of Whiteness*. Minneapolis: University of Minnesota Press, 1993.
Fraser, Nancy, and Linda Nicholson. 'Social Criticism without Philosophy.' In *Feminism/Postmodernism*, ed. Linda Nicholson, 19–38. London: Routledge, 1990.
Fried, Jane. 'Bridging Emotion and Intellect: Classroom Diversity in Process.' *College Teaching* 41, no. 4 (1993): 123–8.
Gadol, Joan Kelly. 'The Social Relation of the Sexes: Methodological Implications of Women's History.' In *Feminism and Methodology*, ed. Sandra Harding, 15–28. Bloomington: Indiana University Press, 1987.
Giddings, Paula. *When and Where I Enter: The Impact of Black Women on Race and Sex in America*. New York: Bantam Books, 1984.
Giroux, Henry A. *Border Crossings: Cultural Workers and the Politics of Education*. New York: Routledge, 1992.
– 'Rewriting the Discourse of Racial Identify: Toward a Pedagogy and Politics of Whiteness.' *Harvard Educational Review* 67 (1997): 285–320.
Gluck, Sherna Berger. 'Reflections on Linking the Academy and the Community.' *Frontiers* 8, no. 3 (1986): 46–9.
Goek-Li, Shirley. 'Feminist and Ethnic Literary Theories in Asian American Literature.' *Feminist Studies* 19, no. 3 (1993): 571–95.
Goldberg, David Theo. 'Introduction: Multicultural Conditions.' In *Multiculturalism: A Critical Reader*, ed. David Theo Goldberg, 1–41. Oxford: Blackwell, 1994.
Grant, Carl A., and Judyth M. Sachs. 'Multicultural Education and Postmodernism: Movement toward a Dialogue.' In *Critical Multiculturalism: Uncom-

mon Voices in a Common Struggle, ed. Barry Kampol and Peter McLaren, 89–105. Westport, CT: Bergin and Garvey, 1995.

Gutzwiller, Kathryn, and Ann Michelini. 'Women and Other Strangers: Feminist Perspectives in Classical Literature.' In *(En)gendering Knowledge: Feminists in Academe*, ed. Joan Hartman and Ellen Messer-Davidow, 66–84. Nashville: University of Tennessee Press, 1991.

Halbwachs, Maurice. *The Collective Memory.* Trans. Francis J. Ditter, Jr and Vida Yadzi Ditter. New York: Harper and Row, 1980.

Hale, Sondra. 'Our Attempt to Practice Feminism in the Women's Studies Program.' *Frontiers* 8, no. 3 (1986): 39–43.

Harding, Sandra. 'Conclusion: Epistemological Questions.' In *Feminism and Methodology*, ed. Sandra Harding, 181–90. Bloomington: Indiana University Press, 1987.

– 'Introduction: Is There a Feminist Method?' In *Feminism and Methodology*, ed. Sandra Harding, 1–14. Bloomington: Indiana University Press, 1987.

– 'Rethinking Standpoint Epistemology: What Is "Strong Objectivity"?' In *Feminist Epistemologies*, ed. Linda Alcoff and Elizabeth Potter, 49–82. New York: Routledge, 1993.

– 'Women, Science, and Society' *Science* 281, no. 5383 (09.11.98): 1599–1600.

Harding, Sandra, and Merrill B. Hintikka. 'Introduction.' In *Discovering Reality: Feminist Perspectives on Epistemology, Metaphysics, Methodology, and Philosophy of Science*, ed. Sandra Harding and Marrill B. Hintikka, ix–xix. Boston: D. Reidel Publishing, 1983.

Harjo, Joy, and Gloria Bird. 'Introduction.' In *Reinventing the Enemy's Language: Contemporary Native Women's Writing of North America*, ed. Joy Harjo and Gloria Bird, 19–31. New York: W.W. Norton, 1997.

Harris, Angela P. 'Race and Essentialism in Feminist Legal Theory.' *Stanford Law Review* 42, no. 3 (1990): 581–616.

Harris, Trudier, comp. *Selected Works of Ida B. Wells-Barnett.* New York: Oxford University Press, 1991.

Harris, Virginia R., and Trinity A. Ordoña. 'Developing Unity among Women of Color: Crossing the Barriers of Internalized Racism and Cross-Racial Hostility.' In *Making Face Making Soul: Creative and Critical Perspectives by Women of Color*, ed. Gloria Anzaldúa, 304–16. San Francisco: An Aunt Lute Foundation Book, 1990.

Hartmann, Heidi L. 'The Family as the Locus of Gender, Class and Political Struggle: The Example of Housework.' In *Feminism and Methodology*, ed. Sandra Harding, 109–34. Bloomington: Indiana University Press, 1987.

Harstock, Nancy C.M. 'Feminist Standpoint: Developing the Ground for a Specifically Feminist Historical Materialism.' In *Feminism and Methodology*, ed. Sandra Harding, 157–180. Bloomington: Indiana University Press, 1987.

Hekman, Susan. 'Truth and Method: Feminist Standpoint Theory Revisited.' *Signs* 22, no. 2 (1997): 341–65.

Herbert, Bob. 'In America, Lessons in Reality.' *New York Times*, 21 February 2000, A19.

– 'In America, Unseemly Alliances.' *New York Times*, 18 January 2001, A23.

Herrnstein, Richard J., and Charles A. Murray. *The Bell Curve: Intelligence and Class Structure in American Life.* New York: Free Press, 1994.

Hewitt, Nancy A. 'Beyond the Search for Sisterhood: American Women's History in the 1980s.' In *Unequal Sisters: A Multicultural Reader in U.S. Women's History,* ed. Ellen Carol DuBois and Vicki L. Ruiz, 1–14. New York: Routledge, 1990.

Higgenbotham, Elizabeth. 'Getting All Students to Listen: Analyzing and Coping with Student Resistance.' *American Behavioral Scientist* 40, no. 2 (1996): 203–11.

Higgenbotham, Evelyn Brooks. 'African American Women's History and the Metalanguage of Race.' *Signs: Journal of Women in Culture and Society* 17, no. 2 (1992): 251–74.

hooks, bell. *Feminist Theory: From Margin to Center.* Boston: South End Press, 1984.

– *Killing Rage: Ending Racism.* New York: Henry Holt, 1995.

– 'Representing Whiteness in the Black Imagination.' In *Cultural Studies,* ed. Lawrence Grossberg, Cary Nelson, and Paula Treichler, 338–46. New York: Routledge, 1992.

– *Talking Back: Thinking Feminist Thinking Black.* Boston: South End Press, 1989.

– *Yearning: Race, Gender, and Cultural Politics.* Boston: South End Press, 1990.

Houston, Velina Hasu. *The Politics of Life: Four Plays by Asian American Women.* Philadelphia: Temple University Press, 1993.

Hunter, Margaret L., and Kimberly D. Nettles. 'What about the White Women: Racial Politics in a Women's Studies Classroom.' *Teaching Sociology* 27 (1999): 385–97.

Hurtado, Aída. *The Color of Privilege: Three Blasphemies on Race and Feminism.* Ann Arbor: University of Michigan Press, 1996.

Jackson, Sue. 'Crossing Borders and Changing Pedagogies: From Giroux and Freire to Feminist Theories of Education.' *Gender and Education* 9, no. 4 (1997): 457–67.

Jaimes, M. Annette. 'American Racism: The Impact on American-Indian Identity and Survival.' In *Race*, ed. Steven Gregory and Roger Sanjek, 41–61. New Brunswick, NJ: Rutgers University Press, 1994.

– *The State of Native America: Genocide, Colonization, and Resistance*. Boston: South End Press, 1992.

Jewell, K. Sue. *From Mammy to Miss America and Beyond: Cultural Images and the Shaping of U.S. Social Policy*. London: Routledge, 1993.

Kadi, Joanna. 'A Question of Belonging.' In *Working Class Women in the Academy: Laborers in the Knowledge Factory*, ed. Michelle M. Tokarczyk and Elizabeth A. Fay, 87–96. Amherst: University of Massachusetts Press, 1993.

Kaplan, Amy. Review of *American Anatomies: Theorizing Race and Gender*, by Robyn Wiegman. *Signs* 23, no. 1 (1997): 220–5.

Keller, Frances Richardson. Review of *American Anatomies: Theorizing Race and Gender*, by Robyn Wiegman. *American Historical Review* 102, no. 1 (1997), 220–1.

Kim, Elaine H., and Lilia V. Villanueva, ed. *Making More Waves: New Writing by Asian Women*. Boston: Beacon Press, 1997.

Kincheloe, Joe L., and Shirley R. Steinberg. 'Constructing a Pedagogy of Whiteness for Angry White Students.' In *Dismantling White Privilege: Pedagogy, Politics and Whiteness*, ed. Nelson Rodriguez and Leila Villaverde, 178–97. New York: P. Lang, 2000.

King, Deborah. 'Multiple Jeopardy, Multiple Consciousness: The Context of a Black Feminist Ideology.' *Signs* 14, no. 1 (1988): 42–72.

Kliebard, Herbert M. *The Struggle for the American Curriculum 1893–1958*. Boston: Routledge and Kegan Paul, 1986.

Kurian, Manju S. 'Negotiating Power from the Margins: Lessons from Years of Racial Memory.' *Women and Language* 19, no. 1 (1996): 27–31.

Lerner, Gerda, ed. *Black Women in White America: A Documentary History*. New York: Vintage Books, 1992.

Liu, Tessie. 'Teaching the Differences among Women from a Historical Perspective: Rethinking Race and Gender as Social Categories.' In *Unequal Sisters: A Multicultural Reader in U.S. Women's History*, ed. Vicki L. Ruiz and Ellen Carol DuBois, 571–83. New York: Routledge, 1994.

Longino, Helen. 'Subjects, Power and Knowledge: Description and Prescription in Feminist Philosophies of Science.' In *Feminist Epistemologies*, ed. Linda Alcoff and Elizabeth Potter, 101–20. New York: Routledge, 1993.

Lorde, Audre. *Sister Outsider: Essays and Speeches*. Freedom, CA: Crossing Press, 1984.

Lorimer, Douglas A. 'Nature, Racism, and the Late Victorian Science.' *Canadian Journal of History* 25, no. 3 (1990): 369–85.

Lugones, María. 'On the Logic of Pluralist Feminism.' In *Feminist Ethics*, ed.
   Claudia Card, 35–44. Lawrence: University Press of Kansas, 1991.
MacKinnon, Catharine A. 'From Practice to Theory, or What Is a White Woman
   Anyway?' In *Critical White Studies: Looking Behind the Mirror*, ed. Richard Del-
   gado and Jean Stefancic, 300–4. Philadelphia: Temple University Press, 1997.
McCarthy, Cameron. 'Multicultural Policy Discourse on Racial Inequality in
   American Education.' In *Anti-Racism, Feminism, and Critical Approaches to
   Education*, ed. Roxana Ng, Pat Staton, and Joyce Scane, 21–44. Westport, CT:
   Bergin and Garvey, 1995.
McIntosh, Peggy. *White Privilege and Male Privilege: A Personal Account of Com-
   ing to See Correspondences through Work on Women's Studies*. Wellesley, MA:
   Center for Research on Women, 1988.
McKee, James B. *Sociology and the Race Problem: The Failure of a Perspective.*
   Urbana: University of Illinois Press, 1993.
McLaren, Peter. 'Decentering Whiteness.' *Multicultural Education* 5 (1997): 4–11.
McPhatter, Anna R. 'Cultural Competence in Child Welfare: What Is It? How
   Do We Achieve It? What Happens Without It?' *Child Welfare* 76, no. 1 (1997):
   255–77.
Matsuda, Mari J. *Where Is Your Body? And Other Essays on Race, Gender, and the
   Law.* Boston: Beacon Press, 1996.
Mazumdar, Sucheta. 'General Introduction: An Woman-Centered Perspective
   on Asian American History.' In *Making Waves: An Anthology of Writings by
   and about Asian American Women*, ed. Asian Women United of California:
   1–22. Boston: Beacon Press, 1989.
Mead, Rebecca. '"We Are Your Sisters."' *Oral History Review* 23, no. 1 (1996):
   47–56.
Merritt, Karen M. 'A Braid of Associations: Ten Years of Women's Studies in
   Wisconsin.' *Frontiers* 8, no. 3 (1986): 20–5.
Mihesuah, Devon A. 'Commonality of Difference: American Indian Women
   and History.' *American Indian Quarterly* 20, no. 1 (1996): 15–27.
– *Cultivating the Rosebuds: The Education of Women at the Cherokee Female Semi-
   nary, 1851–1909*. Urbana: University of Illinois Press, 1993.
– 'A Few Cautions at the Millenium on the Merging of Feminist Studies with
   American Indian Women's Studies.' *Signs* 25, no. 4 (2000): 1247–51.
– ed., *Natives and Academics: Researching and Writing about American Indians.*
   Lincoln: University of Nebraska Press, 1998.
Minh-ha, Trinh T. *Woman, Native, Other: Writing Postcoloniality and Feminism.*
   Bloomington: Indiana University Press, 1989.
Mitchell, Lucy Sprague. *Two Lives: The Story of Wesley Claire Mitchell and Myself.*
   New York: Simon and Schuster, 1953.

Mohanty, Chandra Talpade. 'On Race and Voice: Challenges for Liberal Education in the 1990s.' In *Between Borders: Pedagogy and the Politics of Cultural Studies*, ed. Henry A. Giroux and Peter McLaren, 145–66. New York: Routledge, 1994.

Mohanty, Chandra Talpade, Ann Russo, and Lourdes Torres, eds. *Third World Women and the Politics of Feminism*. Indianapolis: Indiana University Press, 1991.

Moraga, Cherríe. 'La Güerra.' In *This Bridge Called My Back: Writings by Radical Women of Color*, ed. Cherríe Moraga and Gloria Anzaldúa, 27–34. New York: Kitchen Table Women of Color Press, 1981.

– Title of presentation unknown. Paper presented at workshop on cross-cultural feminism, DePaul University, Chicago, Illinois, 1997.

Moraga, Cherríe, and Gloria Anzaldúa, ed. *This Bridge Called My Back: Writings by Radical Women of Color*. New York: Kitchen Table Women of Color Press, 1981.

Morrison, Toni. 'Introduction: Friday on the Potomac.' In *Race-ing Justice, Engendering Power: Essays on Anita Hill, Clarence Thomas, and the Construction of Social Reality*, ed. Toni Morrison, vii–xxx. New York: Pantheon Books, 1992.

Moya, Paula M.L. 'Learning from Experience: Politics, Epistemology, and Chicana/o Identity.' PhD dissertation, Cornell University, 1998.

– *Learning from Experience: Minority Identities, Multicultural Struggles*. Berkeley: University of California Press, 2002.

Moynihan, Daniel P. *The Negro Family – A Case for National Action*. Washington, DC: Office of Policy Planning and Research, United States Department of Labor, 1965.

Mydans, Seth. 'One Last Deadly Crossing for Illegal Aliens.' *The New York Times*. 7 January 1991, A1.

Narayan, Uma. 'The Project of Feminist Epistemology: Perspectives from a Nonwestern Feminist.' In *Gender/Body/Knowledge: Feminist Reconstructions of Being and Knowing*, ed. Alison M. Jaggar and Susan R. Bordo, 256–69. New Brunswick, NJ: Rutgers University Press, 1989.

National Academy of Science, Institute of Medicine, Division of Health Care Services. *Health Care in a Context of Civil Rights: A Report of a Study*, no. 1804. Washington, DC: U.S. Government Printing Office, 1981.

National Center for Education Statistics. Digest of Education Statistics, 2001 [online]. Accessed 30 September 2002. http://nces.ed.gov//pubs2002/digest2001/ch3.asp.

Nelson, Lynn Hankinson. *Who Knows? From Quine to a Feminist Empiricism*. Philadelphia: Temple University Press, 1990.

Newman, Louise Michele. *White Women's Rights: The Origins of Racial Feminism in the U.S.* New York: Oxford University Press, 1999.

Nobles, Wade W. 'African American Family Life: An Instrument of Culture.' In *Black Families*, ed. Harriette Pipes McAdoo, 44–53. Newbury Park, CA: Sage, 1988.

Nora, Pierre. 'Between Memory and History: *Les Lieux de Mémoire*.' *Representations* 26 (1989): 7–25.

Nordstrom, Marisa. Interview with author, April 1995, Evanston, Illinois. Author's notes.

O'Brien, Eileen. *Whites Confront Racism: Antiracists and Their Paths to Action.* Lanham, MD: Rowman and Littlefield, 2001.

O'Meally, Robert, and Geneviève Fabre. 'Introduction,' in *History and Memory in African American Culture*, ed. Geneviève Fabre and Robert O'Meally, 2–17. New York: Oxford University Press, 1994.

Omi, Michael, and Howard Winant. 'On the Theoretical Concept of Race.' In *Race, Identity, and Representation in Education*, ed. Cameron McCarthy and Warren Crichlow, 3–10. New York: Routledge, 1993.

– *Racial Formation in the United States: From the 1960s to the 1980s.* New York: Routledge, 1994.

Pascoe, Peggy. 'Home Mission Women, Race, and Culture: The Case of "Native Helpers."' In *Relations of Rescue: The Search for Female Moral Authority in the American West, 1874–1939.* New York: Oxford University Press, 1990.

Razack, Sherene H. *Looking White People in the Eye: Gender, Race, and Culture in Courtrooms and Classrooms.* Toronto: University of Toronto Press, 1998.

– 'Revolution from Within: Dilemmas of Feminist Jurisprudence.' *Queen's Quarterly* 97, no. 3 (1990): 398–413.

Reverby, Susan, ed. *Tuskegee's Truths: Rethinking the Tuskegee Syphilis Study.* Chapel Hill: University of North Carolina Press, 2000.

Reyes, María de la Ruz, and John J. Halcón. 'Racism in Academia: The Old Wolf Revisited.' In *Facing Racism in Higher Education*, ed. Nitza M. Hildago, Caesar L. McDowell, and Emilie V. Siddle, 69–83. Cambridge: Harvard Educational Review, 1990.

Rich, Adrienne. 'Women's Studies – Renaissance or Revolution? A Paper Read at University of Pennsylvania Women's Studies Conference, November 15, 1974.' *Women's Studies* 3 (1976): 121–6.

Robinson, Victoria. 'Introducing Women's Studies.' In *Thinking Feminist: Key Concepts in Women's Studies*, ed. Diane Richardson and Victoria Robinson, 1–26. New York: Guilford Press, 1993.

Rodriguez, Nelson M. 'Projects of Whiteness in a Critical Pedagogy.' In *Dismantling White Privilege: Pedagogy, Politics and Whiteness*, ed. Nelson Rodriguez and Leila Villaverde, 1–24. New York: P. Lang, 2000.

Roediger, David. *Towards the Abolition of Whiteness*. London: Verso, 1994.

Romero, Mary, and Debbie Storrs, '"Is That Sociology?" The Accounts of Women of Color Graduate Students in Ph.D. Programs.' In *Women Leading in Education*, ed. Diane M. Dunlap and Patricia A. Schmuck, 71–85. New York: State University of New York Press, 1995.

Rosaldo, Michelle Zimbalist, and Louise Lamphere. 'Introduction.' In *Women, Culture, and Society*, ed. Michelle Zimbalist Rosaldo and Louise Lamphere, 1–15. Stanford: Stanford University Press, 1974.

Rosaldo, Renato. *Culture and Truth: The Remaking of Social Analysis*. Boston: Beacon Press, 1993.

Ross, Dorothy. 'New Models of American Liberal Change.' In *The Origins of American Social Science*, chap 9. Cambridge: Cambridge University Press, 1991.

Roy, Beth. *Bitters in the Honey: Tales of Hope and Disappointment Across Divides of Race and Time*. Fayetteville: University of Arkansas Press, 1999.

Ruddick, Sara. 'Maternal Thinking.' *Feminist Studies* 6, no. 2 (1980): 342–67.

Ruiz, Vicki L., and Ellen Carol DuBois. 'Introduction to the Second Edition.' In *Unequal Sisters: A Multicultural Reader in U.S. Women's History*, ed. Vicki L. Ruiz and Ellen Carol DuBois, xi–xvi. New York: Routledge, 1994.

Russell y Rodriguez, Monica. 'Confronting Anthropology's Silencing Praxis: Speaking of/from a Chicana Consciousness.' *Qualitative Inquiry* 4, no. 1 (1998): 15–40.

Russo, Ann. 'We Cannot Live without Our Lives: White Women, Antiracism, and Feminism.' In *Third World Women and the Politics of Feminism*, ed. Chandra Talpade Mohanty, Ann Russo, and Lourdes Torres, 297–313. Indianapolis: Indiana University Press, 1991.

Scharff, Virginia. 'Else Surely We Will All Hang Separately: The Politics of Western Women's History.' *Pacific Historical Review* 61, no. 4 (1992): 535–55.

Segrest, Mab. *Memoir of a Race Traitor*. Boston: South End Press, 1994.

Shanley, Kate. 'Thoughts on Indian Feminism.' In *A Gathering of Spirit*, ed. Beth Brant, 213–15. Ithaca, NY: Firebrand Books, 1988.

Sheridan, Susan. 'Feminist Knowledge, Women's Liberation, and Women's Studies.' In *Feminist Knowledge: Critique and Construct*, ed. Sneja Gunew, 36–55. London: Routledge, 1990.

Sherif, Carolyn Wood. 'Bias in Psychology.' In *Feminism and Methodology*, ed. Sandra Harding, 37–56. Bloomington: Indiana University Press, 1987.

Sievers, Sharon L. 'What Have We Won, What Have We Lost?' *Frontiers* 8, no. 3 (1986): 43–6.

Simpson, Jennifer S. 'Easy Talk, White Talk, Back Talk: Some Reflections on the Meanings of Our Words.' *Journal of Contemporary Ethnography* 25, no. 3 (1996): 372–89.

Smith, Barbara. 'Toward a Black Feminist Criticism.' In *All the Women Are White, All the Blacks Are Men, But Some of Us Are Brave: Black Women's Studies*, ed. Gloria T. Hull, Patricia Bell Scott, and Barbara Smith, 157–75. New York: Feminist Press, 1982.

Smith, Dorothy E. 'Women's Perspective as a Radical Critique of Sociology.' In *Feminism and Methodology*, ed. Sandra Harding, 84–96. Bloomington: Indiana University Press, 1987.

Spelman, Elizabeth V. *Inessential Woman: Problems of Exclusion in Feminist Thought*. Boston: Beacon Press, 1988.

Stanley, Liz, and Sue Wise. *Breaking Out Again: Feminist Ontology and Epistemology*. London: Routledge, 1993.

Sterling, Dorothy. *Black Foremothers: Three Lives*. New York: Feminist Press, 1988.

Stocking, George W., Jr. *Race, Culture, and Evolution: Essays in the History of Anthropology*. Chicago: University of Chicago Press, 1982.

Stolberg, Sheryl Gay. 'Link Found Between Behavioral Problems and Time in Child Care.' *New York Times*, 19 April 2001. (Accessed from the web: http://www.nytimes.com/2001/04/19/-health/19CHIL.html).

Tan, Cheng Imm. 'Thinking about Asian Oppression and Liberation.' In *Skin Deep: Women Writing on Color, Culture and Identity*, ed. Elena Featherston, 40–6. Freedom, CA: Crossing Press, 1994.

Terrell, Mary Church. 'Lynching from a Negro's Point of View.' In *Black Women in White America: A Documentary History*, ed. Gerda Lerner, 205–11. New York: Vintage Books, 1992.

Thompson, Becky. *A Promise and a Way of Life: White Antiracist Activism*. Minneapolis: University of Minnesota Press, 2001.

Thompson, Becky, and White Women Challenging Racism. 'Home/Work: Antiracism Activism and the Meaning of Whiteness.' In *Off White: Readings on Race, Power, and Society*, ed. Michelle Fine, Linda C. Powell, Lois Weis, L. Mun Wong, 354–66. New York: Routledge, 1997.

Tokarczyk, Michelle M., and Elizabeth A. Fay. *Working-Class Women in the Academy: Laborers in the Knowledge Factory*. Amherst: University of Massachusetts Press, 1993.

Tuana, Nancy. 'The Radical Future of Feminist Empiricism.' *Hypatia* 7, no. 1 (1992): 100–13.

United States Census Bureau, Census 2000 Briefs. 'Overview of Race and Hispanic Origin.' 12 March 2001.

– 'The Hispanic Population.' 10 May 2001.

United States Department of Education, Office of Educational Research and Improvement. 'Tenure Status of Postsecondary Instructional Faculty and Staff, 1992–98.' July 2002.

United States Immigration and Naturalization Service. *1993 Statistical Yearbook of the Immigration and Naturalization Service.* Washington, DC: U.S. Government Printing Office, 1994.

Visweswaran, Kamala. *Fictions of Feminist Ethnography.* Minneapolis: University of Minnesota Press, 1994.

Ware, Vron. *Beyond the Pale: White Women, Racism and History.* London: Verso, 1992.

Wheeler, David L. 'A Growing Number of Scientists Reject the Concept of Race.' *Chronicle of Higher Education* 41, no. 23 (17 February 1995): A8–9, 15.

Whelehan, Imelda. *Modern Feminist Thought.* New York: New York University Press, 1995.

White, E. Frances. 'Africa on My Mind: Gender, Counter Discourse, and African-American Nationalism.' *Journal of Women's History* 2, no. 1 (1990): 73–97.

White, Paulette Childress. 'Getting the Facts of Life.' In *Memory of Kin: Stories about Family by Black Writers,* ed. Mary Helen Washington, 129–40. New York: Anchor Books, 1991.

Wiegman, Robyn. *American Anatomies: Theorizing Race and Gender.* Durham, NC: Duke University Press, 1995.

Wilds, Deborah J., and Reginald Wilson. *Minorities in Higher Education 1997– 1998.* Washington, DC: American Council on Education, 1998.

Wong, L. Mun. 'Dis(s)-secting and Dis(s)-closing "Whiteness."' In *Shifting Identities Shifting Racisms: A Feminism and Psychology Reader,* ed. Kum-Kum Bhavnani and Ann Phoenix, 133–53. London: Sage Publications, 1994.

Young, Melvina Johnson. 'Exploring the WPA Narratives: Finding the Voices of Black Women and Men.' In *Theorizing Black Feminisms: The Visionary Pragmatism of Black Women,* ed. Stanlie M. James and Abena P.A. Busia, 55–74. London: Routledge, 1993.

Zavella, Patricia. 'Reflections on Diversity among Chicanas.' In *Race,* ed. Steven Gregory and Roger Sanjek, 199–212. New Brunswick: Rutgers University Press, 1994.

Zelizer, Barbie. 'Reading the Past against the Grain: The Shape of Memory Studies.' *Review and Criticism* (1995): 214–39.

Zia, Helen. *Asian American Dreams: The Emergence of an American People.* New York: Farrar, Straus, and Giroux, 2000.

Zimmerman, Bonnie. 'Seeing, Reading, Knowing: The Lesbian Appropriation of Literature.' In *(En)gendering Knowledge: Feminists in Academe,* ed. Joan Hartman and Ellen Messer-Davidow, 85–99. Nashville: University of Tennessee Press, 1991.

Index